Critical
Communication
Pedagogy

Critical Communication Pedagogy

Deanna L. Fassett
San José State University

John T. Warren
Southern Illinois University, Carbondale

SAGE Publications
Thousand Oaks ■ London ■ New Delhi

KH

For information:

Sage Publications, Inc.
2455 Teller Road
Thousand Oaks, California 91320
E-mail: order@sagepub.com

Sage Publications Ltd.
1 Oliver's Yard
55 City Road
London EC1Y 1SP
United Kingdom

Sage Publications India Pvt. Ltd.
B-42, Panchsheel Enclave
Post Box 4109
New Delhi 110 017 India

Printed in the United States of America.

Library of Congress Cataloging-in-Publication Data

Fassett, Deanna L.
Critical communication pedagogy / Deanna L. Fassett & John T. Warren.
    p. cm.
Includes bibliographical references and index.
ISBN 1-4129-1625-9 (cloth) — ISBN 1-4129-1626-7 (pbk.)
    1. Communication—Study and teaching. I. Warren, John T.,
1974- II. Title. P91.3.F366 2007
302.2071—dc22

                            2006006383

This book is printed on acid-free paper.

06   07   08   09   10   11   10   9   8   7   6   5   4   3   2   1

Acquiring Editor:	Todd R. Armstrong
Editorial Assistant:	Camille Herrera
Project Editor:	Astrid Virding
Copyeditor:	Jamie Robinson
Typesetter:	C&M Digitals (P) Ltd.
Indexer:	Pamela Van Hass

10/5/06

Contents

It's tempting to dwell in the seeming absence of community—feeling out of place, ignored, excluded. But community is what you make of it. In its finest moments, community feels like home, like celebrations and sunshine and understanding. In its finest moments, community feels like the fantasy of coming home, of falling into step, of open arms. But community is so much more. . . . It's the messy home, the argument on the stairs, the scrabble for attention. We've been blessed to find ourselves in communities that support and nurture us: Our families, our alma maters, our institutions, our departments, and our classrooms. And though these places have felt like home to us—in all its beautiful and messy senses—it is in our continued relationships that they come to matter. We don't find communities; we forge them. Each and every day. In our communication. It is this sense of community we'd like to celebrate here, by giving thanks to all the people who helped to shape and strengthen this work: our colleagues—both the ones down the hall and the ones around the country who work in small ways toward great ends—and our students—who model for us in so many ways what it means to love and be loved, to be part of a growing community.

We would also like to thank our reviewers—our work is much stronger for their caring and considerate advice:

Sarah L. Bonewits Feldner, Marquette University; Shannon Broke VanHorn, Valley City State University; Patrice M. Buzzanell, Purdue University; Leda Cooks, University of Massachusetts, Amherst; Keith Nainby, California State University, Stanislaus; Deanna Sellnow, North Dakota State University; Jo Sprague, San José State University; and Kristen P. Treinen, Minnesota State University Mankato

Moreover, we would like to express our deepest appreciation for Amy Kilgard (whose insight, support, and creativity were invaluable to the early designs of our cover art), our copyeditor Jamie Robinson, and the kind folks at Sage, including and especially Todd Armstrong, Camille Herrera, Sarah Quesenberry, Astrid Virding, and Deya Saoud.

Introduction

Stolen Moments in Critical Pedagogy and Communication

One of my research participants for my dissertation, Abel—a student worker in my department, broke into my office and stole two of my books: a tattered copy of Peter Elbow's (1973) *Writing Without Teachers* and a writer's reference. We knew it was him because he'd taken items from other people's offices—pens, books, and other small, beloved items—and then disappeared. I don't know whether anyone followed up on this, whether they called campus police or spoke with his adviser; all I know is my books were gone . . . but perhaps that was a small price to pay for an interesting interview for my dissertation.

The books themselves were nothing remarkable, and I've since replaced them. The writer's reference was something I'd been sent by a publisher—an enticement to use a particular grammar and style text with my students (though I was still years from enjoying a teaching position where I could choose the books I'd ask my students to read). Elbow was in arrears—tattered, a bit stained, and split along the spine so it needed a rubber band to keep the pages together. I had liberated Elbow from the library of the writing center I'd worked in as an undergraduate, taking it home and reading it more than once. It followed me from my B.A. to my M.S., from my M.S. to my Ph.D., only to find a new home with Abel (and then perhaps with whomever or wherever after that).

So Abel stole my book—a book I'd stolen from someone else . . . a book that mattered very much to me at the time I'd taken it. There are a few other books in my collection, "borrowed" as well—books with the names of their original owners inside the covers or written on the spines. Each is problematic and precious; each marks a moment, a covetous urge satisfied in pages

1

and promises and thoughts of what could be or should be. Who I am as a scholar has been built in these stolen books, these stolen moments full of possibility.

Just recently I noticed my own books are "disappearing." I can't find my old copy of Lakoff and Johnson (1980) anymore, the one with all the notes I made during my philosophy of communication course; I'll have to wait for the publisher to send me another copy of Lindlof and Taylor's (2002) *Qualitative Communication Research Methods;* and I can't even begin to know what's happened to my office journal collection, passed on to me from a retired colleague. This would irk me were it not for the sneaking suspicion they'd moved on to better, more attentive homes; their new masters' covetous interests satisfied by a promise, a piece of knowledge that represents a relationship, a connection, a stolen moment.

If we were to carefully examine our own prized personal libraries, I wonder how many of us would find names other than our own inscribed inside, names indicating the original, though not true, homes of these works. How many of us have built our lives around such stolen moments?

* * *

So we missed the Rock and Roll Hall of Fame—we never got to go and, even though that was the draw to Cleveland and the Central States Communication Association annual conference, we never even entered the door. We missed it.

* * *

Conferences are overwhelming—you have to juggle reconnecting with friends, meeting new colleagues, attending panel sessions and learning more, and traveling to a new and often enticing city you'd like to explore. This says nothing of all the other, smaller associated stresses: eating too much or not enough or at the wrong times, delayed flights and lost luggage, grading papers and reading theses in the hotel room between sessions or after dinner, drinking too much, spending too much money, and reassuring your partner and friends and students at home that this is time well spent. I commonly tell graduate students to expect to feel alienated and uncomfortable at first; everyone's busy, everyone's juggling, everyone's trying to make time.

So much of my conferences these days are spent carving out time, making a space for this person or that person in an otherwise frantic schedule.

Relatively new to me is the experience of reconnecting with past graduate students, who are now at other institutions, working with other advisers. I make time for these folks, but also my current students who don't know how to "read" a conference yet, and also my friends from grad school, whom I love and miss and don't get to see nearly as often as I would prefer.

I try to take time, to steal it wherever I can, to get away and talk with my friends, my coauthors, my informal, chosen mentors. With a finite number of days and an infinite number of friends, colleagues, students, advisers, and scenic attractions, we struggle to make time for each other. We steal time where we can find it, and often that means something else loses.

*　*　*

Instead, we sat on our separate beds in the conference hotel, scratching ideas on cheap stationery. To do this, we had to meet in the middle. The middle, the space between and betwixt, the liminal, the stretch of ground between here and there but in no way ever here or there, is an uncomfortable place to be. Turner's (1982) discussion of the liminal as a space where things "seem to have been turned upside down" (p. 27) suggests the middle consists of a struggle, of being without firm ground, perched as it were between two lumpy conference beds.

*　*　*

In our earliest conversations, the idea of this book sounded so simple—a matter of describing the state of the art in critical communication pedagogy (i.e., teaching and research addressed toward understanding how communication creates and may, therefore, challenge sociocultural oppressions—e.g., classism, racism, sexism, heterosexism, ableism, ageism, etc.). But very few matters are easy for academics, and as we discussed the nature and scope of the book, we realized we'd happened on something complex.

On the one hand, the problem was that bringing together critical theory, educational studies, and communication (and the particular and often contradictory subdisciplines within it) was like merging very different bodies of literature together to make one story—the parts have to be smooth and build toward a narrative that we (and others) can believe. On the other hand, to us, communication has always been our lens for understanding both education and critical theory—for it is the careful analysis of the everyday that communication research affords, that we are even able to discern the nature of sociocultural oppressions at all. For us, the limitation of critical pedagogy has always been its failures to examine communication's role in the persistence and maintenance of institutional power.

* * *

A conference I enjoy is hosted by the American Educational Studies Association—a collective of education scholars who examine the philosophical, sociological, and cultural foundations of education. Their work is critical, vital, and timely. Critical pedagogy research is not only present in their conferences and journals but expected. Faced with the country's (misguided and dangerous) obsession with "standards" and "accountability," each questioning the integrity and professionalism of the teachers in our classrooms, these scholars/activists work to examine and interrupt or reverse educational inequities, to promote justice and value in schools. It is a conference I love, but one that frustrates me. In a recent business meeting, the conversation turned to the latest standards exam. In these moments—these conversations about their everyday struggles—I realize I am only a guest here. While welcomed, I still must ask permission. This is not my home. Maybe that is why I have stopped going to that conference.

Two weeks later, at the National Communication Association annual conference; the frantic meeting of my tired body and the communication education/instructional communication/communication pedagogy panels, each featuring researchers of communication apprehension, communobiology, and other work steeped in positivism, reminded me that this is also not my home. And while I have the loving support of some critical scholars, the conversations we share are often limited to ourselves. Our impact is diminished, overwhelmed by statically positivist, socially irrelevant research that measures this factor against some other, never connecting that work to the lives and bodies of students and teachers in classrooms, research that is unable to find a home in my body. But I still choose to go.

* * *

For humans, a perch isn't a particularly comfortable place to rest. It's a temporary respite, a place to gather one's resources before taking flight. But eventually, we have to build nests. This came to a point for us in, of all places, the conference hotel in Cleveland, Ohio. There began the birth of an idea—a labor of love—that marks the origin of this book, this effort to build a home, a place of comfort within the competing and contradictory forces that mark us. And that is why we missed the Rock and Roll Hall of Fame.

Missing the Rock and Roll Hall of Fame is missing an opportunity to escape—to leave the mix of conference panels and conference talk, to leave the bleachy smell of tightly tucked hotel sheets and stale smoke from the hotel bar, to leave the demands of scholarly obligation and find refuge in wonder.

* * *

The Rock and Roll Hall of Fame is a space of comfort—or, at least I imagine it to be, to be one of the places where the stories, songs, images of my childhood are held up as significant . . . where I can gaze upon the instruments and sheet music of musicians who filled my childhood bedroom with warmth and security, with lullabies scratched from vinyl 45 records and whirring from cassette players. Songs do that—they cuddle you and hold you tight, reminding you of the simplicity of Matchbox cars, Cabbage Patch dolls, and the world of imagination. A certain Billy Joel song takes me back to packing my book bag for my first week of middle school; an Elton John song marks my first kiss.

Going to the Rock and Roll Hall of Fame, for me, was about going home. Yet, when push came to shove, we didn't go. We stayed put, holding ourselves accountable for our own decisions to stand on/in the middle. In our careers, in our researching and teaching lives, we made a choice about where to perch, where to mark our own location. To go to the Rock and Roll Hall of Fame and stand in the illusion we had created was to neglect our own commitments. We chose to read and study the things we did. We chose to attend certain conferences, create alliances with certain people, and write the scholarship we wrote. We chose, in full knowledge that what we were doing was not the norm, to be the kind of education-focused communication scholars we became. Choosing the lullaby, a space of illusory comfort and peace, was never going to bring us a sense of real community. To do that— to create a home—was our own job, our own duty to the work we read, the scholarship we wrote, the commitments and promises we made. We did not go to the Rock and Roll Hall of Fame because there, in that hotel room in Cleveland, Ohio, we opted instead to make our work matter.

Book Goals

We are both fortunate to work in departments that feature graduate programs. In this capacity, we often find ourselves talking about our research lives, suggesting possible texts to read, papers to write, questions to ask. It is a privilege to work with dedicated students who care deeply about issues of communication and social justice, communication and the links to classroom inequality, or communication and identity. The students we work with humble us with their critical minds and caring queries. We grow as a result of this kind of interaction.

Our desire here, in this book, is to steal away with them, with you, for a time.

* * *

This book centers on commitments we have made: a collection of promises, of goals that interweave and provide vision for this book. To describe the book by goals (as opposed to some linear timeline or chapter outline) is to frame the book with political and social relevance; we make a commitment here to engender spaces of conversation and dialogue about the meeting of critical theory/pedagogy and communication. We write this book for two major reasons:

- First, we believe the field of communication studies is in desperate need of this conversation. There is no sustained or prominent investigation of the place of critical theory in communication pedagogy.

- Second, as communication studies scholars, we contend that the field of communication studies can significantly revise and extend work in critical pedagogy; the key to examining education in critical ways lies in communication studies-oriented methods, discourses, and perspectives.

A communication analysis illuminates not only the mechanisms of power's production but also hope for change, a hope made from the moment of articulate contact between (educational) subjects (Nainby, Warren, & Bollinger, 2003; Stewart, 1995). Our goals for this book are about a commitment and dedication to this work—a vision we hope to share with those who join us.

Our dedication stems from our personal experiences situated at the juncture of critique and hope:

- *Response to Injustice.* We were graduate students and teaching assistants once, struggling to understand how to better serve our students, students with vastly different backgrounds, experiences, advantages, and disadvantages than us. Assigned to teach students from inner cities, from homes we'd only read about in Kozol's (1991) *Savage Inequalities,* we sought research that would help us survive, that would help them thrive. In this way, a central goal of this book is to articulate a language of critique that accounts for how communication creates and makes possible our ability to see and respond to such inequalities.

- *Epistemological Pluralism.* We developed our way of engaging in academic inquiry in a doctoral program where the majority of communication education faculty had, for various reasons, recently left the university. However, it wasn't as though we were left to fend for ourselves in a void; instead, rather than following a prescribed series of courses and readings, we made meaning for ourselves. Our remaining advisers, committed and caring faculty in educational administration, intercultural communication, performance studies, and philosophy of communication, encouraged us to take risks and build connections across areas of study, both within and outside our discipline. Without a "proper" orientation to the study of the intersections of communication and education, we were free to find our own ways, to pursue the connections that felt most meaningful to us, to see the process of knowledge construction for what it is: a collaborative, communicative, personally meaningful, visceral adventure. In this way, we saw educational phenomena through multiple lenses, making possible various readings and interpretations of what was happening in our classrooms. Thus, another central goal of this book is to put those diverse (and divergent) tools to use, building theory and context for communication study that embraces critique and seeks new ways of imagining educational activity.

- *Disciplinary Pluralism.* Because we lacked traditional communication education professors in our lives, we went to the literature that our trusted critical faculty used to develop their pedagogies: critical pedagogy, feminist pedagogy, performative pedagogy, queer theory, whiteness studies. Our literature reviews featured names like Freire, Dewey, Conquergood, Ellsworth, Butler, Kozol, Lather, hooks, McLaren, Giroux, Anzaldúa, Postman, and Sedgwick. These names and works made sense to us as we saw inherent, but often unrealized, communication-based thinking in them— we drew these authors into our ways of seeing, crafting arguments that were communication based, but influenced by lines of reasoning that were not common in our own journals. We moved from book to book, instead of article to article, from theory to criticism and back again, instead of through the pages of *Communication Education.* For a critical scholar, there can be no better preparation. Instead of learning the field as a linear, purposeful progression (of systematic study of traits and states), we experienced it as something Kuhnian: contradictory, emergent, personally invested, and relationally supported. When we finally came to our reviews of *Communication Education,* we could sense paradigmatic patterns, encampments, alliances. And we could also see where the fissures were forming, where new work could spill forth. In other words, one of the goals of this book is to create a book we ourselves could have used as we pursued our studies.

• *Advocacy in Research.* When we look back across our published scholarship, each article is imbued with a sense of frustration of feeling unprepared, of not knowing what to expect. These moments emerge in descriptions of our work from mentors within and beyond our own graduate programs, in our assessment of how colleagues in our field define and describe the students who might benefit by our work, and in our sense of disciplinary cross-talk that fails to be accountable to the implications of each discipline's perspectives. For instance, scholars will advocate for the use of critical pedagogy (e.g., Sprague, 1992, 1993, 1994); however, such work calls for (long overdue and absolutely essential) paradigmatic inclusion but rarely helps make the connection concrete. This is to say, the call is there, but it is infrequently explored by scholars in concrete, particular instances that, in their specificity, raise the stakes for instructional communication theories and methods. In short, this book is about making those connections, those implications, more substantial and more specific. We move beyond the call for this scholarship and, instead, lay the groundwork for the field as we model one means to pursue it.

• *Research Is Pedagogy; Pedagogy Is Research.* We work with graduate students in a variety of capacities—as TA supervisors and graduate advisers, as chairs and members of thesis and dissertation committees, as professors and mentors. We struggle together with difficult questions, questions about how to live a more meaningful life, how to build research that is ethically sound and makes a real difference with real people, how to engage in scholarship as activism, as a means to challenge oppression. Many of our graduate students are teachers themselves; they encounter racism, sexism, and homophobia in their classrooms as students and as teachers. Critical communication pedagogy is about engaging the classroom as a site of social influence, as a space where people shape each other for better and for worse; it is about respecting teachers and students and the possible actions they can take, however small, to effect material change to the people and world around them. Many of these graduate students will engage in research as well. Our hope is that this text will serve as a model for how to consider and engage in meaningful interdisciplinary work, in work that builds from their own values and commitments. In other words, rather than continuing to pile-drive deep into the logical-positivist instructional communication trench, probing particular traits or constructs as possible veins for scholarly gold, we demonstrate it is advisable to survey the philosophical topography first.

These goals aside, there are also some reasons *not* to write this book: First, there are many in the academy who view books and research on pedagogy, even pedagogy scholarship that is theoretically complex and carefully examined, to be teaching and not research. Since our goal here is to theorize pedagogy, our work may be misread and, as a result, continue to relegate pedagogy-related scholarship to the margins. Part of our commitment here is to make this work (and the work of other people who do this research) matter.

Second, we are not "experts" in the traditional sense. We continue to grapple and struggle and fight with ourselves and with the field. We do not fully know the end result we would like to see, and in that sense, we fall into a similar trap as those overly abstract and utopian critical educators (Ellsworth, 1989). We're pushing toward something we've never known and don't yet fully know how to achieve. But, as we will address in what follows, must critical work know its ends? Or might we address ourselves to the means, the process instead of the product? If the point of critical work is, in Freire's terms, to reveal the process of knowledge construction, to make that process plain and accessible to all (and not just philosopher-kings and academics), then it is most important we reveal the grappling, that we reveal we don't fully know where we're headed. The better for all to participate, to help chart out how to make this work matter.

Finally, wouldn't it seem as though writing a book about teaching is less important than actually teaching well? One of us usually teaches eight classes a year—graduate classes, classes for teachers, for all levels of students—in addition to supervising theses. The other has been a director of graduate studies and remains active dissertation adviser. Would our time be better spent working on course preparation, on making sure each and every day is a meaningful learning experience for our students, on making possible the next generation of scholars/professors for the field? Is writing this book taking us away from our students? Our colleagues? Our advisees? This is one of those quandaries that *feels* true more than it *is* true. Time spent writing can sometimes feel like time away from students and topics. However, time spent writing also sharpens and clarifies the work of the classroom (in much the same way time in the classroom sharpens and clarifies the work of writing).

This book represents our attempt to bridge often conflicting, sometimes contradictory, and, in many other ways, complementary ways of seeing and thinking about educational practice, communication, and how each is influenced by power, culture, and the production of knowledge within institutional contexts. Our effort here is, in part, to craft a vision of what critical communication pedagogy is not—it is not exactly critical pedagogy, not exactly communication education, and not exactly instructional communication, but rather a mix of these methodological, pedagogical, and theoretical traditions. In describing what critical communication pedagogy is, we make possible a meaningful interdisciplinary framework, a potential home for our (and others') work. We aim here to create a context for scholarship and educational practice to flourish—to make "generative spaces" where we can make meaning together (Lather, 1991). We are excited about the potential of this work, excited to learn more about and from the students, teachers, and scholars who will join us.

Organization of Our Book

We begin—in Chapter 1, "Critical Communication Pedagogy: Shifting Paradigms"—by narrating paradigmatic shifts in this area of study and addressing the changing nature of communication research within educational contexts. Our layered, unconventional review of the literature places critical communication pedagogy in context, by showing how it occupies a divergent and diverse position within various academic traditions and within our own scholarly experience. Our next move—in Chapter 2, "Naming a Critical Communication Pedagogy"—is to identify the stakes and claims that one might make when adopting this stance. Our hope is that through a series of commitments, we address, in a fluid and contingent manner, the nature of critical communication pedagogy. From there—in Chapter 3, "Critical Communication Pedagogy in the Classroom"—we move into three instructional contexts, reading those experiences through critically oriented theoretical perspectives (through the work of Foucault, Butler, and de Certeau) and exploring how these perspectives help us to understand how to make sense of academic and intellectual engagement. The shift to the site of the classroom is about locating critical communication pedagogy within the lives and bodies of educational participants, showing how this way of educating and conducting educational research may profoundly influence our lives. We then—in Chapter 4, "Writing, Researching, and Living: Critical Communication Pedagogy as Reflexivity"—shift focus from the classroom to an examination of critical communication pedagogy as research, by exploring our own relationship to autoethnography as tactical (in de Certeau's sense) scholarship. In particular, we are interested in identifying how this work is necessarily contextual, located, and fluid. Our next move in the book—in Chapter 5, "Compromise and Commitment: Critical Communication Pedagogy as Praxis"—is to focus inward, to examine the politics, the ethics, and the demand for reflexivity and accountability in our research and classroom practice. In this, we attempt an unflinching exploration of our successes and failures to do this work in our own classrooms. In Chapter 6, "Nurturing Tension: Sustaining Hopeful Critical Communication Pedagogy," we take seriously the importance of critical communication pedagogy as nourishment, as something that sustains us and propels us to create and celebrate our communities. We illustrate this through our own experiences with communities that sustain us, that keep us honest, that help us remember, that encourage us to care for one another. We conclude—in "Grappling With Contradictions: Mentoring, in and Through the Critical Turnoff"—with our consideration of the mentoring relationships in our lives, in what this work means for the people we nurture and who nurture us. Though we conclude there, our belief is that we are not ending a conversation, drawing to close the dialogue about the nature and purpose of this kind of project; rather, we hope our thoughts here will give rise to continued discussion.

Stealing Away From Here

The idea of stealing time, stealing space, stealing away a moment to envision something new, is exactly what this book aims to do—to make it okay to take time, space, and effort to generate new ways of imagining our work in (and about) the classroom. Sometimes, in the act of stealing away, we might stumble, rouse the guards, find ourselves in confinement; however, we might just as well happen upon a moment, a gathering, a conversation we might join if only we listen carefully. Sometimes, the only way to get something new is to take it, to make it our own. But this sense of stealing is not illegal; it is in the stealing that we gather our resources, find partners in crime, "friends who bust friends out of jails" (Goodall, 2000, p. 193). In this sense, stealing is worth the risk.

Interlude

How to Read This Book
(or, My Dad Read This Book)

Before we get ahead of ourselves, we think it is important to discuss, briefly, how to best read this book, about how to read layered, storied, collaged writing. Long before you arrived, we imagined you; just as you might be imagining us now. We imagined you sitting there, reading this copy of the book, marking the pages here and there with fine lines and colorful Post-it stickies. We imagined you drinking your coffee, listening to the radio, and wondering what you'd gotten yourself into with this class. You didn't know you were going to be a part of this story, did you?

My dad read this book.

My dad read this book.

Whose dad? My dad. One of our dads.

We—that is, Deanna and John—had just finished the entire draft manuscript, printing it into color-coded chapters so that each of our copies was pleasing to our palates, something we'd want to take up and reread and revise. He—that is, my dad—asked to see it, to see the reviews, to get a sense of the process. I left him with my copy one day, but told him not to read it; I told him I'd be collecting it before he'd have a chance to read it. I didn't want to know whether or not he liked it—it seemed like too much weight to bear.

Of course he read it. (I really did want him to, even though I said I didn't.)

He read it carefully, calling out themes the reviewers would note as well, questions about power and voice and ethics. Without my asking, he marked the typos just as I would, with a dark graphite slash in the right-hand margin.

My favorite comment? "Are you using real words?" I love this.

I turn page after page and see his handwriting on my work; he has listed all the strange words, all the academic and seemingly incongruous to the narrative words: *elide, conflate, author, name,* and *reify.* I know these will give our readers pause.

Better still are the questions I don't expect, like, "Is there any such thing as 'unlived experience'?" I am reminded that even when I think I'm accessible, I'm still an academic, putting language to particular ends I cannot always foresee, that don't always make sense outside the margins of my own discipline.

His efforts mark this book, literally and figuratively, as surely as my own voice, as either of our own voices. As surely as our—Deanna's and John's—students' voices and experiences. As surely as your own voice. As surely as what has happened and what might be. And what has never been.

My dad read this book.

* * *

So, maybe you're sitting there, drinking your coffee . . . or maybe it's Diet Coke . . . and you're wondering, "who cares whose dad read this book? I could care less whether it was Del Fassett or Tom Warren, whoever those guys are. . . ." You might also be wondering who's driving this bus—"who's the 'I,' the 'we,' the 'me' who's making my life so difficult?"

Autoethnographic writing, writing that creates scholarly truth and knowledge in stories about our own lives, is a bit of a tease. It tempts us to ask questions about the particulars, about people's "lived experience," even if we don't especially care about those particulars. Before you know it, your scholarly focus on the need for critically oriented, relationally developed instructional communication research is sidetracked while you wonder whether Deanna really stole that book (maybe that was John) or whether John's really old enough to have owned vinyl 45s (hmm . . . must have been Deanna). This scholarship makes possible a host of questions more seemingly objective work masks, and it is these questions that lead some scholars to consider autoethnographic work solipsistic and self-aggrandizing. But, as we would encourage you to believe, it is not the particulars themselves, but rather the relationship between those particulars and the big picture that matters.

Autoethnographic writing invites us to breathe in deeply, to take up and take in someone else's experiences, and so it is no surprise when we become lost in our own senses. Work that moves us to anger and confusion, frustration and celebration does so successfully by inviting us to look inward, to explore how we, as readers, are (or are not) like the person or people we meet on the page. In those comparisons, we can't help but ask, "Is this Deanna? Or John?" "Is she (or he?) talking about Southern Illinois University (or Bowling Green State University? Or San José State University?)?" "Maybe that's Deanna's colleague. . . ." "Maybe that's John's student. . . ." "Oh, I'll bet that's about the panel I saw at. . . ." That's a fun game to play; we play it too (often when we're reading work by our own former professors—our first readings of Pelias's "The Critical Life" were spent trying to decide whether this was really how it happened, whether these were the people we knew in our lives in that insular community).

But don't be fooled. Don't allow your sense that this is somehow more self-disclosive writing—and certainly it is more apparently self-disclosive than the work we see most often in our academic journals—cause you to lose sight of the author's (or authors') goals. Authors rarely share anything lightly, rarely let their guard down unwittingly, rarely share a story that isn't aimed, in some way, at implicating their readers.

Come on, at some level, aren't you just a little bit curious about which of us would tease you, press you, pinch you in this way?

C'mere. . . .

No, come closer. . . .

I'll never tell.

But *we* might.

* * *

This work is a collaboration, one we've been working on, with greater and lesser awareness, for as long as we've known one another. We often see eye to eye, but not always; in these moments it is easy to find our "we." However, even as some of our experiences are shared, others stories are private and ours alone until we choose to share them with one another or with you; of these private stories, some are only John's or Deanna's to tell. Make of these moments what you will.

* * *

One of our dads read this book. My dad read this book. So what does that mean to you? It may not mean much to you, but it means a lot to me, and not just in the way you think. It matters to me because he is an example of something that will happen frequently throughout this book: He will serve a larger purpose, and in so doing, he may no longer be particularly my dad. He will read this book, again, and he may not recognize himself. It matters to me because, like so many of the people you will meet in this book, he did not know he'd become a character within it. And it matters all the more because he (and they) will not have the same power to respond, to push back against or to challenge my characterization of him (or them) here. And what of the dad who didn't get to read the draft? The other dad weighs heavily on my mind; he will read this book too and must know that he marks this work as well, though in less literal ways. If I tell you whose dad read our book, I risk hurting both dads, and quite frankly, you don't really need to know. While we have worked carefully, methodically, and respectfully to render the characters in our book, these people we've (and you've) known in some form or another, it is also *your* responsibility to read them carefully, methodically, and respectfully.

Reading the book in this way means recognizing that just as the "you" you met at the start of this interlude isn't really you, each of these characters is and is not an actual person. In this writing, you will meet Deanna and not Deanna, John and not John. You will meet our colleagues, but you won't. You will meet our students, but you won't. This is more than just the alteration of personal characteristics to protect identity, though we practice that here. Where you encounter others through us, you should know you are not learning about those others as much as you are learning about us, about what we took from those experiences and what that means, in our estimation, for critical communication pedagogy.

Reading the book in this way means recognizing that you have to advocate for these characters' interests, that you have to make them real, that you have to care about how they became the people they are (and are not).

Reading the book in this way means recognizing that it is partial, incomplete, truthful but not necessarily True. You should write too.

Reading the book in this way means recognizing yourself in these characters. Often the characters we meet on the page, including and perhaps especially the narrators, are composites, are collages themselves. Look carefully and you just might see yourself.

1

Critical Communication Pedagogy

Shifting Paradigms

A s scholars, we spend so much of our time thinking about time. . . . How much of it there is until a deadline . . . whether someone is wasting our time . . . how to create and enjoy a spacious sense of time inside a discussion or an activity. . . . Time to regroup, time to change, time's up, a time to every purpose under heaven. Time is always on our minds. But not just time . . . moments. Because the issue is not so much whether there's enough time for a teacher or a writer or a professor, but whether the time was well spent, whether the moment was well rounded, purposeful, or meaningful to us, our students, our research participants. . . . In teaching, we live life moment by moment, looking for patterns, reliving and loving and dreading "key" moments. There are many such shared moments in our lives. . . .

In thinking about the field—the state of communication education, instructional communication, communication pedagogy—we found that time has different shapes than we expected. As fairly linear thinkers, we expected to conceive of the discipline as we conceive of time itself: a moment to moment, processional process beginning with our foreparents and leading us, in a historical line to the present issue of *Communication Education*. After all, it makes sense to us, as communication scholars, to see the past influence and make possible the conditions of the present. And of course, this is mostly true; however, as we began to encounter the field, we noticed that our engagement with it failed to have the expected directionality. Instead of a line, we found the story of the field was told to us in pieces. We read Freire (1970/2003) before we found Dewey (1916/1944, 1938). We learned about the ideology of "blaming the victim" from Kozol (1991, 1995, 2000) long before we read Ryan's (1976) treatise on the subject. We tried to read the pages of our field's journals, but often found distraction in the pages of McLaren's (1999) *Schooling as Ritual Performance* or Fine's (1991) *Framing Dropouts*. Thus, the story of our field became individualized, personalized; we learned the field in pieces, as a rich collage or mosaic that generated meaning through juxtaposition rather than cause and effect.

Of course, this is often how time works—we piece together enough time here or there to accomplish the doings of our lives. We have written this book in stolen moments found in between the preparation of both memos and courses. We smuggle our time with loved ones, carefully extracted from the tasks and to-do lists of our lives. The fact of these moments' stolen nature (like the moments we spent swimming in Ira Shor's, 1980, 1992, 1996 critical pedagogy books) does not mean they are less valuable. Rather, it means that how we make sense of our daily lives is much more like art, like a poem or a mosaic, than like the linear pages of our high school history books. For instance, we learned to drive cars not by the manual, but by the moments stolen from our parents' schedule or the time occupied in the driver's education car. Those moments, as a series of lucky juxtapositions, have created the meaning making of driving—it is in the moments stolen from time and knitted together that we have crafted our driving selves. It is, of course, why we drive differently—Deanna, as a Californian, is a much different driver than John, who learned to drive in Indiana.

Thus, the idea of defining a state of the field is troubling—how do we do this in a way that actually represents or mirrors the nature of how we learn, how we make sense of ourselves as communicators and scholars in the field? Certainly, we could provide a linear description—a timeline that locates Sprague's (1992, 1993) call for critical inquiry or Pelias's (2000) self-interrogation of the critical life within the timeline of *Communication Education*. We could craft a story of the field in this way, but in doing so, we would rob the story of the field of its lived quality. Rather than try to create some order that somehow preexists us as researchers, in this unconventional review of, this interaction with the literature, we strive to steal away these moments from our sense making, to fashion them into an image for others. We paint here the field as we encountered it, offering, as one must, our own impressionistic understandings of how we have arrived at a point in time where we find a need for this book on critical communication pedagogy. In what follows, we take up our own relationships to the intersections of instructional communication and critical pedagogy, considering what each provides that the other does not. In drawing together the two perspectives, we suggest a vision for coming together that extends beyond theory and methodology to the creation of community.

You Think You're a Comm Ed Scholar?

It was my first job interview and I was so nervous. In the moment of the interview, I was asked to define myself in the field. This, I had been taught, was tricky business. I remember in graduate school in a meeting, my faculty asked a similar question: Who do you think you are becoming? I responded confidently that I was a performance studies scholar interested in pedagogy and culture; however, I thought I was also a generalist. When they stopped laughing, they informed me that I was no generalist and I had better begin to embrace it. It was then that I began really publishing; with only the perceived luxury of a generalist position to fall back on, I had better make a stand.

So I was standing in front of the search committee when a communication education scholar I admire asked me to define myself; taking a gulp of air, I said: "I'm a performance scholar centrally, but I also see myself as an intercultural scholar. I also see myself as a communication education scholar." The definition was strategic; I wanted this scholar in communication education to see in me, her potential new colleague, an ally. I wanted her to see, in my definition of myself, an image similar to her sense of herself. I wanted to appropriate the image of communication education so it would help me get this job. And while I had very little idea of what made a communication education scholar at the time (except that I had published in *Communication Education* already and felt this helped me qualify), I had found that definitions matter.

"A communication education scholar? You think you're a comm ed scholar?" Puzzled at this response, I noted my recent publication in the journal of that same name, pulling cut pages out of my bag as evidence. She smiled, "Well, publishing in *Communication Education* doesn't make you a comm ed scholar." It was then that I realized the ground of communication and pedagogy was not as stable as I had previously thought.

Box Checked

My first experience with "communication education" was a box I checked on my application to Southern Illinois University for the Ph.D. It was simple enough in my mind: "I like to study communication. . . . I like to study education. . . . If I check this box, I'll get to study both." Little did I know there was more to it than that. There is a long and well-documented history (see, for instance, Sprague, 1993) of what constitutes communication education, and how that is and is not the same thing as instructional communication. This is a distinction that matters very much to other people, even if it hasn't been an especially salient distinction for me; Sprague (1993) is very eloquent in her call to "ask the questions that are 'embarrassments to theory,'" to ask the questions that other researchers overlook as too practical, too applied, too pedagogical (p. 106). Every time I think about blending together the two areas into an amorphous "CE/IC," Sprague challenges me to consider the ways in which this blurring of the borders is enabling for some and perhaps harmful for others. Too often I find myself quick to focus on the "scholarly," on writing something I think will be "appropriate" for *Communication Education,* and I fail to answer Sprague's call; often, I overlook how teaching communication studies is a distinct area of study in its own right (and not simply something everyone does . . . so no one has to study it).

This distinction poses something of a dilemma for me: How do I define myself in this field? I suppose you could look to my C.V. (my *curriculum vitae*) to see how I label myself. And I suppose that's a function of two considerations: (1) the effects I think that label will have on the reader, and (2) whether or how I want to foreground certain intellectual and political commitments. For a long time, I labeled myself as part of "pedagogical studies," a suggestion from my adviser. At first, I liked how that sidestepped the question of communication education or instructional communication; I made the case that I was concerned with how scholars, in a variety of disciplines, study pedagogy. But the question of how this was communication nagged at me—why not study pedagogy in an education program?

* * *

I first proudly proclaimed I was an instructional communication scholar.

We'd stopped for a Coke at McDonald's. For those of you who know a little about the Midwest, you know that one way to measure the size and stature of a town is to total up the number of McDonald's restaurants it has; ours was a four-McDonald's town, maybe 40,000 people soaking wet, during the school year when everyone's absorbed in classes, eating cheeseburgers, whatever. It was my happy task, as a first year doctoral student, to give tours of the town to the two candidates for our "comm pedagogy" hire. And I was actually happy to give the tours, as it gave me some insight into the process I'd have to pursue myself in a few years.

I'm chauffeuring my first candidate, West Virginia, today, showing her where the faculty live in town, where the students live, what the rec center is like. Most of the day has been pleasant, and she's warmed up enough to talk with me about my studies. She's surprised I don't yet know what I want to do for my dissertation. And it's true, at the end of my first year, I don't know. I do know I don't want to write about "at-risk students," and at this point in my studies, I'm just beginning to strategize as to how I'll work with critical theory. West Virginia asks me what classes I'm taking—an innocent enough question. "Focus Group Methodology, Ethnomethodology, Special Student Populations, and Contrasting Educational Philosophies." And that's when she asks—judges—challenges—"Philosophy? What's that got to do with instructional comm?"

It's not that I don't understand her question. West Virginia has had a very prestigious preparation for her work in instructional communication, including completing a prescribed series of courses in statistical methods and programmatic research. I was supposed to take Inferential Statistics, but was allowed to substitute with a course of my choosing (I chose Performance as Methodology). What I didn't understand was how I was supposed to turn off the Dewey, and Counts, and Freire, and McLaren, and Apple, and Giroux, and all the other educational philosophers who had already shaped my thinking. What I didn't understand was how philosophy wasn't a foundation for the study of instructional communication . . . or really any kind of communication. . . .

* * *

So, I tried on the mantle of "communication education."

"But you're not just comm ed—you do other things too!" My performance studies colleagues, all well meaning, are quick to convince me that I am a performance studies scholar too; their comments suggest that if I would only stop dragging my feet and play along, I would be one of them. Perhaps that's true; perhaps I spend far too much time thinking about what I don't know, what I can't do, what I'd still need to read, say, publish in order to fit in with them. But they're my friends, and it's nice to be wanted . . . and I'd like to believe that if I were to publish in *Text and Performance Quarterly*, they would take it as an opportunity to say "See? We told you so!"

"But you're not just comm ed—you do other things too?" Prospective tenure track hires in my department always seem to come to a crux in our conversations: Either they grant that I'm the "comm ed" person—that one member of the faculty who supervises TAs and asks questions about assessment and publishes exclusively about those endeavors—or they probe for my "real" interest, the motivation that moves me to write while I'm working at my day job of preparing future teachers, biding my time as a "basic course director" until I can have the luxury of tenure and (relatively) uninterrupted time to pursue other, certainly grander questions (perhaps about Buber or Butler or de Certeau or Foucault . . .).

It's the "just" that interests me, a just that implies "those that can, do [certain kinds of research] and those that can't, teach [and teach and teach]." A just that suggests one cannot specialize in pedagogy, that a scholar concerned with pedagogy is, by nature, a generalist (and that being a generalist is somehow less scholarly). A just that suggests pedagogy is not, in itself, research, but rather a synthesis of research, a sharing of what others have done. As someone who refuses to accept that a classroom is "just" a classroom, that what we do there as teachers and students has little to do with the "real world," I cannot accept that pedagogy is "just" conveyance, transmission. If pedagogy is, in the Freirean sense, a process of knowledge construction (or, as Lather, 1991, suggests, a process of working together to create generative, transformative spaces), then the classroom is a site of theorizing, of (re)constituting social, cultural and economic relationships. Pedagogy is research.

* * *

Frustrated, I turned away from labels that didn't quite fit. To call myself instructional communication meant that I would be othered or marginalized by my peers who do similarly termed research. To call myself communication education would mean I would be perceived by my colleagues in other areas of the discipline as having no research focus, as having nothing other than the classroom, as though that weren't a rich enough area of study, replete with cultures, identities, politics, power, pain, and pleasure.

This is to say that the policing of the boundaries between paradigmatic perspectives isn't obvious, isn't a matter of barbwire and unambiguous signs. It's the reactions of a more senior scholar at dinner, or over Cokes at the local McDonald's, or in a letter regarding your latest submission. As Kuhn (1996) taught us, the nature of a discipline is to evolve slowly and socially, not in terms of radical, earth-shattering breakthroughs. Our field grows in terms of who speaks with whom, who can say what and when, and what sense people make of transgressions. And so, policing the boundaries is equally subtle, a matter of asking the well-placed question, of justifying the grade just so, or of whom the editor chooses to review a given manuscript.

* * *

The field came together for me in an instant, sitting with my cat in the midst of stacks and stacks of paper in my cluttered "office," late in the process of writing my dissertation. I could only draw from critical pedagogy work in as much as I could justify it as communication studies scholarship (and not some other field, say, educational foundations). I was writing a dissertation I'd avoided, a dissertation I didn't especially want to write. Early on in my graduate coursework, I took a class on the communication needs of students at risk, a class that exposed me to the vein of scholarship that purports to address these needs, scholarship that casts students as deeply flawed (and, at times, as cancerous or as educational Typhoid Marys). I felt very passionately about challenging this work, making it the focus of a number of conference papers, classroom presentations, and the like, and it wasn't long before my peers started asking me questions like "So, are you writing an at-risk dissertation?" Already interested in language, and especially metaphor, I bristled at the idea of writing a dissertation that would continue to uphold, however well intentioned or unreflectively, a deficit or "at-risk" model of student failure.

I pored over issue after issue of *Communication Education* (before the dawn of sophisticated Internet search engines and our national organization's electronic archive), looking for anything that might help me—pieces on power, which would turn out to be elaborate considerations of behavioral alteration techniques and methods (BATs and BAMs), pieces on culture, which would reveal whether communication apprehension transcended cultural and/or national boundaries—anything that would officially sanction my interest in critical pedagogy so I could keep broad swaths of my idea. Jo Sprague's (1992) essay "Expanding the Research Agenda for Instructional Communication: Raising Some Unasked Questions" appeared to me, as if in a vision, from the unlikeliest of places: a pile of articles in the corner of my then still-prelim-ravaged office. Maybe a year before, one of my professors had passed along a copy to me, saying that Sprague's work would be key; at the time, I couldn't believe that would be so. Nothing in my field looked like anything I wanted to do; remember, I was reading Dewey and Freire, metaphorically resting my feet on the stacks of *Communication Education* I didn't think had anything to offer me. It's worth noting that there's so much to be found between the covers of that journal, if only you know how to look, how to recognize what you're seeing.

Sprague's work—I quickly read every article I could find—brought our discipline's efforts at understanding communication in the classroom into sharp focus for me. Today, when I teach graduate students how to understand the paradigmatic strands of communication education and instructional communication research, I ask them to read Sprague (first 2002, and then 1993 and 1992). And, when I want to help them understand the roots of critical communication pedagogy—where outside scholarship infiltrates and is made meaningful in communication scholarship—I still ask them to read Sprague (1992, 1994). In her work in the early 1990s, Sprague offers us a useful distinction for understanding classroom-oriented work in communication studies: (1) Communication education explores how best to teach communication by considering questions like what is disciplinarily specific about communication instruction that, by necessity, sets it apart from science instruction or art instruction. (2) Instructional communication is the study of communication as it plays out in a variety of instructional contexts, from the one-to-one tutoring session to the training and development seminar to the kindergarten classroom, and it considers the question of how instructors of any subject or student population might best engage communication to educate. Sprague's writings reveal both areas of study to be impoverished, to be overly beholden to particular paradigmatic perspectives that fail to capture the richness of the phenomena we study or to genuinely engage communication scholars in careful consideration of defining foundational epistemological and ontological questions.

Sprague's work helped me understand what constitutes instructional communication, how it is informed by educational psychology work, and how that paradigmatic (theoretical, methodological) influence makes instructional communication ideally suited to answering some questions and neglecting others. Indeed, Sprague's 1992 essay, "Expanding the Research Agenda," does just that: defines the field of study, and then challenges scholars in this area of study to ask heretofore "unasked" questions about the purpose and function of schools and teachers, about the role of language and power in knowledge. In short, she asks the very sorts of questions scholars in other fields have asked, the sorts of questions that have relevance and bearing for our study of communication in classrooms, and to which communication scholars are ideally poised to speak if they would only recognize the questions.

In my dissertation, I could use Sprague's work to support an important claim: Language matters. Descriptions like "at-risk" or "behaviorally disordered" or even "BATs and BAMs," already define what we can see and learn and what we can't. For example, "at-risk," already enveloped in medical discourse, could only illuminate ways to diagnose students' problems and prescribe for them remedies; the first wave of research in instructional communication that aimed to treat "at-risk students" locates students' likelihood of failure in aspects of their identities that are beyond their control (i.e., race/ethnicity, economic class, etc.), in deficits they must look to researchers to fill (Fassett & Warren, 2005). Another perspective on educational failure (Johnson, 1994; Johnson, Staton, & Jorgenson-Earp, 1995; Rosenfeld & Richman, 1999; Rosenfeld, Richman, & Bowen, 1998), an ecological or systems theory-informed understanding of failure as interactional (as located in the goodness of fit between a student and the social systems in which s/he plays a part—the family, the classroom, the school, the neighborhood, the culture, the society), makes an important shift away from deficit under-standings, understandings that blame the victim (Ryan, 1976). A critical pedagogical perspective suggests yet another understanding of educational failure—failure occurs when a student is unwilling or unable to reproduce a given ideology. In other words, the student isn't inherently "at risk" of anything exactly; s/he is placed at risk by (often) well-intentioned partici-pants in the educational system (from teachers to test designers, from scholarly researchers to voters who fail to question and revise property tax allocations to schools).

Such a small change in terms—from *risk* to *ecology* to *resistance*—why give it a second thought? Aren't these "just" words? Communication schol-ars, of all people, shouldn't write off words as "just words."

Reading Freire for the First Time

I remember my first encounter with him—it was in an undergraduate women's studies class. His famous Chapter 2, the concrete image of banking vs. problem posing, became a clear image for me of how and why education was flawed. All my life, I'd been searching for a way to conceptualize my own dis/comfort in education. Time and again, I'd find myself within or out-side various educational experiences and this book, Freire's words, gave me a way to see myself in education.

In high school I took Precalculus with the new football coach—a young, built blond man who had much energy and tried to make math visual. When we, as a class, couldn't grasp the mathematical concept he had traced, again and again, on the blackboard, he moved the desks to the side of the room and created a massive graph on the floor of the room, using the natural lines created by the institutional tiles as markers and points. With tape, he made axis lines that began to chart out the abstract numbers. Each of the students had a problem and, when it was a student's turn, s/he entered the graph—walked into the math problem, sketched out on the floor, and had to be the numbers, to embody the formula and literally walk the numbers into exis-tence. While I don't remember the math of that occasion, I remember the feeling of entering pedagogical problems with my body—to make ideas flesh. Compared with the blackboard, this pedagogical moment embraced me and brought abstract ideas to flesh; that moment of walking the graph taught me what it means to create a problem-posing pedagogy.

It was this moment, the enfleshed moment of taking pedagogy into the body, that stood out to me as I read, for the first time, Freire's (2003) conceptualization of power in/through pedagogy. It was in the memory of that math class and in the reading of *Pedagogy of the Oppressed* that I began to understand that learning did not have to consist of exercises in constraint and rote memory. Learning could, instead, mean entering into the problem, feeling the moment of possibility, walking the lines of abstraction in my tennis shoes, rubber soles on masking tape, on dusty institutional tile.

* * *

There's a lot to resist in critical pedagogy, which is part of what makes that area of study so fascinating. I love the moment of introducing students to critical pedagogy, the moment where they furrow their brows and whisper, with no small amount of irritation, "What's pedagogy?" And, if I'm lucky, we have a conversation about how "critical" does not simply mean locating and naming the bad, the incomplete, the oppressive in a given instance, but also means considering the possibilities, hoping for and imagining something better. Students are very astute in their frustrations; as Elizabeth Ellsworth (1989) noted many years ago, much to the dismay of many famous critical educators (most notably McLaren, 1994), critical pedagogy—at its deepest linguistic roots—is too modernist, abstract, and utopian for concrete situations, fleshed individuals, palpable conflicts. Sure, we all want democracy, we all want to believe we are rational individuals capable of acting in our own and others' best interests. But Ellsworth is right; situated at the juncture of modernism and postmodernism—of grand and vague ambitions regarding the purpose and value of an education and efforts to unravel grand narratives about progress and one's ability to succeed in the face of seemingly insurmountable odds—critical pedagogy is a deeply flawed and yet profoundly moving way of seeing.

But what is critical pedagogy? Wink (2005) spends her entire book teasing apart and weaving together different definitions of critical pedagogy, in many ways working toward the creation of generative spaces (Lather, 1991), places where the reader might build her/his own definitions, own meanings. In this book, we take critical pedagogy to mean efforts by people concerned with education to embrace profound ideological difference and socioeconomic context as constitutive of what happens in schools and classrooms. Critical pedagogy, at its best, is inherently Freirean: efforts to reflect and act upon the world in order to transform it, to make it a more just place for more people, to respond to our own collective pains and needs and desires (Freire, 1970/2003). Critical educators appraise education for pain, for inequity, and seek to act accordingly, which is to say with each other, not *on*, *for*, or *to* each other. Quite simply, critical pedagogy is a journey, not a destination.

But, if many prominent critical educators, including Ellsworth (1989) and Lather (1991), are suspicious of critical pedagogy, concerned with whether critical pedagogy's "very efforts to liberate perpetuate the relations of dominance" (Lather, 1991, p. 16), then why do they draw it into the field of communication studies? Because

> where instructional communication scholars see "at-risk" students, critical educators see students who resist educational contexts that place them at risk.

> where instructional communication scholars work to control isolable variables, critical educators work to situate the classroom in relation to a larger sociocultural context.

> where instructional communication scholars understand identities as amalgams of traits (of race/ethnicity, of gender, of class, of sexuality), critical educators understand identities as multifaceted and fluid, relational selves that emerge in communication (Fassett & Warren, 2004; Hendrix, Jackson, & Warren, 2003).

> where instructional communication scholars see "power in the classroom" as a series of compliance-gaining and resisting moves and countermoves, critical educators understand power as distributed, fluid, and complex (Sprague, 1994; Wood & Fassett, 2003).

> where instructional communication scholars deploy primarily self-report, statistical research methods to understand educational contexts, critical educators engage a broad range of research methods, including ethnography (in its interpretive, critical and performative iterations), interviewing, and discourse analysis.

In effect, a critical pedagogical perspective invites instructional communication scholars to situate their inquiry in relation to larger, macro sociocultural, socioeconomic structures, to explore the ways in which racism, sexism, classism, homophobia, and other forms of oppression permeate classrooms and research on classrooms, teachers, and students.

Communication Intention, in Tension

My friends think I'm a little bit strange (or perhaps it would be more accurate to say quixotic) for using Freire's (1970/2003) *Pedagogy of the Oppressed* with graduate teaching assistants (GTAs) in my department. That may be true; as they're quick to remind me, GTAs need to understand how to fill out a gradebook, need to understand what a B means and how to justify it consistently and clearly with their students, before they question the purpose and value of grading. My response—that even the seemingly apolitical concern of awarding an A or a B is ideological, is a question of power and judgment and reproduction of certain values and not others—is always that the two are mutually informing.

Freire helps me broach the subject of power with GTAs in a nuanced way; together, we consider how best to pose problems for our collective work with students (rather than craft seamless lessons on "good introductions" or "effective transitions"). In reading his work, we grapple with what he might mean by praxis (reflection and action? reflection and action on the world? reflection and action on the world in order to transform it?) and whether such an effort is amenable to our university's general education learning outcome objectives. In his discussion of false generosity, Freire gives us some pause: He suggests that oppressors cannot simply take action on behalf of the oppressed because to do so further disenfranchises them, renders them perpetually dependent on their oppressors.

Situating his work in the context of TA training is exciting precisely because it does not speak fully to this particular, local context. GTAs often ask: Is lecture always part of a banking or "transmission" (Wink, 2005) pedagogy? If we show how we're working with students to create knowledge— if we even broach the possibility that knowledge is socially constructed and subject to change—how do we prove ourselves to be credible, trustworthy, capable of giving a fair grade or offering good advice? As students and teachers both, are we really oppressors? When a student follows me back to the office late at night is he really the oppressed?

This notion of "oppressor" and "oppressed" is a seductive binary, an enabling fiction. For Freire, it is a choice of terms that helps to illuminate something important: that this is our collective project, that, in hooks's (1994) words, "education can only be liberatory when everyone claims knowledge as a field in which we all labor" (p. 14). But this is a language choice that shapes our understandings, shapes our realities. As the GTAs' questions suggest, we are always already both oppressor and oppressed (though to greater and lesser degrees and with greater and lesser consequences, depending on the context, to be sure). At least in U.S. higher education, we all participate in white, supremacist, capitalist patriarchy (hooks, 1994), but we occupy any number of conflicted and contradictory subject positions. GTAs, in general, and GTAs of color, of transgressive genders or sexualities or classes, in particular, are very well suited to exploring these tensions as they live them every day. And, as we come to know our students' lives more fully, we find they are not immune to these tensions themselves, even if we do not explicitly call those tensions into question in the classroom.

But if instructional communication scholars tend to decontextualize and parse classrooms into smaller, discernable, controllable elements, if instructional communication scholars fail to engage in larger, macroscopic analysis of socioeconomic context, then why embrace their work as part of a critical communication pedagogy? Because

> where critical educators wax philosophic about whether someone has false consciousness or participates in her or his own domination, instructional communication scholars look to concrete instances, to how communication functions to create, shape, support, sustain, or challenge existing social structures and oppressions.

> where critical educators address the importance of communication, of language choices and instances of talk, instructional communication scholars are ideally poised to analyze those choices, those instances, through careful and sophisticated methods ranging from experimental methods to ethnomethodology and conversation analysis.

> where critical educators tend toward, as Ellsworth (1989) noted, highly abstract and utopian language, accessible and deemed valuable by only a small segment of the academic community, communication scholars are, through recent innovations in autoethnographic and performative writing as well as a longstanding tradition of audience analysis, well suited to lucid, provocative explorations of communication as constitutive of identity, culture, and power.

In effect, an instructional communication perspective invites critical pedagogy scholars to situate their inquiry in micro, local, discursive instances, to illuminate and explore how larger sociocultural and socioeconomic structures come to permeate, move in and through, individuals through their concrete, mundane communicative practices.

Desire and Critique in Communication Education

Searching, searching, searching for something to help me understand how I'm supposed to react when one of my friendliest students blows up at me during a class. Will "An Attributional Analysis of College Students' Resistance Decisions" (Kearney, Plax & Burroughs, 1991), "Compliance Resistance in the College Classroom" (Burroughs, Kearney, & Plax, 1989), or "Resisting Compliance in the Multicultural Classroom" (Lee, Levine & Cambra, 1997) increase my understanding? In class we were talking about whiteness studies research, and I'd supported an article with statistics from the Department of Justice; you know, the ones that show people of color are punished more than white people for similar crimes? Chris turned a plum color and stormed out of the class. I followed—was I supposed to follow?

"I just won't listen to this any more. . . . You always do this; you find your little moments, you drop something that makes me so angry, and then we don't have time to talk about it!"

Uh. . . . "Chris, why don't you calm down? Of course we can talk about this; I'll give you my sources, you can take a look at them—we can meet and—"

"But that's not true—it's just not true that white people get away with crime!"

Huh? Of all people . . . Chris's brothers are cops, but he's an out gay man—doesn't he know about social oppression? "What do you make of these statist—"

Chris is actually shaking; I'm sure students in the classroom can hear us, we're just outside. Could I have kept this moment in the classroom? Is this a teachable moment?

"This isn't true—my fathers' friends are attorneys and they say to even get out on bail you have to be Mexican or black. You don't even know how it is. . . . "

And I snap. "Are you calling me a liar?"

It's a night class, I'm tired, and I don't know why my statistics aren't good enough. Upon reflection, I understood that we were using different kinds of sources to support our claims, that neither of us was calm enough to reflect upon the strengths and limitations of his sources, and later, when we debriefed this moment, we both apologized for allowing the anger to escalate. In that later, we agreed that even when there are statistical trends, there are always exceptions, but that the statistical trends still matter, but that the exceptions still count, but. . . .

* * *

Searching, searching, searching for anything that will help me make sense of this feeling, that I know I'm going to burst, with pride, with sadness, with. . . . I'm at home now, after a long convocation ceremony. All the students had a minute to speak to the crowd of family and well-wishers:

"Gracias mamá, y Isabel, y Yazmín."

"I guess I just want to thank God because, with Him (and my mom and dad's help), all things are possible."

"I'd like to thank all the professors behind me here tonight, but especially Dr. Fassett. She was the first person I met when I came to San José State, and I wasn't sure I could do it. But she said. . . . "

They went on and on, thanking family and friends, thanking different members of the faculty, thanking people they've lost over the years for all their support. And I didn't know what to do. I'm not religious, but I felt blessed. For every faculty meeting I've bitched about, for every quarrel I've had with a colleague, for every time I felt like I was getting screwed by the state on salary or workload, at that moment I felt blessed. I wouldn't choose another career.

This wasn't even my first graduation. Those were easier; I didn't know anyone very well then, and though I'm a crier, I could sit through those hours dry-eyed. But now I know people, I've seen frosh graduate with master's degrees, I've seen people lose family or give birth—both to children and theses; I've not made friends exactly, but I've found community and made connections, however brief.

How do I get at this experience of pride, of pain, of love, of hope? Will "The Effects of Student Verbal and Nonverbal Responsiveness on Teacher Self-Efficacy and Job Satisfaction" (Mottet, Beebe, Raffeld, & Medlock, 2004) get at this sense of how it feels to know I've made a difference? Will "Immediacy in the Classroom: Student Immediacy" (Baringer & McCroskey, 2000) account for why I wish our community could continue, deepen, grow even when it most likely won't? Will "The Relationship of Perceived Teacher Caring With Student Learning and Teacher Evaluation" (Teven & McCroskey, 1997) help me understand what it is about me that makes for that lasting, enduring connection beyond the class or the semester?

* * *

Searching, searching, searching for examples of interdisciplinary work, work that draws together critical theory and instructional communication. I'm serving two masters, neither of whom I know very well. Each wants something from me; each is dissatisfied. If I challenge racism or sexism or homophobia, I risk being too critical, too biased for the interpretive scholars, and if I fail to call out these injustices, then I'm not critical enough for critical scholars. On my left are researchers who remind me that it is important to remain objective, to pursue scientific inquiry in a dispassionate way, to break a complex phenomenon into its component parts so that we might understand precisely how it works. On my right are researchers who challenge me to take a stand, to see that I'm making a choice, to know that objectivity is an enabling fiction, but one that enables some and disables others; they suggest that complexity is inevitable, that rendering something simple might render it simply dead. I am caught between "scholarship" and "commitment," as though these must, by necessity, be two different goals.

I want to be a good researcher. I want to be a good teacher. But I feel cut off, isolated, incommunicado, spread thin by workload algorithms that treat my writing as a hobby, as something I can do in between my four classes and committee work and service to department and university. Those same algorithms will figure my tenure in numbers, numbers of articles published, numbers on my teaching evaluations. Where should I look, from whom should I seek counsel to not simply survive, but thrive in the next twenty or thirty years of my career? I search for articles and find "Models of Mentoring in Communication" (Buell, 2004), "An Examination of Academic Mentoring Behaviors and New Faculty Members' Satisfaction With Socialization and Tenure and Promotion Processes" (Schrodt, Cawyer, & Sanders, 2003), and "The Impact of Mentoring and Collegial Support on Faculty Success: An Analysis of Support Behavior, Information Adequacy, and Communication Apprehension" (Hill, Bahniuk, & Dobos, 1989). I need to learn to be a critical (appraising, unflinching, hopeful, creative, resourceful) advocate for myself and others. At the risk of seeming immature or unprofessional, I refuse to be compartmentalized. We all exist in this tension, whether or not we pretend otherwise. We all define "scholarly" and "commitment," but for some of us, these are inextricably intertwined. Advocacy is scholarship. Pedagogy is scholarship. Advocacy is pedagogy. Pedagogy is advocacy.

But, we aren't born to mentors, we don't find them lurking about, we make them. We author them, in the collusion between our needs and theirs, in ourselves and with one another.

Mentoring—Getting It, Right? Getting It Right

"Wait—what's the difference between comm ed and instructional comm again?"

"Uhh . . . the first is what we do and the second is . . . what we study?"

These are my students, graduate students in a seminar on communication pedagogy; we've just read Jo Sprague's work (1992, 1993)—her introduction of critical theory and critical pedagogy to the study of communication and instruction—and these students are grappling with the central idea of one of the writings.

Admittedly, I've set them to a difficult task: having read these pieces, they're to embody the central figures in the debate on critical vs. logical-positivistic study of instructional communication. Each student has a name tag: The usual suspects, like Jo Sprague, James McCroskey, and Patricia Kearney, but also bell hooks, Michel Foucault, Peter McLaren, and "community college debate coach," "high school teacher of speech and English," and "parent of an English-language-learning child" are in attendance this evening. They know I'll ask them to engage in discussion, perhaps even debate, over issues central to power and pedagogy, which will be a challenge, especially for the students I've cast against type. And so they're very concerned with reviewing their reading; I have the sense that most of them never thought to consider their particular author's or constituent's perspective before . . . that they have been moving through the course reading for content, for issues, but not for that sense of groundedness in individual commitments and goals. One is grappling with how Foucault, with his discerning eye for discipline and power, might have spoken to instructional communication scholars, while another is tacking back and forth between her understanding of Delpit's (1995) "culture of power" and her own experiences as a "generation 1.5" student to explore what this entire discussion might mean for parents whose children are marginalized in schooling.

But there's more to the difficulty of the task—a fact of which I'm acutely aware. Jo Sprague is, literally, in attendance this evening; she is sitting in a corner of the classroom, apart from everyone else, writing . . . seemingly everything . . . in a legal pad. Just as I can see this, so can these students, and Jo's presence has heightened their concern for getting everything just right. I wonder if I've gotten everything just right too. When I asked her to provide a peer evaluation, for my tenure dossier, of a course she designed and developed and that I'm in my second time teaching, I knew I was taking a risk. And, of all the nights she could have chosen to attend, Jo quite understandably chose an evening where her work was the primary topic of conversation—riskier still. Each time she taps her foot, each time she notes a phrase, each time she steels her facial expressions, I wonder whether I've gotten everything just right. And my students do the same.

While nervous, I have never felt such a sense of promise from a classroom activity. Everybody is perched, precarious—awaiting that moment where something will happen, where everything will come together or fall apart. We walk this line for nearly an hour and a half. Students are tentative, confused—"Sprague" offers: "I think that what 'I'm' saying in this piece is that we should consider the consequences of power. . . . " Students are playful and provocative—as when "Foucault" notes that he was addressing all these issues years before us and that we're all behind the times. And, much to my delight, students become involved in the personal politics behind our scholarship, that sense of snarling, barely suppressed disdain for perspectives unlike our own; they grapple with Buber's (1970/1996) I-it/I-thou in a professional sense, in their sense of professional work, respecting their academic forebears' passion at the same time they are annoyed at how important disciplinary ideas seem to emerge from irritation, as sand in an oyster produces a pearl. This discussion troubles their sense of scholarship, their sense that ideas are produced in smooth sophistication and detached calm; this is perhaps my favorite outcome: They will think twice about theory, about method, about onto-epistemic commitments; they will wonder from whence sprang a particular idea or assumption or value. But I know this isn't necessarily Jo's goal, and I can't help but think about how she feels—her work put to this end—as she sits in the corner of the class.

I haven't asked, but I know my students sense my own anxiety. They're caught in a moment of wanting to please me, and wanting to be right, and wanting to resist the activity itself; they're mad at me for putting them in this position, and perhaps a bit proud of me for finding a way to engage the class that draws from and extends our work with critical pedagogy theorists/practitioners like bell hooks, and perhaps a bit excited at the chance to go somewhere new in their time in class. I can't blame them. I'm angry too, angry because I put myself in this position; I'm frustrated because they haven't prepared better, which isn't entirely their fault; I'm hoping Jo will be proud of me for finding a clever, cheeky approach to teaching the issues present in her foundational work, but I'm also uncomfortably certain she'll find fault with my approach, my values, my efforts in this classroom.

* * *

When you're junior faculty, more senior, established scholars are quick to offer advice—some of it very welcome, like how to plan for early retirement or how to secure modest seed funding on campus, and some of it very unwelcome, like how to dress in an "appropriate" manner or how to show students who's boss (as strong teaching evaluations might suggest an unseemly friendship with students). Most take mentoring very seriously, and most mean well by their efforts. (And, so we're clear: Jo Sprague has always been a very supportive, professional, and kind mentor to me; even when we don't see eye to eye, I treasure her insights.) Recently, one of my colleagues, freshly tenured, observed it was so nice to see an established line of scholarship emerging from my work with graduate students. At first blush, I took his compliment at face value, proud to have someone senior discern and express regard for what I perceived to be important and typically overlooked service efforts. But—and perhaps it is the nature of junior faculty status to question compliments, to read for subtext and to act cautiously—I also mark, in that compliment, an undercurrent of questions: Are you pushing your own paradigm, engineering your own mini-mes, nurturing scholarship the field will not sustain, reward, or tenure?

I hear the questions even as I know my course reader is filled with scholarship the field is publishing and sustaining, however recalcitrantly, from Pelias's (2000) "The Critical Life" to Heinz's (2002) "Enga(y)ging the Discipline: Sexual Minorities and Communication Studies," from Cooks and Sun's (2002) "Constructing Gender Pedagogies: Desire and Resistance in the 'Alternative' Classroom" to Hendrix and Jackson's special issue of

Communication Education on gendered, racialized, and sexualized identities. I am part of a critical community, a chorus of voices growing in both volume and presence. One vision of the field is that Sprague's work (1992, 1993) helped give rise to and garner legitimacy for these questions that had been heretofore overlooked as "embarrassments to theory" (Hendrix, Jackson, & Warren, 2003); a review of *Communication Education* from 1992 until the present shows threads of critical scholarship, authors weaving works back and forth to create a rich, more complete tapestry of communication and pedagogy. For example, authors of critical race theory, in their efforts to engage pedagogy, have helped to lend depth and nuance to our collective understandings of culture, identity and power (e.g., Cooks, 2003; Giroux, 2003; Martin & Davis, 2001; Warren, 2001a, 2001b, 2003; Warren & Hytten, 2004). More voices will continue to join in the conversation.

On Joining the Community

"Pretentious and absurd. But well written." Our first efforts to join in the conversation met with mixed reviews. Each of us has stories of work we've attempted to place in journals like and including *Communication Education,* stories of editors torn between an enthusiastic supporter (a "revise and resubmit" or, perhaps, "accept with revisions") and an angry critic (somewhere between a "reject" and a "stop wasting my time"). Admittedly, many of our first attempts were characterized by the usual rhetorical limitations of critical theory: We went after other scholars as though we were killing snakes, beginning our pedagogical conversations on a more finely worded equivalent of "you know what's wrong with you?" It's much easier to deconstruct than to build, to criticize without a hopeful and generous sense of possibility; we wouldn't have appreciated the insinuations either.

And indeed, we don't—at a recent conference, we were sitting in the pub enjoying a conference beer or two when some former and current graduate students of ours joined us. As relatively new faculty members, we still marvel at the desire of students who actually want to talk to us. When a student approaches and notes s/he liked or used our work in a class paper, we blush, we dismiss our efforts because we are still so new to being known beyond our small group of friends and former graduate school colleagues. So here are these graduate students, awaiting us, pulling up chairs, gathering their brews and lighting their cigarettes, ready for our wisdom. And as performers in our own right, we step up—we ask them to position themselves carefully, to think contextually, to not begin with their own sedimented opinions, but to ask questions and listen. We do this because in their talk, in their excitement about this reading or that panel, they want to begin with "let me tell you what's wrong with you"—and we know this trap, we feel this trap, we have been caught in this trap and know the exclusion of feeling one believes s/he knows but no one listens; most often this exclusion is because s/he (I, we) haven't listened in the first place. Those moments of "let me tell you . . . " are often the result of not listening. Yet, here are the graduate students and we know they will need a place, a location to go to, a community they can build, trust and affirm. And while we, Deanna and John, may or may not be that community, we do know they will need to find one.

Perhaps one of the most refreshing moments of our academic careers occurred in those panels or email exchanges where we trade ideas about pedagogy and ideology with scholars who share common commitments (even if those ideas have divergent avenues or paths or processes). In those moments, we can think together, build ideas together, and imagine futures together. Looking for rewards from people who can't see beyond their own ideological short-sightedness will always produce disappointment, regardless of who they/we are or where they/we stand. The key, then, is to create community where you are, build alliances and hold on to others you know to be both thoughtful and humane.

And in this moment at the bar, with these students, we spend time—we welcome their ideas and plant seeds for collaborative efforts—plant suggestions about what it means to seek community where you can find it. Community is the lifeblood of critical work: If we displace collaboration in favor of "being right" or showing others how they are irretrievably wrong, we engage in violence; we reconstitute education, scholarship, and intellectual engagement as necessarily contentious, necessarily aggressive, necessarily dismissive. Instead, we must forge this community together; forging necessitates heat, requires conflict, but must also be tempered, by understanding, by curiosity and by respect.

2

Naming a Critical
Communication Pedagogy

Prologue: A moment, a turn of the phrase, an opportunity

"Why can't we talk through this, rather than around it?"

It was a simple critique of my course—even as it was coded and couched as anything but. That is, the critique wasn't supposed to be directed at me, but there, in a sense, was my body and in this moment, this turn of a phrase, I found myself looking at what I hoped to be an opportunity. The context doesn't matter as much as the phrase—put it in any context and it seems to work—the call for more talk about "it." Sometimes this question refers to "real issues" or "something real"—like a mystery novel, one searches for the whodunit, Professor Plum in the library with the candlestick. The mysterious "it" is illusive indeed, just beyond the reach of the fingertip, on the tip of the tongue, or perhaps in the back of the mind. Like if you just tried hard enough, you could find it, say it, know it, and call it what it is. Yet, the "it" escapes. Like the "real world," so romanticized in the contexts of these academic walls, one never has "it"—we desire to have "it" when we feel uncomfortable or disengaged. The student wanted "it" and his desire chafed against my frustration with illusions—I don't trust the "it" and suspect such desires are easy ways out of the conversation at hand.

"Why can't we talk through this, rather than around it?"

It was a simple critique of my course—the suggestion that I, in some diabolical scheme, had taken us astray, off topic, occluded their view and stolen precious time away from talking about the important stuff. This is the point of my classroom—to engender first the critique and second the opportunity to talk about these issues; I want them to struggle with the questions, the issues, the complex matrix of sex plus race plus gender plus class plus power plus. . . . I have worked to build this space, with their support, their questions, and, to some extent, their indulgence, to make this moment possible. I want them to discuss the "it" embedded in this student's question for, perhaps, the question of "it" is exactly the point they . . . we . . . need to address.

"Why can't we talk through this, rather than around it?"

My response: "Ok. Let's talk about that—let's begin with the assumptions that make such questions possible. Perhaps it's there that we might find out what we're even talking about."

* * *

In a sense, we have spent considerable time exploring what critical communication pedagogy is not: It is not exactly communication education, although a dedication to the communication classroom, as a point of analysis and examination, remains. It is also not exactly instructional communication, but the site of communication within classroom interaction continues. It is also not exactly critical pedagogy, even as we persist in our effort to maintain a critical orientation. Rather, critical communication pedagogy, as both a field of study and a pedagogical practice, is somewhere in the nexus of the overlapping areas of interest.

It is, perhaps, the tendency of critical educators to set forth their work as an agenda, in terms of a set of tenets or commitments that name, organize, and call for action. Even that critical educators should work toward agenda setting is consistent with their values; that other scholars, other researchers or scientists, do not seem to follow suit does not suggest a lack of advocacy or political vision or agenda setting on their parts, but rather a series of tenets or commitments that call for a different kind of (and language for) action (often couched in scientific method). In what follows, we draw attention to the interconnected commitments that constitute critical communication pedagogy, that connect it to and distinguish it from other scholarly areas of inquiry. We are drawn to commitments for their sense of duty, for the way they charge us with certain tasks and remind us of certain agreed upon (and often taken-for-granted) assumptions; commitments remind us that we have responsibilities, promises to keep. Promises are relational, we make them to and with one another. Like promises, commitments don't fall from the sky fully formed; we (re)create them in and through our work with others (in our classrooms, our offices, our journals, our families, and our communities). Here are the fundamental commitments that draw together critical communication educators:

Commitment 1: In critical communication pedagogy, identity is constituted in communication.

In their *Communication Education* special issue introduction, Hendrix, Jackson, and Warren (2003) report the results of their review of the journal, from its inception as *The Speech Teacher* until 2003: This area of study lacks "prolonged, systematic investigation of the influence of race or the interplay of multiple cultural identities in academic settings . . . [instead] we only see periodic sparks of light" (p. 177). Historically, the overwhelming majority of instructional communication research has emphasized a programmatic, positivistic approach to educational phenomena, identifying and situating in relation to each other (a) a variety of psychobehavioral constructs (such as communication apprehension or verbal aggression), and (b) seemingly stable or natural demographic factors or traits, such as race/ethnicity, gender, or sexuality. For example, one might study whether "at-risk" students (ostensibly students of color, students from working-class backgrounds) are more communicatively apprehensive than other students. Or, one might study whether students perceive GLBTQ (Gay, Lesbian, Bisexual, Transgendered, and Questioning) graduate teaching assistants as more or less credible than seemingly "straight" graduate teaching assistants. Doing so embraces the modernist promise of clarity and order; this approach works to carve complex communicative phenomena into discernable, isolable component parts, which are then subject to manipulation. And while there is value to this decontextualized, dispassionate approach, its relative dominance over instructional communication contexts has left us with an impoverished sense of how communication constitutes identity, power, and culture. In effect, "the continual (and repeated) pattern in [instructional communication] research constructs educational identities as static—identities only measured, graphed, and counted in order, ultimately, to be fixed—and such work inevitably narrows our understanding of these students [and teachers] and the needs they have, failing once again to truly listen to them. . . . Before we create students as 'communicatively apprehensive,' 'verbally aggressive,' 'compliant' or 'noncompliant,' or 'at-risk,' we would do well to consider how our own scholarly discourse elides our role in perpetuating the phenomena we study" (Fassett & Warren, 2005, pp. 253–254).

Critical communication educators look to postmodern and poststructural understandings of human identity, to senses of students and teachers as relational selves produced in collusion and collision, to theories and methodologies that help them account for identities as produced in cultural—and therefore inherently ideological—contexts. One possible direction is ethnomethodological, an understanding of human identity as accomplished (Fenstermaker & West, 2002; Garfinkel, 1967). In particular, ethnomethodologists study "situated conduct to understand how 'objective' properties of social life achieve their status as such" (West & Fenstermaker, 1995, p. 19). Rather than assuming an aspect of identity as given and simply enacted, ethnomethodologists call for us to observe that we create and sustain aspects of our identity in concrete, mundane activity (i.e., communication). This is to say, identity is not assigned at birth but rather made possible, accomplished, through communication; it is through repetition that this "communicative residue of assumptions and beliefs" (Fassett & Warren, 2005, p. 242) comes to seem natural or inevitable.

Another theoretical perspective that illuminates how identity is communicatively constituted is performativity. Scholars who embrace this perspective, such as Butler (1990b) and Warren (2001a, 2001b, 2003), advocate an understanding of identity as performatively accomplished—echoed in Butler's (1990b) claim that gender is "a stylized repetition of acts" (p. 270). For example, all the minute and mundane choices we each make—how we hold our books, how we phrase a question, how we form letters with a pen or pencil—create us as male or female, or as neither, or as someone in between. Warren's (2001a, 2001b, 2003) work extends Butler's observations regarding gender to a consideration of racial identity as performative accomplishment, which might, at first, seem a more difficult argument to make; yet even something as enduring as a person's particular skin tone is the result of day-to-day communicative actions (including, for example, prohibitions on interracial relationships).

For critical communication educators, interested in how best to engage the classroom (and research on the intersections between communication and classrooms) as a space for social justice and change, this shift in thinking about identity is not simply a change in language. If, as Freire (1992) observed, "changing language is part of the process of changing the world," then how we talk about identities shapes how we understand those identities, and, more importantly, the actions we take to respect the role of our communication, as researchers, in defining and obfuscating that process (p. 68). Calling out a more complex, nuanced understanding of identity as emergent from communication commits us to more complex and nuanced understandings of power, privilege, culture, and responsibility.

Commitment 2: Critical communication educators understand power as fluid and complex.

Because critical communication educators situate identity as relational, as emergent from (always already ideological) contexts, then they must, by necessity, understand power as similarly so. For example, when a student is described by her university as academically "at risk," a critical communication educator will no doubt raise a series of questions: What is the purpose and function of the label "at risk"? Who finds that discourse empowering? Or disenfranchising? Who is the author of this discourse, and who does it author? How does the student make sense of this expression? Does she understand herself to be "at risk?" Or, would it be more appropriate to say that a well-meaning institution has placed her at risk? An instructional communication scholar operating from within a positivist logic is likely to identify different aspects of this student's identity—for example, her race or ethnicity, her socioeconomic status, whether she is an English-language learner—and apply to her the cultural category of "at risk." However, the critical communication educator, committed to the perspective that these seemingly stable aspects of identity are residual and taken-for-granted as stable, will ask: What is it about the classroom's (or school's or teacher's or community's) culture that places this student at risk? Is it that she is African American in a university dominated by white, upper- or middle-class privilege? Is it that she is a woman in a field historically and discursively dominated by men? How does her identity as "at risk" emerge from the collision of multiple ideologies? How does the very expression "at risk" author the student in ways that privilege the institution, that privilege the scholars who invoke it, and disenfranchise her further? As Sprague (1992) challenges, "Does our current approach to scholarship have a liberating or dehumanizing effect on students and teachers?" (p. 5).

A point of illustration: Power in the classroom research (McCroskey & Richmond, 1983; Richmond & McCroskey, 1984; Kearney, Plax, Richmond, & McCroskey, 1984, 1985; McCroskey, Richmond, Plax, & Kearney, 1985; Plax, Kearney, McCroskey, & Richmond, 1986; Richmond, McCroskey, Kearney, & Plax, 1987) has a foundational place in the study of communication in the classroom. Indeed, it is an established line of instructional communication scholarship, along with other constructs such as communication apprehension, teacher immediacy behaviors, teacher efficacy, and verbal aggression. Working to serve the classroom teacher, by helping her or him put communication toward effective classroom management, this line of research draws out behavioral alteration techniques (BATs) and behavioral alteration methods (BAMs). These techniques and messages help clarify the complexities of power, in part to help someone acquire skills s/he may not possess intuitively; through the effective application of BATs and BAMs, a teacher should be able to acquire her or his students' compliance. In other words,

> power, then, is seen as another tool that teachers have at their disposal to use wisely or poorly, but in the students' best interests to facilitate instructional goals. If a teacher is skilled in the selection of BATs and BAMs, and if the teacher displays the quality of *withitness*—a variable measured by the teacher's ability to deliver "desists" promptly and "on-target" to the right student immediately after the "deviant behavior" (Irving & Martin, 1982, pp. 314–315)— then one's classroom should be orderly. (Sprague, 1992, p. 15)

However seemingly neutral this work seems, though, it encourages an ideology of individualism (Sprague, 1992), and a vision of power as a "flat plane of disembodied practices and seemingly naturalized traits" (Wood & Fassett, 2003, p. 291).

In attempting to reduce power to a tool or skill set, instructional communication researchers have, in effect, cast student (or teacher) resistance as deviance, as decontextualized (mis)behaviors that, at first blush, may seem arbitrary or irrational. Such a perspective elides the ways students might have legitimate reasons for feeling and behaving as they do; moreover, such a perspective fails to call out the ways in which student resistance might be (dis)organized against an authority that objectifies them for the purposes of order and compliance. Critical communication educators bear the responsibility of exploring power and privilege, even—and especially—if that process implicates our own work as teachers and researchers.

Commitment 3: Culture is central to critical communication pedagogy, not additive.

Perhaps the most dangerous phrase I hear in my undergraduate communication criticism courses is that there is "too much culture stuff" in my materials. Because I choose texts that feature—indeed, centralize—various groups deemed by students as "cultural," I have been accused of drawing upon material irrelevant to the purposes of my class. That is, because I draw into the center the lives and experiences of people other than the white, straight student body in my classroom, my course and, by association, I am suspect. In times of growing pressure on education and teachers to remain "neutral," to strive for a "fair and balanced" approach, the location of culture (or, at least, the site of cultures not part of what Audre Lorde [1984, p. 116] would call the "mythical norm") is anything but apolitical. Recognizing and interrogating cultural as central to any classroom or curriculum is to complicate the tendency of positivist scholars to define that space as neutral and "objective."

* * *

Because we take identity to be complex, emergent, and relational, and because we take power to be fluid, omnipresent, and oft overlooked, critical communication educators take culture to be central to pedagogy and research regarding pedagogy. As all introductory communication studies textbooks teach, cultures are created, sustained, and altered in communication; that, in itself, is not an especially controversial notion. However, when students correctly discern culture to be imbued with ideology—what they think of as politics or values, and often values that fly in the face of their own assumptions and experiences—they react with frustration, anger, and pain. It is perhaps worth noting that many critical pedagogy scholars would consider this false consciousness, would suggest that students have been effectively duped into believing that their relatively privileged perspectives (or their belief in the value of certain state-sanctioned privileged perspectives—e.g., meritocracy or whiteness) are somehow apolitical, neutral, transparent. We would argue, however, that to assume this stance is as dangerous as suggesting power is a tool we can manipulate at will; it, too, suggests that students, in their resistance, are (mis)behaving irrationally. Lather (1991), in her critique of critical and feminist pedagogies, reminds us that an expression like false consciousness continues to author students in disempowering ways; it forecloses our ability to create transformative, generative spaces of dialogue with students. Though it might be tempting to tell ourselves that certain students are naïve or confrontational or even deluded, we must work to listen to our students, to understand why they consider some topics inappropriate or irrelevant, so that we and our students might more fully understand each other.

Commitment 4: Critical communication educators embrace a focus on concrete, mundane communication practices as constitutive of larger social structural systems.

Every time I chair a thesis to completion, I must attach a letter justifying the author's use of first-person voice. This is, I'm told, a formality, that no one has ever had her or his thesis returned as insufficiently scholarly, so long as there is this accompanying memo. Colleagues have explained that this is a battle I don't want to fight, that tenured professors have tried and failed to make changes to this policy more than a decade ago, that, as an assistant professor, I should maintain a low profile. They suggested I create some boilerplate about the value of first-person voice to my student's choice of research method, so as to limit the number of changes I'll have to make when I use the memo again . . . and again . . . and again. Revising this memo, year after year, is having an effect on me, though I can't say yet as to whether that effect is positive or negative, whether my growing frustration is productive or destructive. When I call up the file, I'm going through the motions, sucking it up, playing the game, accepting the hand I've been dealt . . . in short, I'm not who I want to be in that moment. What should be a simple gesture— get the file, change the name and the date, print it on letterhead, and hand it to the student—makes me a child, makes me a pet, makes me a bureaucrat (especially, I fear, in the eyes of the student who must then take it to the graduate school). In writing an "exception" for first-person voice—an exception for who the student is in the world and her or his choice of research methods—I (re)affirm that this is somehow less scholarly than other, perhaps more statistical, work. In my (in)action, I fail to challenge: Why not make the people who mask their choices, who excise every last trace of themselves from their work, account for their decision?

* * *

Conversational performance, as an area of study built on the analytical work of scholars like Emanuel Schegloff (1984) and Harvey Sacks (1989) and extended in work by Nathan Stucky (1988) and Bryan Crow (1988), studies, through conversational analysis (one sort of ethnomethodological method), the micro structure of every talk—finding patterned, logical, and systemic repetition within the taken-for-granted nature of daily interaction. Analysis in this vein might involve transcribing a 5-minute segment of talk using a highly stylized code that marks breaks in talk, overlaps, particles of laughter, pauses, and drawn-out or emphasized words. A very close reading of the transcript would demonstrate conversational norms leading to a (re)performance of the conversation that showed the analysis and commitment to the tape as recorded. A good friend of ours once described his love for conversational analysis in this way: "It is like sifting through sand with a fine comb; you can appreciate each unique crystal of sand, but also the similarities and repetitions in how the crystals organize themselves in nature." This is an elegant metaphor, one we're drawn to here because it underscores the importance of communication-centered analysis: the ability to look deep into the muscle of everyday life and see the fibers, the movement, and the invisible structures that make our everyday conversation possible (and are made possible in our everyday conversation). It is a method that shows how the concrete, mundane moments of our life work.

But such analysis choices do much more than point to the workings of everyday practices. As Victor Turner (1982) would note, our everyday rituals—those mundane and repeated moments of our lives—from wedding ceremonies to the craft of making a morning cup of coffee—work to (re)produce our sense of self. In Turner's words, ritual is "making, not faking"; that is, these everyday life experiences are not about simply displaying or pretending, but are, in themselves, acts of production (p. 93). Understanding ritual in all its vast detail is more than seeing patterns for the sake of seeing patterns; in identifying and analyzing the detail in the most concrete scenes, we are better able to understand how we function collaboratively to produce our social reality and render it meaningful. For critical communication educators, the value of analysis is that, through it, we might more readily discern that it is the mundane communication practices in our lives that work to make larger social systems possible.

When we fail to note happenings in the classroom (e.g., students' hands raised to ask questions, the presence of the teacher at the chalkboard, the nature and shape of the desks, the use of space and the regulation of movement) as mundane, taken-for-granted practices of communication that are often ignored as neutral or natural, we deny the lens of analysis that communication researchers can bring to the conversation. In effect, we ignore that it is in our communication practices that we produce knowledge, define how identities are negotiated and maintained, and imply that power is something only the powerful possess. If we do not engage communication as constitutive, if we continue to see communication as a mirror (however cloudy) for reality, we fail to see the mechanisms of production in the classroom. A critical communication pedagogy needs, relies, and benefits from research and analysis that begins in the site of our concrete, mundane communication practices, for it is in those moments that the social structure emerges.

Commitment 5: Critical communication educators embrace social, structural critique as it places concrete, mundane communication practices in a meaningful context.

Mary stands in my door with a look that can really only be described as confusion laced with subtle contempt. We have had a good working relationship—she was a great student in my classes, a great advisee, and, under my supervision, produced one of the best thesis projects I've read at my institution. Her work weaves personal experiences of sexism with the institutional pressures that serve to bind her; in one powerful part, Mary shares a complex narrative about her own relationship to body image, drawing on scholarship that talks about the raced, sexed, and weighted body in culture. Mary is a good student; yet, in this moment—when her look can really only be described as confusion laced with subtle contempt—I am faced with explaining why she must now carry my letter defending her choices to the graduate school. She looks down at my form letter defending the first person, the letterhead featuring the university seal, departmental stats, and my freshly inked signature. She is, of course, wondering about how this letter—this seemingly mundane, routine, ritualized communication moment—works with and against the logic of her scholarship and her study. I can't read her mind, but I suspect she is thinking about the sharp social critique featured in her thesis and the ways this letter works to marginalize that story—her story—even more. She knows the ways everyday practices work upon and in her body. She knows that the justification, the legitimizing gesture of this letter in her hand, will mark her work, both in the graduate school and in the field she hopes to enter. This form letter is not form for her—it is a highly politicized act in which social systems of academic and institutional norms—the weight of "social science"—crash down on her; her inevitable failure to make that particular grade will mean she (and others) will never really see the value of her effort.

"It's no big deal—just one last hurdle." Even as I say it, even as she heads off to the graduate school, even as I turn back to the other everyday lives and bodies scattered in the forms on my desk, I don't believe my own dismissal. Each time I repeat this sanction, I add to the institutional markings that work against my own scholarship. And what choice do I really have in this moment? Mary deserves to graduate and I deserve to get tenure for my work. Yet, the cost is real.

* * *

Given that we constitute ourselves in and through our communication, what better argument is there for extended and detailed study of everyday communication? Communication scholars are well versed in a variety of research methodologies (from conversation and discourse analysis to ethnography and participant action research) that are ideally suited to this task, to exploring how minute, often overlooked or taken for granted, performances create, sustain, and alter social phenomena. Autoethnography (also related to—and often conflated with—other areas of study, including autobiographical ethnography, the new ethnography, and performative writing) is one such method. There are an increasing number of autoethnographic writings in communication studies (Goodall, 2004; Jones, 1998; Pacanowsky, 1988; Pelias, 1999, 2000, 2004; Tillman-Healy, 1996; Warren & Fassett, 2002; Wood & Fassett, 2003) that effectively illuminate how the author is both product and producer of culture, how the author's very (in)actions create and sustain complex social phenomena, including how s/he understands identity, power, and culture. Communication studies scholars are ideally positioned for autoethnographic work, situated as we are at the nexus of performance, poetics, rhetoric, and methodology. Indeed, it is the autoethnographer's attention to the makings of everyday life that demonstrates the power of examining personal experiences in order to understand culture—it is through the everyday, argue the autoethnographers, that we can explore our own roles in making the social structures that bind us.

Perhaps most scrutinized are autoethnographers' efforts to draw in readers, to engender their empathy, to write research as evocative and provocative pedagogy. Ellis's (1995) *Final Negotiations: A Story of Love, Loss, and Chronic Illness* points to this central value of autoethnographic work: It reveals something all our other methods together cannot. Its value is in how it creates contrast, in how it illuminates our decisions as researchers, readers, and writers. Another example of autoethnographic research is Corey and Nakayama's (1997) groundbreaking (and extremely controversial) essay "Sextext." In this essay, Corey and Nakayama attempt to talk about desire by writing desire; this is to say, their essay creates desire, of a particular kind, and asks the reader to participate in that sensation. The subject of many academic arguments about legitimacy (Gingrich-Philbrook, 1998; Gray, 1998; Kellett & Goodall, 1999), the topic of this particular autoethnography (and, as a result, all autoethnography as method) remains a hotly debated issue. The critics of this form of research are many (e.g., Parks, 1998; Shields, 2000; Wendt, 1998). The very question of whether autoethnography is sufficiently scholarly illuminates the assumptions each of us in the academy (whether student or professor) holds about what matters, about what's real. Autoethnography as a research method is a contested space of whether we seek truth or truthfulness and about what constitutes either. This is not to suggest that people who rigorously and thoughtfully use other research methods fail to be critical, nor is it to suggest that autoethnography should dominate critical research on classroom communication. However, it is to suggest that these choices, and how we communicate these choices to our students and colleagues, are mundane and reiterative, and they constitute the values and politics and people of our discipline.

What does this discussion of method tell us? How does it inform this commitment within critical communication pedagogy? Our use of method in research is to point to specific ways of thinking, ways of seeing, ways of framing what counts as effective approaches to our work in researching communication in the classroom. Critical communication educators seek to place discussions of mundane communication practices (i.e., grades, research methods, test taking, and the like) within—always, without exception, within—institutional and social setting contexts. For instance, autoethnography, taken out of context, may not measure up to particular markers for scholarship; as a personalized, narrative approach to research, it cannot typically meet, for example, the criterion for generalizability to larger audiences. Of course, if a scholar's goal is to locate and create emotional connections and complex portraits of a self in culture, then the statistical essay—however reliable and valid—will inevitably miss the mark as well. However, any examination of institutional practices (irrespective of method) must reflect the local and immediate context of members' experiences and situate those experiences in relation to larger social (cultural, economic, historical) circumstances for it to be critical communication pedagogy.

Even our most routine interactions with others, whether providing students with conciliatory letters for the graduate school or offering another account of power in the classroom research in order to make observations about the importance of understanding power as distributed and fluid, are reproductive—of relationships, of institutions, of disciplines. In learning what is (and is not) our discipline, not only are we disciplined by others, but we discipline ourselves; it is careful analysis of this interplay that characterizes critical communication pedagogy.

Commitment 6: Language (and analysis of language as constitutive of social phenomena) is central to critical communication pedagogy.

Perhaps this commitment feels most profound when we are reading students' writing. Or, perhaps more accurately, when we are explaining why a student's choice to use one term instead of another has suggested her or his incomplete or inaccurate understanding of a concept, resulting in a grade the student disputes. We might, for instance, call out how "reflective" and "reflexive" are not the same (the first suggests a mirroring or accounting of the past, while the second suggests an important motion, back and forth, between one's actions and how those implicate one in social phenomena), or that "pedagogy" is not just a fancy way of saying "teaching" (that "teaching" calls forth assumptions about someone who provides information for students to learn, while "pedagogy" is more open and potentially dialogic, potentially subversive and suggestive of other ways of being in the classroom). In arguing for "plurivocity" in our scholarship, Langsdorf (1994) argues that "there surely are more characteristics assertable of experiencing a lunging tiger, an unfolding sunset, a starving child" (p. 6). Poignantly, she reminds us to consider the possibilities that surround any assertion, that our assertion masks any number of other, possible assertions, and that we must make space for multiple readings. This is to say that particular selections of words create particular worlds; moreover, each selection of words, each world, implies other possible words, other possible worlds.

An example: Each of us fought writing and the languages of our dissertations. You might be able to anticipate some of these, for example: simply not wanting to write, both dreading and desiring feedback from our advisers, and struggling with learning communication studies discourse and making it our own (getting our minds used to expressions like "purposive convenience sampling" or "the extant literature reveals" or "interviewees were asked a series of seven questions"). But we also struggled with the process of naming, of invoking terms we did not accept or want to perpetuate. John struggled with definitions of method: Did he do "critical ethnography" or "performative ethnography"? He did not want to suggest that discourse—the verbalizing of ideologies and the reiteration of languaged norms—is dispassionate or aloof, somehow divorced from the ways ideas play a role upon and within our bodies. This became most clear when writing his research upon graduation; in an article for *Communication Education* (Warren, 2001b), he described his approach to ethnography as critical, but in an article for *Western Journal of Communication* (Warren, 2001c), he made the case that he was engaged in performance ethnography. This was the same data set from the same study, but he resisted a simple naming of his method—the method section itself eliding the ways ideological commitments influence, shape, and conflate a variety of methods and methodologies. Deanna struggled with naming as well, fighting her dissertation for years; though she'd learned about communication studies approaches to (the possibility or likelihood of) educational failure, she did not want to write "an at-risk dissertation." She did not want to continue to participate in naming students as such. In classes on "special student populations" and "communication needs of the at-risk student," she learned to discern different metaphors for educational failure; each metaphor, whether deficit oriented or resistance oriented, called out researchers' assumptions. Each new naming made possible new understandings of the experience; most poignant were students' own namings of their experience (namings that emerged from their own metaphors). Juxtaposing these namings, placing them in tension, helped illuminate the contest between them, helped illuminate the contested spaces, the conflict in voices, in communication pedagogy.

*Commitment 7: Reflexivity is an essential
condition for critical communication pedagogy.*

Discerning how our communication, our performances and our language, creates who we are and defines our work as teachers and researchers is a reflexive act. It is not simply an act of reflection, an ordering of what was said when and to whom, but rather a process of reflexion, an ongoing effort to call out, to illuminate the (re)creation of our selves, our values, assumptions, and practices. Reflexivity refers to the interrogation of the self—the locating of the authoring self in research or teaching, working to understand how that subject comes to be and who that subject authors in return (Warren & Fassett, 2002). Reflexivity locates the (re)construction of identities in the eye/I of the person who discerns them. Consider Melvin Pollner's (1991) call for "referential" or "radical" reflexivity:

> In the reflexive mode . . . the primordial suppositions and practices allowing for the constitution of the very field or domain of study become the phenomena, with the full recognition that whatever is produced is itself an 'achievement'— including, of course, the characterization of them as an achievement. (p. 379)

This is to say, reflexivity is the process of exploring how we, as teachers and researchers, create the phenomena we observe, through our assumptions, values, past experiences, language choices, and so on. An analogy may clarify: Engaging in reflexivity is like constantly twisting around and around in the mirror, seeking glimpses of the small of your back; you know it's there, it undergirds your action, but it is very difficult to apprehend unless it causes you pain, someone helps you see it, or you're particularly flexible.

Pollner's call for reflexivity involves more than just understanding the ground from which we speak—it is more than a paragraph in every monograph or classroom lecture stating our childhood memories of our subject and how that brought us to our positions. Reflexivity is not something we do, but something we practice, not an end result, but rather a process; reflexivity is not simply about ourselves, but about locating ourselves in relation to the phenomena we investigate. Reflexivity is the critical communication educator's ethical relationship to or with the phenomena and participants of our scholarship, whereby we situate knowledge, locating it in temporal, personal, and sociopolitical contexts that extend, enrich and seek out multiple readings of our work.

*Commitment 8: Critical communication
educators embrace pedagogy and research as praxis.*

As with "reflection" and "reflexion," the distinction between "practice" and "praxis" merits our careful consideration. Most casual understandings of "praxis" take it to be theory and practice intertwined: Without action, what good is theory? Without theory, how might we take informed action? Both "reflexivity" and "praxis" connote process—an important reminder—and neither is a destination or an end result. Perhaps most relevant for our work as critical communication educators is Freire's (1970/2003) definition of praxis, which calls for teachers (teacher-students) and students (student-teachers) to reflect and act together, collaboratively, in order to transform the world. But it is essential to note that, in our desire to improve on the human condition, we must not take that action *on* others, *for* others, or *to* others; a pedagogy of the oppressed, in the Freirean sense, is work undertaken together, *with* one another, to improve our collective lot in life, to work toward what Freire described as our ontological vocation, our reason for being: to become "more fully human" (p. 44). That is to say, our reason for being is "to be a Subject who acts upon and transforms his [or her] world and in so doing moves toward ever new possibilities of fuller and richer life individually and collectively" (Shaull, 2003, p. 32).

Central to critical communication pedagogy is its commitment to pedagogy as praxis, to teachers and students working together to locate and name the taken-for-granted in pedagogical contexts, to decenter normative readings of a given phenomenon, experience, or idea. This occurs through an emphasis on multiple readings, readings that deconstruct and challenge preestablished, seemingly inherent theoretical or phenomenological stability. For example, in embracing performativity (Butler, 1993) as a conceptual lens, we shift from an understanding of the subject as a product—stable and fixed—to an understanding of the subject as a process—continually (re)created in relation, in communication. But this conceptual shift is not just about the work we do or the concepts we foreground and engage as scholars, it also challenges us to (re)consider the nature of our own lives as subjects in general. In our classrooms, when we work with students to understand the nature of racial or gendered or sexual identity, it is to more fully understand how our most mundane and (un)intentional (in)actions make us complicit in racism, sexism, or homophobia; we work to understand how racism, sexism, homophobia, and other oppressions are not simply fully formed and given to us, but rather something we create and sustain through communication. Pedagogy as praxis is working with others to examine the possibilities implicit in constitutive theories of communication; it is to suggest that if we build our identities in contest and collusion with one another, if we create our pains and pleasures in communication, then perhaps we can interrupt those processes and shape them anew in meaningful ways.

Equally central to critical communication pedagogy is its commitment to research as praxis, to working with others (i.e., colleagues and co-investigators, community members, research participants) to locate and name, reflexively, the taken-for-granted in theoretical and methodological contexts, to decenter our own normative readings of given phenomena, research participants, or possible outcomes or actions that might follow from our work. Critical communication pedagogy is explicitly reform oriented; researchers in this vein aim to change our world for the better. But please note: This is not a mandate for researchers to do as they see fit, to engage in some act of false generosity, whereby they would, yet again, assume authority for how the world, how our lives, ought to be. As Lather (1991) charges us, we must work toward research with the people whose lives might profit or lose most by our collective efforts.

Commitment 9: Critical communication educators embrace—in their classrooms and in their writing, within their communities, and with their students, research participants, and co-investigators—a nuanced understanding of human subjectivity and agency.

As we described earlier, ethnomethodology strives to "analyze everyday activities as members' methods for making those same activities visibly-rational-and-reportable-for-all-practical-purposes, i.e., 'accountable,' as organizations of commonplace everyday activities" (Garfinkel, 1967, p. vii). That is, ethnomethodology strives to identify the sense-making process involved in a given act or set of acts. Embracing this perspective involves believing that others' behaviors are purposeful and logical, even if that logic is not readily apparent. In critical communication pedagogy, this means we acknowledge that those with whom we interact have important or formative reasons for how and why they engage in everyday actions as they do. This is to say, people are not "judgmental dopes," duped by and unaware of their participation in oppressive social systems, but instead subjects in their own right, subjects who author and render sensible their experiences in ways that are meaningful to them. Awareness of this is especially important in conversations regarding culture or power where we may find ourselves or others engaged in classist, heterosexist, racist, or sexist discourse; in order to work together to examine and perhaps undermine those power structures (those power structures we build, the acts of building that elide our participation in those structures), we must not move to critique the action without understanding how they and we, as subjects, make sense of how we came, over time, to value or perhaps accept those actions as normal or inevitable. This is why Freire (1992) asks us to remember that critical pedagogy is not just a language of critique or deconstruction, but also a language of change, hope, growth and community.

In other words, we cannot, as scholars, begin to engage others (whether our colleagues, communities, families, or students) in a conversation that begins, "You know what's wrong with you?" When a student says she is offended by bell hooks's (1994) assertion that white women continue to struggle with forging lasting alliances with women of color, when that student argues that, as a white woman, she has never "kept help" or personally oppressed women of color, when that student dismisses hooks's assertion as fallacious opinion, we may be tempted to show that student how she is deluding herself, how she engages in considerable discursive work that effectively blinds her from recognizing her investment in whiteness (and a particular, liberal, progressive vision of "the good white person," someone who, as Thompson, 2003, suggests, has friends who are women of color and believes that people of all races and ethnicities are, or should be, equal). It is well within our power, as educators, to tell that student how she is acting and how she should act instead; it is well within our power, as educators, to tell her what ideology she should embrace and that she will face consequences if she fails to do so. We might accept this as one possible vision of teaching, but it is not critical communication pedagogy.

There is no one critical communication pedagogy, but rather a series of commitments that give rise to unique and local practices, moments, collaborations. But, respecting the centrality of communication to both oppression and liberation, respecting that knowledge is not given but rather built and made meaningful in relationship, respecting that seemingly stable assumptions and values are patterned and enduring (and thus cannot change in an instant), and respecting that every single person works very hard (in reflective and unreflective ways) to assemble a meaningful life from a bricolage of contradictory and confusing experiences, means the teacher cannot author (or, perhaps more accurately, write off) that student as misguided, deluded, or irrational. Because we strive to explore communication in discerning and careful ways, we must engage that student (and her colleagues) in a dialogue: How does hooks's writing name her experience? How does it fail to capture that experience fully? Who might find hooks's assertion compelling? How does hooks's writing name their experience? What experiences might lead you to your assessment? What experiences might others bring to their reading of hooks? How might those experiences lead to multiple readings? What are the different consequences those readings bring to bear and for whom? If we accept hooks's assertion, what might that mean for our work in classrooms? What might that mean for our work as researchers? What are the consequences of dismissing hooks's perspective outright and for whom? Your dialogue with this student needn't incorporate all these possible questions, and, you (and this student) would have no doubt considered other relevant questions as well. What is important about dialogue is not that we see it as dispassionate, as politically or culturally neutral (to do so would elide all the ways we are products and producers of institutions and roles), but rather, that we explore dialogue for what it is: the communicative construction of knowledge, collaborative reflection and action upon the world in order to transform our understandings of the world. What is important, in this instance, is that we recognize that this student is engaged in authoring herself (as feminist, as progressive, as antiracist) in relation to the texts she is reading and the conversations she is having; to short-circuit or circumvent that process is to disempower her.

Commitment 10: Critical communication educators engage dialogue as both metaphor and method for our relationships with others.

Critical communication educators are drawn to the notion of dialogue as metaphor for our interactions with others because of the collaboration it implies; because of our commitments, we work toward a reflexive relationship with others (where we see ourselves as working in concert with others rather than lecturing to or studying others). This is consistent with Freire's (1970/2003) understanding of dialogue:

> the encounter between men [and women], mediated by the world, in order to name the world. Hence dialogue cannot occur between those who want to name the world and those who do not wish this naming—between those who deny others the right to speak their word [their beliefs about reflection and action] and those whose right to speak has been denied them. (p. 88)

It is important to note that power, in Freire's example, is not simply assigned to the professor (the teacher, the researcher, or some other seemingly powerful someone). As each of us, as members of human society, is aware, anyone may attempt to deny someone else's naming of the world. A dialogue is characterized by open acknowledgement of each person's naming of the world, though that acknowledgement need not imply acceptance. So, for example, a student might not agree with the instructor that identities emerge in communication; she may, instead, believe her identity to be an extension of the soul, as something given at birth and not achieved. A professor does not serve this dialogue by proving to the student that she is wrong; by focusing on proving her wrong, by showing her that she has been duped by a particular collection of ideologies, this professor engages in violence. This sense of dialogue is very similar to Buber's (1970/1996) in that this dialogue is an act of love, an effort to maintain one's own commitments while remaining open to the other (Spano, 2001). For Buber, "Love is responsibility of an I for a you. . . . Relation is reciprocity" (pp. 66–67).

This reciprocity does not extend to false generosity, however. Freire (1970/2003) cautions us against paternalism, against a responsibility that suffocates and further dehumanizes the oppressed by doing and thinking for them. Freire argues that, for critical educators,

> dialogue characterizes an epistemological relationship. Thus, in this sense, dialogue is a way of knowing and should never be used as a tactic to involve students in a particular task. We have to make this point very clear. I engage in dialogue not necessarily because I like the other person. I engage in dialogue because I recognize the social and not merely the individualistic character of the process of knowing. (Freire & Macedo, 1995, p. 379)

This notion of dialogue as epistemic is key to critical communication pedagogy, given our emphasis on communication as constitutive of identity, culture, and power and given our commitment to humans as Subjects, authors of meaning. So, while false generosity affirms domination, so too does unquestioning acceptance of worlds we believe to be harmful to ourselves or others. We are always already oppressors and oppressed (Freire, 1992); our efforts at praxis must be, therefore, concerned with exposing and creating generative spaces to work with one another in naming our social, material circumstances and acting together to change them. To this end, "dialogue cannot exist without humility . . . faith in people is an *a priori* requirement for dialogue" (Freire, 1970/2003, p. 90). It is presumptuous to assume we hold authority over someone else's experience, that we know more about it than s/he does. Dialogue is not a matter of negotiation and not a process of friendship building, though both may occur; it is a process of sensitive and thorough inquiry, inquiry we undertake together to (de)construct ideologies, identities, and cultures.

Because this final commitment emerges from and builds upon the other nine, this bears repeating:

> Interpreting other peoples' actions has a moral dimension: such interpretations are social acts that take place in a dialogical situation in which the interpreter accepts responsibility for the accuracy and consequences of her interpretations. Only if we are willing to allow their beliefs to call ours into question can we enter into a dialogue that is sufficient to garner the evidence necessary to interpret their way of life. This same moral responsibility may involve criticizing ourselves and others, as well as proposing new possibilities of interpretation. (Bohman, 1991, p. 218)

Commitment to critical communication pedagogy is predicated on the significance of human communication as constitutive, as the means to produce, maintain, and interpret our worlds. And, when worlds collide, when we must speak across what may feel like profound ideological difference, we look to dialogue—to loving inquiry and unflinching self-reflexivity—to render that difference meaningful and (re)act, in relation, to it.

Implications: Living the Commitments of Critical Communication Pedagogy

In classrooms, the teacher is open for students' assumptions, students' questions, and students' critique. Teachers are texts—students and colleagues read their bodies for weakness and cruelty, for race, gender, and sexuality, and for any sign of deviance (Bordo, 1993). I remember my own studenting behaviors—my own eyes peering at teachers, wondering about the lives they led outside the room and time we shared. In high school, I had a Spanish teacher who refused to stand during the pledge of allegiance—we always wondered why that was the moment he chose to resist (was it for religious reasons? cultural? political?). Another teacher in high school we all assumed to be gay: Her mannerisms, her body language, her choices were ours to critique. In college, a professor always came to class late, his beet-red face suggesting to us that he drank too much. In each instance, I participated in the reading of teachers and, now that I occupy the once-mystical location of teacher, I am certain that I, too, am read by my students, my own body a text for assumptions and charges of deviance. And sometimes I suspect they're right.

My body, in the decade since I began teaching, has been a target. Secure in my marriage, I have had the luxury of pretending that student readings of my body as sexually suspect are just inaccurate; however, I know that sexuality is anything but an either/or. Recently, I've become rather accepting of terms like "queer" or "bi" precisely because they seem to fit me more accurately; in these terms, I've discovered a kind of freedom that does not restrict or place unnecessary boundaries on my own desire, but rather allows me a freedom to accept myself for who I am. It is a freedom I have grown to need. However, this said, I have found it difficult to articulate this in my classroom; how should this identity—this way of seeing myself—affect my pedagogy?

Recently, I taught a gender communication class; the focus of my approach is to examine gender as a communicative accomplishment. In this course, we work to name common assumptions about gender and its taken-for-granted status in our culture. For many students, this means letting go of a number of formative assumptions about gender, including biological determinism, and heteronormativity. Historically, biologically, and socially, our collective assumptions about gender are outmoded, but the point here is that I decided, as a male professor of this class, that the best way to play with, to complicate, gender, was to occupy a position of sexual ambiguity (Warren & Fassett, 2004). That is, my sexuality became a question—I forced it to be a question so students would have to read this text, this body, my body, as a question mark and not a stable, easily recognizable, and comforting period. And for a while it worked; my use of "partner" rather than "wife," my use of queer texts and readings on queer issues made students wonder about me, question me. I could see it in their faces.

One day, we were talking about gender and language; I was trying to help them see the power of forms of address and how gender is encoded and regulated through naming. The perfect example was of my own partner who, while working in a high school, was marked specifically because of her gender. While making her security name badge, the front desk assistant asked a fairly simple question: "Are you a Miss or a Mrs.?" My partner, quick on the uptake and sensitive to the issues at stake in such a seemingly innocent question, replied: "I prefer Ms." The assistant examined her left hand and replied, "Ah! You're a Mrs.!" and, without debate, my partner's name card, a visible document that hung around her neck for the duration of her time at that school, framed and shaped her identity there. So I used the example; I used it to frame our talk of gender as production because it was such a vibrant and clear instance of the power of naming.

After class, one of my students, Joe, approached me; all semester long, he had been perhaps the most resistant to the underpinnings of the course, the most suspicious of me as a professor, the most suspicious of me as a sexually ambiguous professor.

"Professor?"

"Yes?"

"I wanted you to know that I just don't agree with all this stuff—it makes me uncomfortable."

"The power of language? Really? That seems to be central to communication studies. What is it about that idea that bothers you?"

"No—the gay stuff. I just think it's all wrong. Those people make me sick."

By the time Joe got to "Those people make me sick," I admit I was more than a bit stunned. I mean, could he have so easily discarded my performance in class—the complex, ambiguous identity I'd so carefully rehearsed? Was he really willing to assume that the mention of my partner's gender makes me a confidant, an ally? Or was this performance more about his own (in)security—his own outing? And how should I have responded to this moment? How could I have responded? Should I have said, "Well, sorry

I make you sick. You're no treat either. Good day to you." I could have, I guess, but that seemed too easy, too simple, for this moment.

I opted instead to explore the source of his concern—once I'd shot down all the reasons, he finally settled on religion. I noted the mixed messages on sexuality, reminding him of earlier classes where we learned that "gay" and "straight" are relatively new historical identities, not at all relevant in earlier times or across cultures. He refused to engage, talking of sin and casting stones (from his carefully crafted and protected glass house, I suppose). In the end, he left and I never told him that my own body bears the bruises of his stones. But seeing his panic, I felt sad for him, sad for his overwhelming need to claim an unequivocally antiqueer location, so I let this one go. Perhaps I missed an opportunity. Perhaps I sought to protect myself, gathering stones in the garden behind my own glass house.

How do you understand this story? Is it too personal—have I said too much? Do you need hard facts, prevailing trends to garner its significance? Does it bother you that I have an agenda for my courses? Do you think that agenda is too edgy, too political? Do you think I'm just replacing one ideology with another? Is it ever possible *not* to replace one ideology with another? Do you think I let Joe off the hook too easily? Should I have spent more time with him? Should I have gone out for a Coke with him, chatted with him a bit about how we make each other sick? Do you think I let myself off the hook too easily? That perhaps, in gathering stones, I walled myself in? That perhaps I should spend more time with Joe, learn from him so that he might learn more from me? In what ways do you think I've made good on my promises? Do I still have promises to keep? To whom? To Joe? To myself? To you?

* * *

This chapter is about living the commitments that guide our vision for critical communication pedagogy. It is about establishing that, while critical communication pedagogy might be about opposition (opposition to methods we feel leave us wanting, opposition to ideological underpinnings that we sense are untenable, opposition to groundless claims and baseless labels), it is also about hope, about committing ourselves to a way of engaging in educational practice that matters and educational research that suggests we can and must work together toward a better tomorrow.

We attempt to articulate critical communication pedagogy because we believe separating "power" from "identity" is not as easy as we'd like it to be. Inevitably, pedagogy is a nexus of both, from the moment we learn to smile at our caregivers to the last ballot for school board we cast. The choices we make about education, the identities and power relationships we constitute in our (in)actions, matter. As Foucault (1977) reminds us, we all feel power's effects (as a system of moral and physical discipline) in our lives, in our bodies:

> But we can surely accept the general proposition that, in our societies, the systems of punishment are to be situated in a certain "political economy" of the body: even when they do not make use of violent or bloody punishment, even when they use "lenient" methods involving confinement or correction, it is always the body that is at issue. (p. 25)

The body, where identity meets the politics, the assumptions, the policing of the other, remains the site of power's enactment, where disciplinary mechanisms play out in our flesh, our hearts, and our minds. We articulate a critical communication pedagogy because, left opaque, we fail to hold accountable educational practice, and, as a result, we fail to fully examine education as an agent of social, structural change and possibility.

Consider Foucault's most cited premise from *Discipline and Punish,* his analysis of the panopticon—the architectural image of a prison guard tower that draws its force primarily from inmates' fear of and desire for being watched. In an interview following the publication of his book, Foucault describes the panopticon as follows:

> The principle was this: A perimeter building in the form of a ring. At the center of this, a tower, pierced by large windows opening onto the inner face of the ring. The outer building is divided into cells each of which traverses the whole thickness of the building. These cells have two windows, one opening on to the inside, facing the windows of the central tower, the other, outer one allowing daylight to pass through the cell. All that is then needed is to put an overseer in the tower and place in each of the cells a lunatic, a patient, a con-vict, a worker, a school boy. The back lighting enables one to pick out from the central tower the little captive silhouettes in the ring of cells. In short, the principle of the dungeon is reversed; daylight and the overseer's gaze capture the inmate more effectively than darkness which afforded after all a sort of protection. (Foucault, 1980, p. 147)

This structure, so apparent in large lecture halls with fixed chairs and the silhouette of the professor who is able at any moment to identify the bodies of inmates/students who are disruptive, easily manages bodies and requires they conform in/to/with the institution's power. Of course, this structure, like all of Foucault's work on discipline, relies on the idea of repetition; with-out the expectation of surveillance, the disciplinary structure would never work. In Foucault's argument, the guard need not be present in the tower at all—it is the threat of him or her that produces power. Such threat is affirmed and sustained through lived experience, the knowledge that, in the past, such threats have resulted in punishment. In the lecture hall, the teacher need only mark her or his authority a few times before it is the threat of admonishment that produces the effect of power s/he desires. In this way, power, for it to reproduce, must be ongoing, cyclical, repeated.

It is, of course, power's repetitive nature that creates the disciplined subject—that body/person who conducts herself or himself in institutionally desired ways. Consider, for example, the student in the lecture hall: What kind of behavior is the desired effect of power in the setting? Quiet? Responsive? Notetaking? Respectful? How do we know what kinds of behavior are rewarded? We learn this through tradition—in the repeated celebration of "good students" and the "correction" of "problem students." For effective discipline, one must be able to trust in the repetition of these norms or types. The result is a kind of subjectivity—a type of person who works to produce the communication, the behaviors, the attitudes we desire.

The power of education (and, indeed, communication) to do this—to make the selves in our classroom—represents what inspired us to write this book. As students and teachers in education, we feel the reading, the marking that occurs (on us and in us) each day we enter that door, each time we take up the chalk and begin to address our students, each time we think to write about our experiences with education. And rather than acquiescing quietly, or leaving the profession in frustration, or ignoring the implications of our work in the classroom as we go about the decontextualized and sterile research that could potentially sustain our lives in the academy, we take a stand here; we lay our cards on the table and say we believe we have a strong hand, that this way of viewing the world has both merit and hope. We demonstrate that these commitments, while not easy and certainly not the norm in our educational experiences, constitute critical communication pedagogy as a humanizing vocation.

3

Critical Communication
Pedagogy in the Classroom

anguage names our reality—even where our most introductory
textbooks fall prey to representational understandings of language
(the old saw, "language is abstract, arbitrary, and ambiguous"), we can
recognize instances where language isn't simply representational. We bristle
when we hear our students retort "But that's just a word" or "If the author
means 'teaching,' then why not just say that?" or "'Handicapped' or 'person
with a disability'—same difference—one's just more 'PC' than the other."
Sometimes it's their tone that makes us bristle—our felt sense that they think
we're wasting their time or playing games—but more to the point, it's that
the words we use really do matter. Words do more than state fact, do more
than engender meaning; words make experiences real. They may do this in
revelation or obfuscation, by clarifying the truth or by masking it. Most
upsetting to hear from students and colleagues is "the real world," as in,
"When I get out into the real world, what will this mean for me?" or "This
would never work in the real world" or "There are a lot of real-world appli-
cations for this theory." Implicit in this talk is the suggestion that what
happens in the classroom, even that what we do as researchers, is a "false
world," a world without import or consequence. Perhaps this is the result of
educators' own efforts to create "safe" places for dialogue and sharing; perhaps students feel these spaces are a "time-out" from more competitive or
divisive arenas. But a "time-out" is not the same thing as a "false world."

The notion that what happens in the classroom isn't real is intriguing,
especially given how often we cite former teachers or classroom experiences

as central to our growth as individuals or leaders or community members. One of our earliest means of socialization is the classroom; it is one of the first places where we confront difference in all its forms. In this space we are judged, by teachers and peers, on our effort, our citizenship, and our competence. We "raise" egg babies and drop them from the roof of the school to see whether the shelters we've built can withstand the landing. We make or purchase valentines for the entire class, slotting each into "mailboxes" we make carefully from shoeboxes and Elmer's glue and glitter. We learn how to spin the dreydel, how a four-square court can teach fractions, and how to say the days of the week in Spanish. But we learn so much more . . . . We learn about envy and pride, deception and defiance, the competitive edge and sour grapes, violence and growth, disappointment and inspiration. The world of the classroom is not a false world, but rather a microcosm of all the worlds we know, intersecting and interlocking in metonymic relationship to one another. This is to say, any attempt to cast the classroom as a false world ignores the classroom as a site of violence, tension, social justice, and change.

Perhaps the easiest way to put this is to consider your own experiences in college. Was your life on hold? Your "real life" on "time-out" so you could be in school? We all want to achieve our educational goals, and sometimes that causes us to feel like we're waiting for our "real lives" to begin. But, are all those friends you made in school "false friends"? Is what you learned useless, without value? Were you never embarrassed, called out, frightened, harassed, abused, celebrated, challenged, loved? Did you only study, all the time, forsaking relationships with partners or children or parents? Did time stop? In school, each of us found love and lost it, made and ended relationships, felt the ever-present squeezing of our time and resources in the face of state legislation, found vision and power and lost it . . . time and again, saw our families grow and watched loved ones die. Even though a pervasive cultural emphasis on degrees and diplomas foregrounds the destination rather than the journey of education, schools are not holding pens where we spend time waiting for our lives to begin. We are always already living our lives, whether we realize it or not.

In making reference to "the real world," we neglect something very important about communication. Communication creates all possible worlds; we render our experiences sensible through language. Words aren't "just words," but rather our means to interpret and act on our experiences. What is most dangerous about drawing distinctions between a "real" and some other world is that it dulls our sense of justice, our need to be active, to resist, to effect change. What advantage is there to us to change a "false world"? If we're waiting to emerge into "the real world," then might we just bide our time a little longer until we get there?

If the classroom is a microcosm of worlds, a metonym of the cultures we'll encounter throughout our lives, then it is also a site of social change. It is a meaningful environment for engaging difference, for creating community, and for envisioning the kinds of social organization we want for ourselves. We don't forget the ideological lessons we learn in school, and if we presume that, in the classroom, we cannot build a more just society, then we have already abdicated our agency; we have lost ourselves to a series of false worlds by never knowing how to make them real.

* * *

An education professor once asked me why I was engaged in communication research and not education research. My answer was at once simple and complex. Simple because I replied that I was already doing education research—I was publishing in education journals and attending education conferences. That is, how was I not already doing education research? How could I see myself as doing anything other than that? However, embedded in her question was an important distinction that, while perhaps not obvious, was undergirding the complexity that did in fact mark me as communication and not education. This very moment—this question between us—signaled why I research and teach communication; it is for the careful ability to unpack this discursive moment that I sought a set of degrees in communication and not in education. That I'm interested in how we draw these distinctions in such a small, everyday sort of question indicates why, when I seek a community of scholars, I look first to communication. And while her question marks my choices, this is not to say I don't appreciate education research, scholars, or departments. It is that the questions I ask, the ideas that spark my interest, the concepts that guide my thinking, and the perspectives I think and work from are solidly and completely communication oriented. This is never more obvious than when I'm working with education scholars who note the way I "think everything is communication." And indeed, I do. It is the focus that marks my sense of optimism and critical point of view.

Though it is difficult for critical communication scholars to draw distinctions between critical communication pedagogy as grounds for our research and for our teaching (more to the point, we resist this distinction throughout this book), we will focus in this chapter on what critical communication pedagogy means for our efforts as teachers and students. In what follows, we will explore the relationship between pedagogical moments and the critical theories that inform our understanding of the communication in those moments. In doing so, we show how critical perspectives (i.e.,

Foucault, Butler, and de Certeau) inform our understanding of classroom communication (and communication classrooms). Our efforts as critical communication educators center on illuminating how, in our communication, we work to produce knowledge and power; while an analysis of communication as constitutive of power (and so, too, oppression) might seem, at first, to be the equivalent of an academic postmortem, we find that critical understandings of communication as constitutive reveal hope for our collective ability to enter the conversation of educational process and seek change, justice, and social accountability.

Shaping and Taping: Reading Critical Communication Pedagogy Through Foucault

This was the worst—the worst semester of my life. I was in graduate school—a master's student just struggling to keep my head above water, trying to make it to the end of the semester and the sigh that happens when you turn in your work and your calendar is, blissfully, blank. And at the worst possible time—at midterm—my body gave out, was overtaken and left in ruin. In all my life, I had never before had a sinus infection; I didn't even know what they were. Of course I had heard others say they had them, but without the sensation, I was left without the bodily knowledge of the experience. And so, when it happened to my body, I was clueless as to what it all meant.

The body remembers and, I'm sure, had I ever had this mythical condition in the past, I would have known to take care of it early; yet, here I was, not sure of what was happening to me, and it was only getting worse. The Dayquil didn't work; the Afrin only teased my nose, providing me only hints of relief. It was when I woke up in the morning and smelled what can only be described as infection—that rotting smell that makes you cringe—that I began to think that something was profoundly wrong. I called the student health center: "We have an available appointment on Tuesday." Four days away, but what could I do? I waited. Those days, as I waited, were among the worst of my life: the smell, the aching in my head, my face, and my eyes, the constant effort to blow my nose to no avail, the inability to concentrate on anything. It was, in a word, terrible.

I took antibiotics (two doses to find comfort), and time did pass, if unbearably slowly. In the meantime, I walked through the halls of the communications building with my box of tissues and a plastic grocery bag tied to my belt loop to collect my waste. I was miserable and the members of my departmental community would meet me with sad eyes and kind words. In class, I would blow my nose, so sore, and the room would fill with a loud noise as I struggled to find air. Those weeks, I called attention to myself,

I disrupted and irritated every class I stepped into, causing many to begin to comment on the dysfunction of my body. I began to see people look upon me with disdain, angry with me for allowing my body to disrupt their quiet classroom contemplation. I began to imagine conspiracies—were people plotting against me, avoiding me, trying to find excuses to escape my presence?

Toward the end of the semester, my nose finally disappeared into the background of our social setting. As the final project for a course, I was asked by my group members to allow my nose, my body, to be a point of focus for our final group performance project. The idea was to address the idea of the body in the classroom—to conceive of how we are to understand the nature of the body in the site/sight of others. The performance would go like this: We would perform a classroom, one where the teacher abuses his power in managing the classroom, in keeping students in order, in maintaining the kind of civility that produces knowledge—the knowledge educational systems desire. My body, the body of the dysfunctional student, would be too much for this moment, this space. The teacher (as teachers are wont to do) would discipline me, ask me to adhere to the limits of this socialized, regulated space, this classroom. When I failed (my nose too loud, my body too active, my presence too much), the teacher would finally react and duct tape my body to the small student desk, forcing my body to adhere. This was not only a metaphor of what "normally" happens in classroom— we do discipline bodies in order to achieve certain, desired effects; this performance would help us see that process in vivid detail. And it did: The tape on my arms, the eyes on my body, the desk top in front of me, this performance, while admittedly heavy-handed, worked to put on display the mechanisms that mark, shape, and direct who we are and how we act within the lived spaces of our classrooms.

* * *

Foucault (1977) reminds us that power is never a one-to-one relationship—that power is never housed easily in one site; rather, power is fluid, flowing through all of us all the time. Indeed, it is because power is so slippery that it makes it hard to pinpoint, hard to undermine. As Foucault's work so carefully illuminates, power's greatest effect on bodies is to make them conform even when no one is watching; power works not because we are being watched—but because even when the powerful aren't watching, we, as educational subjects, still perform on cue. Foucault calls this effect of power a disciplining of the body—a type of social control whereby, over time, we craft ourselves in the image of the oppressor. The effect is the making of bodies that conform, that are docile and complacent in the production of culture: "These methods, which made possible the meticulous control of the operations of the body, which assured the constant subjection of its forces and imposed upon them a relation of docility-utility, might be called 'disciplines'" (Foucault, 1977, p. 137).

Foucault (1977) argues that power consists of an uninterrupted exercise of control, the sort of constant authority a lone individual is unable to inflict. Thus, the social norms that we share with others and are shared with us over time, our fears of being caught or scrutinized and the mechanisms of punishment (both physical and social), are what mark our bodies and affect how we move through our surroundings. Foucault makes clear that our bodies must conform: "A disciplined body is the prerequisite for an efficient gesture" (p. 152). Like invisible tape that binds students to classroom desks, the body must be controlled in the classroom, must be kept under wraps, must be trained in order to serve educational needs (Corrigan, 1991; McLaren, 1999; Warren, 2003).

Foucault notes that power functions along several different axes. First, he articulates "the art of distributions," which he describes as the "distribution of individuals in space" (1977, p. 141). Here, space—how it is organized, who is in it (and in what manner they position themselves), and what they can do there—becomes the object of analysis. Space, argues Foucault, is one of the ways we control individuals. Consider, for example, the spatial arrangement of desks in a typical classroom. In most traditional classrooms, desks are organized in rows, aimed toward the chalkboard and/or a larger teacherly desk, and students perform certain kinds of communicative rituals while in this configuration (i.e., raising hands to ask questions, not talking with neighbors, taking notes on what the teacher says). The arrangement of space is one of the ways that schools discipline students so as to control them with greater ease and efficiency. Desks themselves are rife with spatial significance—the small amount of space and the molded chairs position students, regulating and marking their experiences in class. In the case of students who find that kind of bodily encasement restrictive, the system of education connotes their performance as out of order, as irregular. The act of confining the body through institutional space is one of the ways bodies are marked in and through education.

Second, Foucault notes that power can be generated through "the control of activity" (1977, p. 148). For instance, timetables that regulate student movement or posture or gesture control that regulates student speech are examples of how schools manage students' and teachers' activity. In explaining the power of setting time schedules, Foucault notes: Power's "three great methods—establish rhythms, impose particular occupations, regulate the cycles of repetition—were soon to be found in schools, workshops and hospitals" (p. 149). Reading Foucault suggests understanding time in school in the following way:

The entire school day is structured in such a way as to keep the mass of students where they are supposed to be. Students are "slotted" into hard plastic chairs (McLaren, 1993, p. 101), shuffled into rows, stacked in levels, and directed toward the front of the room where a teacher stands lecturing knowledge to note-taking students. Movement is highly regulated: bells dictate the beginning and ending of the class session, students must rapidly gather their possessions at the end of the hour and rush to the next subject, teachers stand in the halls to ensure safe and efficient use of "free" time, and so on. Even the ability to use the restroom depends on the student's request, hopefully leading to the willingness of an instructor to allow passage to the restroom, legitimized by a hall pass that narrates permission to be 'out of place' when caught by a school official. (Warren, 2005, p. 89)

The control of time, as a way of marking the body's activity in schooling, is one of the major ways of seeing how disciplinary systems work upon and within educational subjects. Such control marks educational environments, as it disciplines inappropriate uses of time (i.e., the right or wrong time to be sick, pregnant, or uncomfortable) and is one way to ensure institutional processes proceed without interruption.

The third way power marks our everyday life is through "the organization of geneses" (Foucault, 1977, p. 156). Here, we see how social systems work to segregate and classify people, establishing relationships and hierarchies. Foucault's (1970) *The Order of Things* deconstructs the idea of classification as a systematic formulation of ideology and power; his understanding of disciplinary mechanisms also addresses the effects of creating classification markings as a way to establish social control, especially as it marks individuals' progression through institutionalized spaces. In education, this kind of progression is highly regulated: "It is this disciplinary time that was gradually imposed on pedagogical practice—specializing the time of training and detaching it from the adult time, from the time of mastery; arranging different stages, separated from one another by graded examinations . . ." (Foucault, 1977, p. 159). One need only to think of moving from sixth grade to seventh, or from the last week of classes into finals week, to see this at work. When the body suffers dysfunction (is sick, is hyperactive, or can't be otherwise contained by the institution), it is the location of the student body, and the location of the body within an institutional ordering, that gives rise to discipline. Indeed, even when the teacherly body is itself excessively present, its erasure occurs, moving that body in line with expectation—for it is not an actual or specific teacher body that owns that space, but the idealized constructions that precede and supercede the location of particular bodies in particular classrooms.

Finally, Foucault (1977) examines what he calls "the composition of forces" (p. 162). While the point of this section of his text is an exploration of the changes that have occurred in the military to accommodate the changing nature of conflict, the impact of composing and configuring bodies of institutional members into the most efficient force relates to other systems of power as well. The central thrust behind "composing forces" is to move from individualistic thinking to a more institutional mindset. That is, how can the members of a given system move and function in the most efficient way possible? In large part by having members within each classification help form and mold others to the institution's desire. Foucault argues:

> the complex clockwork of the mutual improvement school was build up cog by cog; first, the oldest pupils were entrusted with tasks involving simple supervision, then of checking work, then of teaching, in the end, all the time of all the pupils was occupied either with teaching or with being taught. (p. 165)

In the end, we have what Foucault (1977) calls "tactics": "mechanisms, in which the product of the various forces is increased by their calculated combination, are no doubt the highest form of disciplinary practice" (p. 167). Control, then, is about making institutional members function as a machine—a well-organized and precisely fluent process that repeats and regenerates itself. To have the institution re-create itself in its own disciplined image is a powerful way of maintaining order. A specific example of this might be the process of schooling itself: Imagine bodies in schools when they arrive, young bodies in kindergarten running and playing. It is in the process of schooling that we train bodies to sit still, to become the docile bodies we need in order to be productive; we regulate bodies, regulate their access to "free" time (i.e., recess) and slowly mold them into figures that can sustain long times in sedentary positions. To have bodies that can sit in a night class for hours or that can survive in an office cubicle, we must train those bodies. Further, we are participants in, parts of, a seemingly well-wrought and balanced machine; as such, we require and desire docile bodies, (re)creating ourselves as products for consumption. Educational subjects, like the bodies metaphorically taped and shaped in the classroom by social and pedagogical pressures, are the products of these institutionalized practices. Indeed, for consumption to occur without question, our finely disciplined and organized bodies must enter the world ready to be sold.

Given this synthesis of how power works in/through us as members of cultures and systems, how are critical communication educators, situated in the nexus of communication and critical pedagogy, ideally suited to the task of understanding power in the classroom? Foucault's four characteristics are not only communicative, but it is in and through communication that we come to see how they function and to what end. It is this that signals the "Why communication?" when seeking to understand power in the context of education. As in any classroom performance (from a project on the body in the classroom in which a student is literally taped to his or her chair, to everyday, mundane classroom performances like raising a hand, taking notes, or appearing in a professor's office with an add/drop form), it is communication—the repeated and sedimented set of carefully scripted acts—that serves as education's most enduring lesson.

Just A(nother) Rehearsal: Reading Critical Communication Pedagogy Through Butler

The thing about a rehearsal is that many believe it is just preparation for the show—the real run before an audience. That is, the rehearsal is how you learn the show—how you practice in order to get it right . . . later. As a performer, I've discovered this is often how directors and teachers ask me to think about the nature and substance of rehearsal—I'm asked to try things out, to pretend in order to be ready for the opening night. In many ways, this is how we've asked teachers and students to think about the classroom—to imagine that it is the classroom that is our play practice—the opportunity to try out our roles without any threat that what happens there is real, has consequences, or has effects. So many times students offer the pithy "What does this have to do with the real world." It is, of course, always a sentence—it is never a genuine question; already they've shown their hand, already they've told me that the critique has little to do with asking me my opinion or rationale. It is commentary on my choices, on my pedagogy, on my rehearsal process. And, in the moment of their statement—the antitheatrical bias against my educational process—my educational goals are actualized. Indeed, their remarks call into question the nature of the classroom space—revealing it (or, rather, naming it in the moment) to be a site of pretense.

But then there are those who talk back to this critique—who say, "Wait, it is not fake or make-believe. It is real, my life and my work is real, my efforts matter." These are the voices of teachers usually. Those of us who desperately cling to the idea that our efforts are important, that they matter, that we matter.

A bit of an aside: I was once in a production where I played a college student. He was the best friend—there is always a best friend, every play has one. In this one, I served as a foil for the lead—a woman who was recovering from an assault. She was hurt—more emotionally at this point than physically. My role was to represent the problem she faces—to be the guy who believes he can solve all the problems. Here, I was to be the traditional guy, to represent all things oppressive about men, about masculinity, and about the nature of misogyny. To be this guy, to embody this figure on stage, I had to learn how to be him, to embody him, to take up his actions in order for her to be who she had to be.

In rehearsals, I struggled. I understood how to speak the way the script called for, but my body struggled to accommodate, to become the person the director wanted me to be. I sat wrong: my legs crossed, my arms folded. My everyday gender performance was not quite what they expected, not quite correct for the part. In one scene, I sat at a bar, my body occupying that space, attempting to play it right (straight?). To correct me, the director would call from the darkened theatre, "this character . . . how should I put it . . . is a real guy, you know? He doesn't sit, walk, stand, or move like you—can you try to be more of a guy here?" I would nod, trying to force my body to adhere to expectation. In once particular moment, the director crawled on stage and shifted my body, crafting my existence according to her desires, her needs, her expectations. My legs felt the touch of her hands, moving my knees apart and exposing me, making me the "guy" she desired in this moment. But these are rehearsals, right? The performance is just for now, just show, just something for an effect with no real consequences, right?

I think I was at the bar on campus when I realized what had happened to me. I was sitting there with my friends—the show long over, but the production still in effect. I was sitting there and I noticed myself shifting, turning my body into the shape of that character, assuming the requisite position. I began to feel the director's touch, the pressure of her fingertips on my legs, moving me into place. I had begun to embody the image I had struggled against. It would take a new set of rehearsals to remember—to re-member my own body and my own sense of who I was.

Back to my classroom. Like a rehearsal, my classroom is a place for imagining, for searching for possibility, for refiguring our lives toward some kind of future. It is play, but it is not simple, in as much as the classroom is a site for placing our bodies and minds, our theories and our actions in tension; the classroom, like the rehearsals that (re)made and (re)figured my body, stands as a site where we (re)make and (re)figure our own minds and bodies. Just as the power of the play rehearsals changed my own sense of self, repositioning how I understand the nature of my gender, my ways of being, my ways of thinking about my own everyday life performances, the site of the classroom has effects. The classroom can be a site of profound oppression. I see this in the life of each student who enters my classroom or my office marred by other classrooms, other students, other teachers. This teacher told her she was stupid, this student called him fat or lazy, this teacher touched her, this moment changed his life forever. The classroom, like the theatre space, has consequences. To accept the notion of the classroom as "just" anything (just academic playtime, just intellectual masturbation) is to deny that the effects of the classroom are real. But the classrooms in our lives are not play—teachers and students leave fingerprints on the lives they touch in pedagogical settings, perceptible impressions that will have lasting effects on us. We are fooling ourselves to imagine them happening in any other way. The theatre is a space that makes things happen—call it magic, call it play, call it imagination, call it what you will—the point remains: The theatre produces . . . produces identity, produces norms, and, as a result, produces possibility. So, too, does the classroom. In rehearsing for social change, we are not practicing for the performance, we are already performing.

* * *

Critical communication pedagogy is about identity, about subjectivity, about who we are as people, people who are invested and produced in the process of education. To help us clarify a processual, reiterative sense of identity, we turn to gender philosopher and cultural critic Judith Butler. We choose Butler for a number of reasons (her body of work, her critical view of identity production, her common association with communication studies, etc.). In the end, Butler's vibrant theory allows a reader to see culture as processual, as a constant set of doings, and in that move, that theoretical vision of who we are, we can see a glimmer of hope, a possibility for change.

Butler succinctly states her theory of gender: "Gender is in no way a stable identity or locus of agency from which various acts precede; rather, it is an identity tenuously constituted in time—an identity instituted through a *stylized repetition of acts*" (1990b, p. 270, emphasis hers). Butler, in asserting that gender is a performative accomplishment, illuminates identity as created in communication (rather than as the origin of our communication). We will take her claim in separate steps to clarify.

Gender is in no way a stable identity . . . . This first assertion seems simple enough: Gender is not stable, gender is in flux. On the surface, this can seem apparent—people each perform or enact their genders in a variety of ways, demonstrating that what counts as "woman" or "man" is subject to interpretation. Applied to a performing body on a stage, this kind of critique can be quick and have profound consequences. However, Butler's logic is much more complex than this notion of variation on a theme—it is to say that gender is the effect of communication, not its origin. To clarify, I'll invoke a common student argument: "Well, gender may be social, but at least sex is fixed—a matter of chromosomes and such." Not so; Butler argues that sex, too, is fluid, a social matter: "'Sex' is an ideal construct which is forcibly materialized through time" (1993, p. 1).

When we ask students which came first, gender or sex—the social or the biological?—they frequently argue that biology precedes gender, the social effects of our bodies. However, this presumes we had microscopes before dresses and pants, prior to social understandings of and sanctions regarding gender. We didn't; we had gender long before we had the technology to "discover" the biological components that guide our science. As Anne Fausto-Sterling (1987) notes, science began with assumptions about the bodies of men and women when the study of genes began. Society constructed gender—it is gender that writes the premise for the study of sex; to begin with gender as a concept to investigate means gender is the decontextualized variable that preceded analysis. Nowhere is this clearer than the new desire to find the "gay-gene"—that biological marker that some claim determines sexuality. The problem, in both the biological study of sex and such studies of sexuality, is that causal assumptions precede and therefore dictate the findings of the study, continuing to reify gender and sex categories. Here, we see the import of asserting that gender is not a stable identity—such reframing is a radical reconsideration of how we see and understand ourselves. Reading common identity markers as contingent and shifting is a radical departure in how we understand the self; this departure informs critical communication pedagogy (Nainby & Pea, 2003; Warren, 2003). It means that the rehearsals of our life, just as the moments before a production opens on a stage, are informative and, indeed, formative.

Gender is in no way a . . . locus of agency from which various acts precede. . . . This, too, is a radical departure from our expectations. As a scholar invested in feminism, Judith Butler focuses on agency as a way of understanding the (gendered) body within culture. For her, a locus of agency is the place or location from which we are able to act; to say that gender is no longer a place from which we act is to deny that gender causes us to act/perform/live in certain ways. Most unsettling to students is that what they once believed to be the basis of their actions is an illusion; consider this from Butler:

> The distinction between expression and performativeness is quite crucial, for if gender attributes and acts, the various ways in which a body shows or produces its cultural signification, are performative then there is no preexisting identity by which an act or attribute might be measured; there would be no true or false, real or distorted acts of gender, and the postulation of a true gender identity would be revealed as a regulatory fiction. (1990b, p. 279)

Here, Butler asks us to not assume that it is gender that causes us to act; instead, by examining our lived experiences, we might learn how we use and construct gender in and through our communicative acts. Like the voice from the theatre that announces the failure to adhere to expectation, it is only from within the logic of gender that her expectation and ultimate critique can even be articulated.

Rather, [gender] is an identity tenuously constituted in time . . . . We begin our analysis of this segment by pausing, if for just a moment, halfway through her thought to consider the nature of the word "tenuously." This one word says much about the importance of Butler's theory for communication studies scholars in general, and for critical communication educators in particular. When identifying gender as a performative accomplishment, she notes that gender is a highly crafted enactment with clear consequences for failure: "Performing one's gender wrong invites a set of punishments both obvious and indirect, and performing it well provides the reassurance that there is an essentialism of gender identity after all" (1990b, p. 279). The idea of tenuous, of being in a moment of tension, of existing within, ultimately demonstrates that gender—that identity—never finds stability nor rest. The success and failure of these seemingly "natural" categories shows that one's performance is contrived, put on for/because of a public, established to generate perception and cultural knowledge. It is always contextual and under a particular amount and kind of social and cultural expectation. And of course, as a result of this contextual frame, such tenuousness is, in the end, subject to time—the use of time, of time in history, and the reiteration (and habituation) of acts over time. Butler argues that body is a historical artifact: "a manner of doing, dramatizing, and *reproducing* a historical situation" (1990b, p. 272). In other words, the very taken-for-grantedness of the body as a site of gender, of identity, is situated in time, in context, in a moment of larger systems. The body, alone on the stage, is never ever really alone—s/he exists within traditions, patterns, situated and contextualized practices, the history preceding this moment, and the futures we anticipate to follow. As one reiteration, this performance will have effects, will have consequences, and will regulate the body within and against expectation.

[Gender is] an identity instituted . . . . The idea of institutionalization demands attention—to be institutionalized, to be grounded within systems of authority, power, and influence, is to be subject to the processes of regulatory practice. Butler (1990b) contends:

> The act that gender is, the act that embodied agents *are* inasmuch as they dramatically and actively embody and, indeed, *wear* certain cultural significations, is clearly not one's act alone. Surely, there are nuanced and individual ways of *doing* one's gender, but *that* one does it, and does it *in accord with* certain sanctions and proscriptions, is clearly not an individual matter. (p. 276)

Of course, the premise behind such a statement, complex as it is, is that while one may do gender with variation, that one does it within a repeated and rehearsed manner demonstrates the degree to which the pattern is, itself, markedly institutionalized. And while one might easily remark that such processes exist, it is the added component of, the verbed nature of "instituted" that illuminates this power—put into play and taken on by members of a given culture. Turning to a schooling example, we might consider the student who arrives in my night class, ready for the 3 to 4 hours of advanced communication theory. In order to be a student who can sit still and learn for that duration, to have *that* kind of studenting identity, s/he must undergo, must take up that subjectivity. This behavior of sitting in this way, in these chairs, in this fluorescent lighting, in this attentive and alert manner is not natural—rather, it is an identity one practices and prepares. Like the moment of training little boys how to use the restroom or little girls to sit with their legs closed, schooling makes, institutes, and inducts bodies into model educational subjects. In these ways, identities, through the ongoing (re)production of their norms and patterns, become naturalized, made mundane through the consistent and reiterative enactment of them. Like layers of sand that become rock, our identities are sedimented—they look like rock only if we secret them from time, failing to imagine how they were formed in the first place. There are various ways one rehearses for any show—one can be the class clown or the honors student—but identities (like a show's cast) are all prescribed prior to our arrival. Typecasting is a learned process, instituted through time and within systems of punishment and reward, but nevertheless categories constructed in and instituted through time.

[Gender is] instituted through a stylized repetition of acts. To say that gender is instituted through a highly regulated and systemic process is to say that it is stylized, that it is crafted, that we practice it—over and over—in both overt and covert and mundane ways. How I do my gender is crafted, taught to me by my mother as she pulled up a dress or straightened a tie; the acts of gender are products of carefully maintained productions:

> Gender is not passively scripted on the body, and neither is it determined by nature, language, the symbolic, or the overwhelming history of patriarchy. Gender is what is put on, invariably, under constraint, daily and incessantly, with anxiety and pleasure. (Butler, 1990b, p. 282)

Gender, like the location of a knee or the swoop of a gesture, is a series of choreographed maneuvers that hide and obscure their rehearsal, masking the sweat taken in making it just so. I see this stylized production when my graduate students perform the "Will you be my adviser/major professor/ committee member?" dance, mixing careful (and, often, scripted) compliment with serious (and, again, crafted) scholarly care. This moment is not natural, even if predictable. And this stylized performance is predictable, as suggested throughout this section on Judith Butler's work, because it is repeated—to such a degree that it becomes sediment, becomes the natural(ized) foundation that we assume has always been there. The key to a good play in the theater lies in its ability to look natural—even as we recognize the mechanisms of production made visible because of the stage, the lights, the bow to the audience in the end. Because the student does not bow at the end of a performance (an act that is no less contrived), we have been taught to assume this moment—this moment of her or his risk and my professorial power—is *just* the way things are.

What could looking at the practices, the everyday communicative moments of the classroom through performativity, do to/for us as critical communication pedagogy researchers and educators? Giroux and Shannon (1997), in discussing the value of the performative in educational theory, note:

> the performative becomes a site of memory, a location and critical enactment of the stories we tell in assuming our roles as public intellectuals willing to make visible and challenge the grotesque inequalities and intolerable oppressions of the present moment. (p. 7)

In the end, the reason performative theories are valuable in education is because they help us see the stable, the taken-for-granted, the assumed as enactments, as processual, as historical, and as contextual. Such a way of seeing the world affords infinite possibilities to the critical communication educator/intellectual; such a way of seeing means that is if identities and educational subjectivities are constituted in and through our communication, we might be able to change them. If we think education can harm, then with this theoretical frame, we have a vehicle for change. Paulo Freire (1992) knew this—he argued that "changing language is part of the process of changing the world" (pp. 67–68). Language, that communicative moment that brings discourse in and through the body, shapes and fills us as educational subjects. Change in this way, if we know the modes of production, is a new rehearsal for hope.

Caught in the Current: Reading Critical Communication Pedagogy Through de Certeau

This writer is drowning, and it's very difficult to watch.

I'm at a thesis defense; it's an interesting project—something to do with relational dialectics in interactions between strangers. It's not something I would do, but it's clever enough, and the author, when he's not choking, seems to enjoy what he's doing.

But he is choking, swallowing "scholarly" discourse, word by word, until his throat is full and the slightest motion sends words spilling across the conference table in a gush. And still he tries to swallow more.

The thesis is appropriately succinct. I read it quickly, marveling at the number of sources and few grammar errors. I read it slowly, looking for traces of the writer. And though it's clear as water, I can't find the bottom, it's like reading for detail beneath waves.

* * *

The writing is characterized by its own dialectical tension, situated between claiming to value plurivocity and yet following a dispassioned, passively voiced positivistic voice.

I ask: "Why write this in the third person, in a passive voice?"

He burbles, but there are no words at first.

I say: "We always ask critical scholars to explain their use of first person, but we don't usually ask the same of scholars with other choices."

He pauses and answers honestly: "You know, that's a good question. I hadn't thought of that. You think the writing's passive? I know when I started it was 'I this' and 'we that,' so it seemed like a good idea to make it consistent."

The colleague to my left offers: "You know, I didn't think of it in those terms either. I had the sense that this was you trying on a scholarly voice . . . . You being scholarly . . . ."

This doesn't get at the depths enough for me, so I continue: "You know, that's really interesting to me in light of this thesis. Your work is characterized by its own dialectical tension between what I think may be two paradigms. You have the emphasis on heteroglossia, on this postmodern understanding of multiple voices situated against each other, and this writing style that casts you apart from the study. So, let me ask: Why not create this as a critical study?"

He burbles, but there are no words at first.

And after a long pause, he answers: "I didn't really think of that, and I've had some bad experiences with critical work in this department."

I know who he means, I know what he means, but he doesn't get to have that. Even if I want for him to have that, that moment, that fissure in the defense, that place that calls out the experience, the structure of being a part of this particular department. We've all known hypocritical critical theorists (or, as my colleague Keith Nainby would call them, "venture criticalists"); we must learn from those experiences, to name them and make them our own, but to temper our response with compassion, to understand that no one ever becomes any way without reason. Our challenge is to throw out the lifeline, to avoid becoming the people we criticize, the people who are quick to call out hypocrisies in others even as they offer another glass of water to someone who's drowning.

* * *

The academic defense has the potential to be a pedagogical moment, and, perhaps in its finest hour, it is. But more often it is a rite of passage—a place to demonstrate one's mastery of "good scholar" . . . whether student or faculty member, writer or adviser.

"On page blah-blah, where you blah-blah, did you use the word 'blah-blah' intentionally? Yes? Did you notice how that undercuts your claim about blah-blah?"

"I notice you're using So-and-So's definition of blah-blah here . . . that's an unusual definition . . . . What would happen to your study if you used a definition of blah-blah like So-and-So's?"

"Blah, blah, blah, blah . . . relativism . . . blah, blah. How do you know you're not just seeing what you want to see?"

"Blah, blah, blah, blah . . . might . . . blah . . . need . . . blah . . . major . . . blah . . . revisions . . . blah . . . no . . . blah . . . graduation . . . blah."

"Yes Dr. So-and-So, you raise an excellent question. I attempt to address that on page blah-blah where I blah-blah . . . ."

Perhaps this is not entirely fair. But we are, as scholars, constituted in our discourse, constituted in our moments of praise and confusion and candor. Constituted as (un)scholarly as we define what counts as scholarly.

* * *

My first instinct is to say,
"You don't get to have that as your answer."
"That doesn't tell me what you think 'critical' means."
"Yeah, I know that 'scholar' too, and I can't even begin to talk about what a hypocrite s/he is."
"It's okay to let your experiences shape the work you do if you think carefully about those choices."
"You should have done this as a critical study."
"But didn't I also introduce you to critical work? Wasn't that meaningful?"
"The defense is not the place to get defensive."
"I don't care who or what told you to do or not do critical work, you have to act like that was always a careful decision on your part . . . like this was the best possible way to do your study."
"Let's talk about those negative experiences . . . what happened there?"
"This writing isn't who you are. Please use your voice, let us hear you in this document."
"Can you breathe? Do you need help?"
"I'll expect a silkier response next time."

* * *

de Certeau makes much of cooking metaphors, poaching metaphors, wandering and window shopping metaphors, ocean metaphors. None of these gets at the experience of drowning in strategies, of seeing tactics in the mirror of the sun—as collage, chimera, mirage. Desperate to stay afloat, we cleave apart strategies, lashing them together to form an intellectual life raft—engaging in the important scholarly work of identifying how institutions seep into and permeate the self, the selves that matter to us. But a tactic is the stroke against the wave; the wave is forever altered, but the ocean reclaims both all the same.

This student, drowning, choking, swallowing, throws water in our faces. He finds a moment in the structure of the defense and offers up something unexpected, or, if expected, easily cast as immaturity or nervousness or some other performance of "bad prospectus defense student." It is a moment, an interruption or fissure in the motion of the meeting, a statement that illuminates, calls forth the structure of that meeting, calls forth the question of particular someones who serve as arbiters of "good" or "bad" answers. It is a vulnerable moment, characterized by the sort of personal and political experience we've carefully crafted academic defenses and scholarly writing to protect ourselves against. He says what I have never been able to say; he calls out a negative experience with a particular someone. We have all had negative experiences with particular someones, with people we meet every day, with people who hurt us and who hurt students.

And in that defense, I immediately rush to calm the waters: "It's okay to not have an answer yet; it's a complicated question; we can talk more about your theoretical and methodological commitments later." The moment is gone, the meeting continues, and it's as though I'd never asked my question in the first place.

But I am forever altered. My own bloated discomfort may have helped to wash over the shoreline, but for that instant I could feel it, could perceive the sand beneath my feet, however briefly. What counts as scholarly, what counts as true, what matters in those moments is fluid; it slips and slides in and through and around people, tossing them about, against each other. But in this ocean, am I the swimmer? Or, am I the wave?

* * *

In wax and wane, ebb and flow, I drink deeply, drawing the transparent, clear fluid into my eyes and ears, into my lungs and through my pores. This writer is drowning, and it's very difficult to watch.

* * *

It's relatively common for people to strategize for an important meeting (say, an academic defense), to use strategies in approaching a professor or an employer for a better evaluation, or, as a number of universities do, to engage in strategic planning; similarly, we might try to locate the tactical advantage in a game of chess, or worry about whether someone will use dismissive tactics against us in an argument. In these senses, strategies and tactics are tools, something we can consciously and handily identify, deploy, and resist. French philosopher Michel de Certeau (1984) offers us an important revision and reconsideration—a respecification, in the ethnomethodological sense (Garfinkel, 1967)—of strategies and tactics in his germinal text *The Practice of Everyday Life*.

A strategy, in de Certeau's sense, is "the calculation (or manipulation) of power relationships that becomes possible as soon as a subject with will and power (a business, an army, a city, a scientific institution) can be isolated. It postulates a *place* that can be delimited as its *own* and serve as the base from which relations with an *exteriority* composed of targets or threats (customers or competitors, enemies, the country surrounding the city, objectives and objects of research, etc.) can be managed" (1984, pp. 35–36). In other words, a school, as a site of organized will and power, may delimit and define its territory; students and teachers, though they move through this site, are the targets (or threats?) to the school's authority. There are a number of mechanisms the school, as a site, can engage to manage those targets: school uniforms; structuring the school day as a series of periods of time (often idiosyncratically named—e.g., 2:06–2:58), with small, highly regulated and policed breaks in between; the location of classes in bland, smooth, institutional spaces with equally bland, smooth, institutional (read: interchangeable) desks. Of great interest to communication scholars are the ways targets or subjects (in this example, students, but really anyone) will absorb and enact these strategies themselves, often in unreflective ways.

Nakayama and Krizek (1995), as communication scholars, bring a distinct focus to de Certeau's articulation of strategies and influence our own exploration of his work (Fassett & Warren, 2004, 2005). In locating their analysis of whiteness in strategic rhetoric, these authors underscore the role of communication in creating and sustaining racist social structures. This is an important pedagogical shift, as scholars like McIntosh (1988) and McIntyre (1997) have argued, because conversations about racism must move from identifying particular racist individuals and asking them to change their ways (or prove their innocence, or purge their guilt) to a discussion of how well-intentioned people (of all social groups, classes, and cultures) participate in social systems that privilege some (i.e., whites and other light-skinned people) at the expense of others (i.e., people of color). And though the emphasis, in this example, is on whiteness and racism, we might raise the same analogy with respect to classism, sexism, and heteronormativity or homophobia.

The academic defense is a rich site for analysis of this process; for those who participate in it, the defense is highly ordered, rife with traditions (though these vary somewhat from campus to campus and department to department) and often linked, usually outside of the defense itself, to initiation, to a rite of passage, or to hazing. The defense, though it might not seem so at first because it is located outside the classroom, is overtly pedagogical; it is most certainly about the reproduction of certain values, behaviors, and discourses. If we view the defense from de Certeau's perspective, strategies are not tools or plots for faculty or students to deploy or deflect, but rather the everyday instances of communication that render an institution—a department, a university, an academic community—stable, that help that institution manage its participants; in the defense, this may involve the tradition of asking the student to leave the room while the committee deliberates (the student, in this case, is not considered part of that committee, but rather an object of their evaluation), particular questioning practices (for example, the effort of a faculty member to ask questions that attempt to undermine the student's project—and her or his confidence—precisely to see how s/he will react), or perhaps even practices meant to prepare the student for a successful defense (for example, an adviser may spend hours with an advisee, drilling her or him with questions so s/he will remain calm, "objective," and "clear" in the defense itself).

Moreover, Nakayama and Krizek's shift from strategy to strategic rhetoric is powerful precisely because it offers a more nuanced understanding of the interdependence between individuals and social systems. It is difficult for many of us, in our day-to-day communication, to explore this interdependence; our tendency is to reify, to render social systems as fixed, when they are fluid, pervasive, and constituted and stabilized through our mundane communication. For example, when a student notes that she does not want to become a teacher because "It won't be long until you get beat down by the system," her use of passive voice (i.e., "get beat down") and her personification of a social system (as though the system is an agent itself, capable of physical and emotional punishment) help to elide her participation in the very social system she critiques. Admittedly, it feels awkward to say "Choreographed relationships between well-meaning people (who have pets and drink coffee and go to the movies) help (re)affirm and (re)constitute processes, discourses, and movements that will make it hard for me to feel good about what I'm doing in the classroom." And perhaps it feels even more awkward to say, "I'm one of those well-meaning people." de Certeau's notion of strategy helps us understand that it is the day-to-day interdependence of people that helps to create and solidify structures (that, at different times and in different ways, both enable and disable us). Nakayama and Krizek further illuminate that it is our own discourse (the words we say, our gestures and movements) that re-creates those structures (whether of whiteness, of heteronormativity, of capitalism, etc.) and renders them seemingly natural, inevitable, and apart from ourselves.

To further clarify: It is tempting to suggest that we are a part of a social system in as much as we recognize our participation in that system. For example, we are a part of an educational system when we are students or teachers, when our children are in schools, and so forth. Or, we are part of an economic system when we work in finance, or when we choose a mutual fund for our retirement plan, or when we make a choice to purchase coffee at an independently owned shop. Though tempting, such language is misleading; it suggests that we are not part of those social systems when we are not participating in those ways. It is misleading because it suggests we can escape the inescapable: that we can break with systems, choose to opt out or refuse to play the game, so to speak. Instead, as this analysis suggests, the ideological lessons we learn, we never forget. This is to say, as Nakayama and Krizek assert, "strategic rhetoric is not itself a place, but it functions to re-secure the center" (1995, p. 295); if strategic rhetoric can be said to have a place at all, it is in discourse, in our day-to-day communication. If what builds and affirms a social system is discursive, then we cannot opt out; a strategic rhetoric of whiteness (or heteronormativity or capitalism or . . .) is always already a part of our language, whether or not we're in the classroom or boardroom or coffee shop or outside in the sun. As de Certeau (1984) challenges,

> since one does not 'leave' this language, since one cannot find another place from which to interpret it, since there are therefore no separate groups of false interpretations and true interpretations, but only illusory interpretations, since in short there is no *way out*, the fact remains that we are *foreigners* on the inside—*but there is no outside.* (pp. 13–14)

One of the greatest assets of a communication studies approach to critical theory is that the notion of language as a tie that binds needn't discourage or feel disheartening. Equally important to de Certeau's analysis of power is the notion of a tactic, a means to interrupt or challenge strategies, however briefly. A tactic, in de Certeau's sense, is

> the space of the other . . . . It operates in isolated actions, blow by blow. It takes advantage of "opportunities" and depends on them, being without any base where it could stockpile its winnings, build up its own position and plan raids. What it wins it cannot keep . . . . It must vigilantly make use of the cracks that particular conjunctions open in the surveillance of the proprietary

powers. It poaches in them. It creates surprise in them. It can be where it is least expected. (1984, p. 37)

Particularly concerned with consumption, de Certeau explores how everyday practices are active efforts at meaning making; this is to say activities, like reading, listening, sightseeing, and so forth, are not passive processes of absorption, but rather characterized by subjects' own work to author their experiences, to make these experiences their own. We are not, therefore, dominated by strategy or strategic rhetorics; though those forces move in and through us, we are capable of pushing back, of naming those strategies for what they are and authoring a response.

However structured the academic defense (and, more to the point, *because* of the structure of an academic defense, because of the way that discourse structures participants' actions to affirm particular institutions), there are a number of opportunities to push back, to resist strategic rhetorics. So, for example, the student in the defense might attempt to make that space her or his own (e.g., using clothesline and pins to hang relevant artwork throughout a conference room, arriving early to the defense and praying in the room beforehand, or selecting a seat s/he finds comfortable, irrespective of—or perhaps because of—traditional seating arrangements). Or, this student might subvert the discourse of the meeting (e.g., asking an overt question about how s/he should behave, creating uncomfortable silences, or framing her or his opening remarks so as to anticipate, and perhaps co-opt, faculty critique). Moreover, as no one can exist outside the discursive construction of the institution, the faculty members may engage in tactical rhetorics as well. For example, they might challenge the nature of the defense process (e.g., by posing scheduling dilemmas and "dragging their feet," by arriving late or leaving early, or by offering their questions to the student in advance of the meeting). In any event, what de Certeau teaches us is that strategies and tactics are not readily located in particular groups of individuals—for example, strategies with professors and tactics with students—but rather, that strategic and tactical rhetorics permeate all human communication. A tactic is always contingent, always reliant on a strategy for its success; tactics are always in relation to some discourse. For example, while a student might respond tactically to a professor's discourse, both professor and student might respond tactically, together, to institutional—departmental, university, or disciplinary—discourse.

One of the central difficulties in exploring de Certeau's theory for pedagogical practice lies in the language of strategies and tactics; not only do we commonly use these terms in many other casual senses, but the very language of describing the two in relation to each other is binaristic. This is to say, we are drawn to writing that a tactic is a response to a strategy, or that strategies give rise to tactics, when it is more accurate to say that tactics and strategies exist in tension with one another: One cannot exist without the other. Just as there is no freedom without constraint, or liberation without oppression, there is no tactic apart from a strategy. It is not possible to ignore strategies, or to excise them from our lives; nor is it possible for us to purposefully sustain a tactical response indefinitely (in so doing, the tactic is co-opted, normed, and rendered strategic). For example, critical approaches to pedagogy must, by necessity, exist in relation to traditional or conservative approaches to pedagogy; we argue that critical pedagogies are most effective as means to interrupt, to call out and call into question the traditional. Most important to remember in discussions of this sort is that strategies are not, by their very nature, immoral, oppressive, painful, or unjust; strategies, in and of themselves, are not always "bad." (Again, what would freedom mean if we did not also understand and appreciate constraint?) Similarly, tactics are not always liberating, meaningful, or comforting.

One of our professors in graduate school, Kathy Hytten, lectures compellingly about what she calls a "survive and subvert" pedagogy; for us, this is a pedagogy that appreciates and draws strength from the co-presence of strategies and tactics. As Heidegger (1962) observed, we are thrown into circumstances not of our own making, but that we must negotiate nonetheless. We are born into social worlds of expectations and values, worlds that are not natural or inevitable but rather (re)created in our movements through and talk in/about these worlds. We do what we need to survive, but there are many, many opportunities for us to subvert, to read our experiences critically. This is to say, the defense candidate may see that academic context for what it is—a site of ideological reproduction—but s/he will often engage those rhetorics that will achieve success, and then later, in discussions with her or his adviser or peers or family, complicate or critically frame those rhetorics, that success.

Reading Critical Communication Pedagogy

Our use of Michel Foucault, Judith Butler, and Michel de Certeau to read critical communication pedagogy is, on some level, arbitrary. We could have traced the works of Pierre Bourdieu (1991), bell hooks (1994), or Jean Baudrillard (1981/1994). We could have called upon many others who have critical theories regarding the nature of social process or power. The issue is not that these intellectuals have magical powers that make their perspectives better than others. Rather, they represent ways of seeing that we have found productive for critical communication pedagogy. The key is not that one takes up theory (how can we ever do otherwise?)—it is that one struggles to occupy positions that are *in relation* to power, that demand that social actors (including teachers and researchers) place themselves within cultural and social contexts and reread the natural and inevitable as inescapably social and coauthored.

We care about seeing lives, behaviors, and ways of being as residue of reiterative and regulated practices (Butler). We care about seeing our normed subjectivities as products of institutional memberships derived from ongoing disciplinary mechanisms (Foucault). We care about seeing our choices as always already located in the inevitable tensive relationship between resistance and persistence of power (de Certeau). And, as we have argued here, such ways of imagining our social world consistently and powerfully locate identity in relation to (an)other, who is always already a participant in (re)assertions of power, who is both framed within and a framer of institutional norms and patterns. Research that strips subjects from contexts, that reduces lived bodies and experiences to soulless, apparently culture-free variables, sustains power(ful) relationships, keeps them in place by measuring emotions without feeling (i.e., "fear appeals," "communication apprehension," "efficacy"), power without consequence (i.e., "compliance gaining" or "teacher misbehaviors"), and bodies without life (i.e., "verbal aggression" or "immediacy").

Critical communication pedagogy asks that we acknowledge that real people, with complicated and difficult lives, who risk carrying the weight of our research only work to reaffirm our own location within and as subject to institutions of power. A commitment to critical communication pedagogy means no longer knowingly using these lives for intellectual profit, no longer knowingly writing violence into flesh in our classrooms. Critical communication pedagogy, in any language, always works against these tendencies. And where it fails, where we fail, we must hold ourselves accountable.

4

Writing, Researching, and Living

Critical Communication Pedagogy as Reflexivity

In the July 2000 issue of *Communication Education,* I realized a new sense of hope. And while, perhaps, I was giving too much power to the editorial decisions of a journal, I must admit I was more than a bit excited when I reached into my mailbox and found the pages of Ronald J. Pelias's "The Critical Life." Pelias's (2000) essay began with an abstract—"This autoethnographic essay follows . . ."—and I was hooked: I wanted to see autoethnography in those pages, to know that a journal that has often felt ideologically narrow could offer new ways of imagining our scholarship. The speaker in the piece, a familiar voice that resonates with the reader, that seduces the reader into what feels like a personal relationship, calls the reader into the story in an immediate way. You feel like you know the speaker, you know Ron, even if Pelias is someone you've never met. And in the second-person narrative voice of the piece, you become Ron for a time— Ron is someone you know intimately. Ron is you.

Ron's essay, a narrative of living the critical life, of doing one's work, of doing the work of critique in and through our everyday actions, resonated with me; I, too, had been trying to live an ethical life, to do the work of being a critical scholar, researcher, teacher. I wanted to like Ron's essay in part because, in its careful reflection—not simply called for but lived—it gave me some hope that it would help me toward that end. And in his failure, in the moment where his competing desires end in tension, with neither ease of privilege nor the sacrifice of one ethical belief for another, I see the potential, the significance, of reflexivity even as I realize that it can also be painful, disappointing. If reflexivity is what enables us to perceive how we are both products and producers of communication, of strategies and tactics, if reflexivity is what enables us to perceive the stroke against the wave, then it will be, by necessity, a perpetually unsettling process. As de Certeau (1984) makes clear, tactical forms of power are ephemeral, are shadows; they are usurped or denied quickly, their interruptions are flickers that illuminate, but briefly. "What [a tactic] wins it cannot keep" (de Certeau, 1984, p. 37). So I understand, feel, Pelias's final thought as he comes to see the impossibility of living critically every moment: "You will continue to evaluate yourself. And when all is said and done, you will know that you are not critical" (2000, p. 228). Living the critical life, lest we suggest otherwise, is not easy, is not consistent, is not prescriptive, and is always subject to others' interpretations, assessments, judgments.

In this chapter, we use Ron's "The Critical Life" as a framework for how we came to reflect on what it means to be a critically oriented teacher-scholar. Indeed, to do critical communication pedagogy is to do reflexivity, to imagine the role one plays within systems of power. In his essay, Ron takes it upon himself to sketch out a day in the life of an academic doing (or failing to completely do) critical work—to live the critical life. In the recounting of his day, Ron's persona faces moments in which he succeeds in living up to the standards of critical thought; he also faces moments in which he fails. This piece is particularly meaningful to us and to our work because it shows how one works to be reflexive, while noting that one never completely lives up to the ways s/he idealizes critical work. As Ron reflects, we see ourselves also trying (and at times failing) to be everything we want, everything we feel we need to be.

* * *

I first read Ruth Frankenberg's (1993) book *White Women, Race Matters* in an undergraduate feminist theory course, my last course in the Women's Studies minor sequence at Indiana State University. I remember being stunned—as a well-meaning white guy from the Midwest, I had never felt implicated in racism until I read that book. This is, of course, the foundation of racial privilege. I now know, given the amount of reading, reflecting, and listening I have done in the last decade, that my own locatedness in systems of privilege and advantage mark me in ways I can't yet imagine. Privilege surrounds me, soothes me, moves in and through me in palpable ways.

Privilege, like a cloak or a soft down comforter, keeps me warm and safe. Privilege, invisible and weightless (McIntosh, 1988), frames my every move, guides my every step, and approves my every fantasy. As I read Frankenberg, I began to feel the weight of her words, the burden of my own ignorance. Whiteness, as a system of power, would allow me the luxury of forgetting these feelings, but in the moment of reading that book and hearing the voices of those women, I felt very much visible, very much subject to that critique.

As with so many other brushes I'd had with self-awareness and privilege, I moved on, promptly put the book back on the shelf and continued living my life, kept up with the "same old, same old." Comfortable. Safe. Or so I thought. While there were moments when I would look at a situation, a moment in my classroom, a mediated image from film or television, or some other moment and could discern it was reproducing a luxury of privilege, I must admit my life went on pretty much as it did before. But that would change in a few years.

In graduate school, for a class, I picked up Frankenberg's (1993) book and reread it. I recalled the moments of awareness the book inspires, the peek under the comforter, beneath the hooded cloak; but more than that, I could perceive something I hadn't the first time. I sought to acquire every book, article, video, and argument I could on whiteness and critical race theory. I began to turn all my energies toward this work; I felt compelled . . . I felt that doing this work might make me feel better. Like it might mean relief. From class assignments to conference papers, to my dissertation, to my first book, to my research agenda, whiteness and critical/cultural communication became my work, my invocation, my mission. I felt my eyes were open for the first time and I needed to do the work, the research that might provide hope.

This has affected my sense of self—my own performance of self in places and ways I do not always expect. For instance, during a recent trip to Chicago, I took the train, riding on Amtrak for the first time from Toledo to Chicago, a 5-hour journey on the rails across northern Indiana. Since this was my first train ride, I didn't know the rules, the etiquette, the mundane routines of life on the train. Sitting in the Amtrak station in Chicago, awaiting the start of the trek home, I was met with a moment in which my class, my socioeconomic privilege, became palpable. While never upper class, I almost always had the ability to travel by plane, and the airport, while still a travel venue of the public, is not the same as a train station. I watched a woman drag her screaming toddler through the station, warm and wet and smelling of rotting food and close bodies; he screamed through the announcements, louder still after each time his mother shook him. As we began to gather our belongings and make our way to the train, through a press of people in worn clothes carrying everything from babies to plastic bags of food from home, I heard her screech, "And now it's your fault I don't know where we're supposed to go! Are you happy?" As I listened to my inner dialogue, an undercurrent of privilege, comment on the happenings within that train waiting room, I felt my class assumptions and values closing in on me, marking me, making me feel uncomfortable. What does it mean for me to expect air conditioning, clean clothes, tickets with seat assignments, calm order, and rational discussion? What does it mean for me to define calmness, cleanliness, order, and rationality on my terms? It is in moments like these when I pause to reflect on what it means to live in my world of privilege, my world of ease. Wound up in, bound by, my own assumptions, I still tried to acknowledge how and in what ways this moment could teach me about subjectivity, about living the life of classed privilege.

As a critical scholar, I feel like I should have known better in that train station. This is the artful guise, the lure, of critique; in engaging it, you imagine that you actually are a better person because of the work you do. But while I celebrate, or at least respect, those moments in which I learn about myself, learn about what it means to be gendered, raced, classed, sexed, nationed, and all, I think what these moments tell me is that the desire to do this research, to be free, to escape "the system," is just another illusion of privilege. It is just another layer that encourages you to feel safe, to believe you've found or become what you most desire. Being a critical scholar is not about escaping, it is not about being or feeling better, and it is certainly not about doing easy research. Being a critical scholar is about always being accountable for not only what you intend but what kinds of effects you put in motion. It is about holding yourself responsible even when privilege tells you are not, about listening to others even though you feel you are entitled to speak.

I pursued research on race and privilege because I thought it offered hope—and it did, but not in the way I had originally thought. I believed such research would allow me to not ever feel the weight of my privilege again . . . that because of this work, I could escape my location. I wanted to be like Peter McLaren (1997), disavowing his whiteness and claiming, as a unity seeking effort, to be brown. But being a critical scholar, as McLaren would do well to remember, is not about escaping your implication or complicity in systems of power, but, rather, about living there in that uncomfortable space, in that tension, and seeking change not just from those around you but from yourself as well. Instead of the ease, the self-assuredness, I sought from engaging in critical work, I found struggle. But it is the struggle that represents hope; it is only in and through that discomfort that we learn to listen and seek community, seek possibility. Ease is isolating in scholarship, but discomfort is communal, a place and sensation that demands collaboration and dialogue. That change in mindset is where hope begins.

This chapter is our attempt to be reflexive. This is to say, we strive here to find a way to see our experiences in relationship to others (academic voices as well as the voices of our students and teachers). We aim here to model a mode of writing, a way of engaging in the living of our pedagogical lives in ways that open up experiences, that illuminate how power and social structure move through us and shape us even as we strive to promote social justice. Reflexivity is not linear—one rarely maps out a life in history, in an artificial timeline of this, then that. So in this way, our chapter is more of a collage of moments, mediated through Ron Pelias's (2000) "The Critical Life." In the end, we argue that doing critical communication pedagogy is about holding ourselves accountable for the ways we exist within the institutions that have shaped us. We might better understand the nature of power through engaging in what Ron Pelias (2000) describes as an effort to "call into question the individual's relationship to criticism and its presence in the ongoing process of doing one's job and living one's life" (p. 220). Our task in this chapter is, in many ways, to name the (im)possibility of critical communication pedagogy, to suggest that one always falls within the tensive relationship between success and failure, between good and bad, between strategies and tactics.

* * *

Favorite moments from Ron's (2000) "The Critical Life":

What does it mean to live with a critical eye, an eye that's always assessing, always deciding questions of worth, always saying what's good or bad? (p. 220)

You wake up in the morning with a cat in your face. (p. 220)

You begin to grade a set of papers you've promised back to your students. The first paper you select begins with the sentence, "In my speech, I want to do a poem I always liked a lot." You cringe, wondering how a student majoring in Speech Communication could misspell "speech." (p. 221)

You think to yourself: My friend is caught; my students are caught; I'm caught. Everyone is caught in the same critical grind, giving out and taking in comments designed to say how we are positioned, rated, ranked. (p. 222)

You thumb through *Communication Monographs*. You see five articles, most by more than one author, on topics of interest to you but located in a paradigmatic logic you find less than convincing. . . . During the next several months, you will keep skipping over it until you finally put it on your book shelf along with the other unread *Monographs*. (p. 223)

Writing articles is; it is what you are supposed to know how to do. It is what you were trained to do. It is what you claim is essential to an academic life. So, when one of your articles is rejected, when the reviewers point out the silliness of your ideas, when the editor doesn't even have an encouraging word, you feel as if you have been punched. (p. 224)

You would like to run from all, from all the words that pin down, for better or worse, person after person. (p. 225)

History is saved. (p. 226)

You are open to criticism. You revise to get at the heart of the matter. You think the piece was better than it was. You wonder how it will be read: too detached? Too cynical? Too sentimental? You will continue to evaluate it. (p. 228)

* * *

Recently, *Communication Education* published an essay we wrote in which we sketched out a strategic rhetoric of educational outcomes (Fassett & Warren, 2004). This essay, emerging from our work with critical approaches to the study of educational risk, made possible a competing narrative of educational subjectivities; that is, we wanted to offer a different story about how and why people succeed and fail in schools that avoids the labeling and categorizing so prevalent in our field. We wanted our work to give rise to a different way of understanding this phenomenon, an understanding that promotes a deeper, more nuanced exploration of students' and teachers' (and scholars') communication. Rather than sorting students, diagnosing their limitations, and offering prescriptive solutions, we listen as they tell us what they think educational success means. And then we try to learn from them.

Our second essay in this line of scholarship was published by *Communication and Critical/Cultural Studies* (Fassett & Warren, 2005). In this piece, we take the frame from the first article—that strategic rhetorics make possible or legitimate hegemonic beliefs about success and failure—and worked to illuminate how Jane, a student we interviewed, made sense of her own experience as an "at-risk" student. In the end, Jane crafted a complex image of herself; she was not the one-dimensional character who is captured so often in literature on the communication needs of at-risk students. We found that it was impossible, inappropriate to reduce Jane to a number or statistic; doing so would only inflict violence—her story was too rich, her struggle too visceral, her identity too intricate. We invited Jane to teach us about what it means to be (and not be) an educational subject in crisis; in doing so, we also learned something about ourselves. She taught us that when we become vulnerable, even for an instant, change is possible. The moment Jane makes herself vulnerable is the moment we find hope. Of vital importance here is to recognize that vulnerability, that hope, and embrace it; if we fail to perceive vulnerability, to name it as such, then we will most certainly lose it.

We found strategic rhetoric, as a theoretical frame, useful in teasing apart how power moves in and through communication in these educational contexts. That is, we grounded our work in the efforts of Nakayama and Krizek (1995), who, in their essay "Whiteness: A Strategic Rhetoric," argue that embedded in our everyday talk are systems of power—logics that we rely on and reproduce even without our direct intent. A communication-centered extension and application of de Certeau's (1984) philosophy, an analysis of strategic rhetoric, illuminates how discourse "functions to resecure the center" of a system of power (Nakayama & Krizek, 1995, p. 295). Whiteness—as a system of racial power that works to sustain privilege and inequality—served as the locus of Nakayama and Krizek's study. In our writing, we named education as a system of power—a system that maintains carefully, through our everyday talk, educational identities. Thus, identities such as "successful student," "problem child," "honors student," "at-risk youth," and "dropout" are identities not written in DNA, but crafted through our everyday talk—discourse that inevitably reproduces the cultural systems that make these identities not only possible, but necessary. Given this, we take as our responsibility a careful analysis of, engagement with, and response to research in communication studies literature that addresses educational identities. Moreover, we also take as our responsibility a careful analysis of, engagement with, and response to our own lives, our own experiences with teachers and students in educational settings.

In the first essay, we sought, though a focus group research project, to study the mechanisms of power in students' talk. We applied that understanding to an individual, to Jane and her complex understanding of and relationship to the schooling of her body. We ended that second essay with the realization that we needed to more fully explore acts of resistance, what Nakayama and Krizek (1995) call "tactical rhetorics." These are oppositional modes of engagement—ways of, as bell hooks might suggest, talking back. Because tactics are "calculated action[s] determined by the absence of a proper locus," because they are the "space of the other," they operate "in isolated actions," functioning as an "art of the weak" (de Certeau, 1984, pp. 36–37). de Certeau makes clear that a tactic's significance is its ability to make visible what typically lies just beneath the surface; power, de Certeau

(1984) asserts, "is bound by its very invisibility" (p. 36). In effect, tactics make the structure of power available for interrogation. Nakayama and Krizek (1995), for instance, describe their essay as a tactic—an effort to render visible the invisible center of whiteness. Similarly, we could assert that our effort to cast the production of identity in educational systems as a problem worthy of scholarly investigation is a tactical response; however, we still seek more rigorous, varied, and systematic analyses of the reproductive structure of power in instructional communication research. When we met Jane, when she revealed she had given serious consideration to suicide, we were confronted with the systemic nature of power, with our participation—as students, as teachers, as researchers, as parents, as children, as members of countless communities—in the invisible mechanisms that come to rest on, to weigh down, to push back Jane and us all. Her vulnerability, her citation of the most visceral escape possible, calls us all—including scholars—to develop a more nuanced and responsive understanding of power and resistance.

While they do not specifically invoke the language of strategies or tactics, one can examine work by Butler (1990a) on the performativity of gender, Bennett (2003) and Gingrich-Philbrook (1998) on sexuality as performative, Warren (2003) on whiteness as performative accomplishment, Nainby and Pea (2003) on contradiction and class identity, and Alexander (2004) on racialized identity as tactical—as relatively fleeting, time- and context-bound efforts to disrupt power by identifying how power manifests in particular experiences. These works function as tactical in that they articulate the brief, situational, and ephemeral actions that make visible domination and power. It is here, in the site/sight of performance, that we find a number of parallels to what we might productively consider tactical scholarship. Of note is Butler's (1990a) assertion that performance allows us to more fully discern the mechanisms of systemic reiteration of power. She offers parody as a critical response to the performative accomplishment of gender—a subversion or reimagining of mundane performance that marks the creation of identity as repetitive, patterned, emergent, and constructed:

> Indeed, when the subject is said to be constituted, that means simply that the subject is a consequence of certain rule-governed discourses that govern the intelligible invocation of identity. The subject is *determined* by the rules through which it is generated because signification is *not a founding act, but rather a regulated process of repetition* that both conceals itself and enforces its rules precisely through the production of substantializing effects. In a sense, all signification takes place within the orbit of the compulsion to repeat; "agency" then, is to be located within the possibility of a variation on that repetition . . . it is only *within* the practices of repetitive signifying that a subversion of identity becomes possible. (Butler, 1990a, p. 145; emphasis hers)

Parody, like a tactic, must always already stand in response to some discourse, must call out a structure in order to subvert it. Drag as parody, for instance, is not just a performance of a man in woman's clothing, but rather a performance that plays with, challenges, or calls out gender as structure, as performed differently by men and women through clothing, makeup, and so on. Though such parodic performances may receive social sanction or dismissive laughter, each stands as an interruption or fissure in what might appear an otherwise smooth and heavy discursive fabric. As Shugart (2001) notes, accumulation of these tactical responses helps to increase their subversive potential.

Vulnerability, then, is a way of constructing a parodic politic, a purposefully subversive stance, in the classroom. When we reveal ourselves as vulnerable, we also reveal the mechanisms of power's production; we show the strategic rhetorics of educational practice as constructed, as repeated practice that regulates and mediates our communication, and, therefore, our relationships with one another. Such performances of vulnerability constitute, in effect, a performative pedagogy that, as Pineau (1994) suggests, allows the classroom to be a space of the trickster, a space where the politics of our subjectivities are called into question. As a result of experiencing an accumulation of these subversive, vulnerable moments, we become better suited to the task of retheorizing educational activity. As a result of these accumulated moments, we might effect educational change that is responsive to and reflective about the ways social systems move in and through us; moreover, we might cultivate in ourselves the sort of reflexive attitude that makes possible meaningful dialogue and collaborative work. Our task in this chapter is to explore the (im)possibility of critical communication pedagogy, to reflect on the practice of research, to reflect on our research, and to consider the potential of research as compliant, as resistant, as pedagogy.

* * *

When I reflect on my enthusiasm at seeing Ron's essay in *Communication Education,* I am struck by the degree to which my celebration was premature. That is, what was really radical about this one essay in this one journal? Did it open up space for others? Did it cause a revolution against the dominance of social scientific research in that or any other journal? Did it receive such support from the academic community that our assumptions and beliefs about research, about the nature of authorial voice, have changed since its publication? Not exactly. But, in order for an effort to matter, it need not change the world; resistant, tactical responses are often momentary, often a flicker that calls attention to the status quo.

One need only consider the uproar over the 1997 publication of "Sextext" in *Text and Performance Quarterly* to see what happens when an essay goes against the grain. In that writing, Corey and Nakayama offer a desirous essay about desire, an erotic consideration about eroticism. The piece was scandalous, causing some to laud the piece as responsive to and reflective of paradigmatic plurality and the advance of critical, evocative scholarship; others dismissed the article as pornography, writing to *The Chronicle of Higher Education* and *Spectra* to decry the essay as evidence of deviance, of a decline in our discipline's professional standards. Of course, we could read this essay, its portrayal of queer-themed content in an "alternative" style, as deviant in more ways than one. The critiques came fast and furious (Parks, 1998; Wendt, 1998), often ignoring the argument of "Sextext" and instead advocating more proactive intellectual gatekeeping and discipline. Like some conservatives' efforts to fight marriage equality, these critics worked to deny others the basic right to express their paradigm, to locate their message, their argument in their experiences and in their voices.

And Ron's piece was not free from that critique either; perhaps the marker of tactics is the effort made by gatekeepers to silence you.

* * *

A common problem when we teach de Certeau (1984) in our classes is the overwhelming tendency to cast tactics as good and strategies as bad. Students' first movement through this work is, typically, to name strategies in their lives, to call out institutions as oppressive and regulating. While understandable, this move misses the central thrust of de Certeau's work, especially as extended by Nakayama and Krizek (1995) where they shift the emphasis to discursive patterns in our everyday talk. Rather than imagine strategies as only a product of evil institutions, it is useful to think about how these rhetorics move in and through all of us, all the time. Indeed, many times strategies are useful; they organize experience and make complex phenomena accessible. Tactics, what we would call upon to resist particularly harmful strategies, are those moments in which we call attention to the structure. So, for instance, we might view the use of APA style, our use of it in this book, as a strategy that works to mark our academic voice as a particular kind of scholarship while also working to credit those scholars who preceded us. One might see bell hooks's (1994) writing as tactical, her choices to not cite others in the familiar way, as a way of resisting a particular vision of what counts as scholarly. And while we agree with Bazerman (1987) that APA is rhetoric, does shape how we understand our relationship to the published (and unpublished), it is also a helpful, systematic means of organizing those voices into our argument.

Our work certainly has strategic elements working in and through it, some we recognize and others we have surely overlooked. Our use of APA, or our choice to publish in academic venues, our efforts to write our scholarship in a fairly conventional format (i.e., literature review, method, findings, etc.), and our choice to pursue human subjects approval for each study, show how our work reproduces order, rules, and institutions. Moreover, it is important to us, in a sense, to know our readers' expectations, to know that we have some things in common.

We also made some choices—for practicality? for survival?—that we think worked to keep things in place, rather than to frustrate them. For instance, our piece on Jane, perhaps the most damning critique of some instructional communication research, is published not in *Communication Education* but in *Communication and Critical/Cultural Studies,* for an audience who are likely to agree with the conclusions we offer. Almost all of our scholarship has been published in academic journals; we have not sought to publish in policy journals or with popular presses or submit our findings to institutional offices that make direct changes to how universities label or regulate student identities. Rather than rocking the boat, we've put everything in its proper place, lest we find ourselves swimming.

* * *

I remember one student entering my office with a copy of Ron's essay—she was fuming, more angry than I expected. I had assigned "The Critical Life" in a methods course and, while I was hoping for dialogue about the piece, I wasn't expecting this kind of response:

Isn't this a white guy? Wow, more stories from a white guy—I haven't heard any of those before. . . .

How does this guy not just reproduce us as victims of a trapped system? Am I just supposed to feel totally screwed as a result here? How is this even remotely helpful?

I'm glad he actually allowed some dialogue here—it's good to know he doesn't really need to include anyone else or talk to anyone. . . .

For a critical guy, he sure doesn't actually address major issues of power—race, class, gender, sexuality? I sure don't feel he went very far. It is like 'The Critical Lite,' half the length, half the critique.

And while I tried to take some of these away, tried to balance her critique with suggestions that it was Ron's essay that made possible her questions, she remained unconvinced. I tried to suggest that perhaps he was speaking to a particular audience—that he wanted to make sure his argument was clear and that perhaps her frustration meant there was more work to do. Regardless, I left that meeting knowing that as resistant as I found Ron's work, others did not find it resistant at all. Like any piece of scholarship, it calls to some audiences and leaves others unmoved.

* * *

When we were in graduate school, we both had the same response to certain kinds of research—often we would stir anxiously in our seats, brooding at some line in an essay, some curious claim, some theoretical or methodological failing. Our bodies, as if sewn from the same thread, would cringe. This is not to say that our reading or critique of these works was correct, but rather that we shared a sense of what chafed, irritated us in research. For instance, the passive voice, so often celebrated and recognized as "scholarly" or "objective" or "unbiased," struck us as a choice with real costs for the reader, the argument, and the people who stand to profit or lose most by the writing. The passive constructions effaced all agency from the person seeing (not to mention the person being seen) and left us wondering who was responsible for the claims within the work.

Further, we grew frustrated by the same kinds of ethical questions. In a class on education and culture, we read Carger's (1996) *Of Borders and Dreams,* an ethnographic study of Alejandro, a young Mexican-American student who is overwhelmed by life and schooling in inner-city Chicago. This is, frankly, a remarkable book. I begin, in and through her telling of the tale, to love this little boy, to care about his successes and worry about his failures. I become invested and want to know where Alejandro is now, how he is faring, and whether he's happy. Of course, this is evidence of good writing and we celebrate Carger for creating a text that is both so rich and enriching. Further, we celebrate her argument; the schooling system fails Alejandro repeatedly and it is from Carger that we learn an important lesson about the effects of education on the bodies of its subjects. But in the course of the book, we become troubled by Carger's decisions as an ethnographer. She becomes, at times for us, overly involved in Alejandro's life, leaving us wondering about what happens to this little boy (not to mention Alejandro's mother, whom Carger assists several times during the course of the book) who has become dependent upon Carger's influence, her efforts to defend him, tutor him, and care for him. We can't help but wonder about the role of the researcher in the lives of the researched. In these moments, we both fear that in our celebration of Carger and her book, we may neglect the ways our love of this tale effaces the effects of scholarship, both positive and negative, on the boy who did not just live in the pages of her tale but lives in our world.

One day, in a graduate class on the communication needs of special student populations, we both became incensed at one essay, Rosow's (1989) study of Arthur, a boy who is struggling to learn to read. During the reading of this essay, we both recoiled at the assumptions embedded in the author's rendering of this boy and his family. She grants, from the outset, that academic skills, such as reading, were a life necessity, that school (abstractly) was a moral virtue, and that any family who felt otherwise irresponsibly reduced that child's chances of succeeding. Rosow, we felt, took the position (whether intentionally or unreflectively), that anyone who might question intellectual assumptions about the purpose and value of schooling (assumptions that are thoroughly and always classed, gendered, nationed, raced, and sexed) was just as dangerous as the demonized family she describes in her essay. In class, we questioned her assumptions. One of us asked: "Where does it end? If we tell Arthur's family they have to teach him to read, then where does it end? What about the court decisions that force Mexican-American families to speak English in the home? Where does it end? What would it mean to replace reading with, say, Catholicism, or homonormativity, or athletic accomplishment? We need to talk about this—some values may be more important than others, but who decides?" At this, one of our classmates smacked her desk: "Don't you get it? Arthur can't read! Don't you see what his family is doing to him? Somebody has to *do something!*" Let us be clear: We are not suggesting that literacy is unimportant, that it is not a skill we'd wish for our own children, that it is not a skill children from marginalized cultures must cultivate in order to understand and survive the "culture of power" (Delpit, 1995). However, the value we place culturally on reading (or on compliance, or on criticism) is just that . . . a cultural value, not a moral imperative, not above question.

More frustrating still are the values that mark our discipline's textbook industry, the production of introductory texts that suggest, in both form and content, that the story is fixed and solid, linear and unproblematic. The presence of developmental editors, who work to achieve consistency and "appropriate" content, has made possible a wide array of books that suggest the field moves in a simple progression from communication models to perception and self-concept to verbal and nonverbal communication to (some) intercultural theory (mostly stereotyping and ethnocentricity) to public communication. These well-worn, reiterative patterns have consequence for our students, for their understanding of and ability to read primary texts, for their sense of stake and contention with respect to communication theory, for their sense that these, too, are values not givens. What does it mean when we save questions about the relationship of culture, power, and oppression for the latter third of our classroom communication texts (if we address it at all)? What does it mean to cast interpersonal relationships as primarily heterosexual, relegating members of the GLBTQ community to the end of the chapter, to the footnotes, to a quick claim that there really is not that much difference at all? What does it mean that our textbooks still maintain silence on issues related to economic class or class conflict? These are choices we (re)make as a field, choices that function to create our field, choices that, by necessity, authorize certain values and discourage others; we must begin to recognize them as such.

But to what end? The bottom line for us, as critical communication scholars, is that we believe research should and does matter—that research itself is pedagogical. Whether shared in our textbooks or at conferences, in publications or lectures, research teaches. Our frustration about passive voice reflects our desire to mark authorship and agency, to hold human actors accountable for the things they (don't) do. As a writer, I must be present in the document in order to identify *from where* I, as a critic, speak. Our concern with the ethnographer who oversteps her or his bounds is a reflection of our belief that we must engage in scholarship (in and out of the classroom) always with the awareness that our (in)actions can have consequence for the minds, bodies, and spirits of our research participants. Our concern with unreflective assumptions that elide values, leaving them decontextualized and unquestioned, is that such essentialism implies that learning and the process of knowledge construction are apolitical, neutral, uncontested. Our concern with homogenization in our discipline's textbook industry is that it makes it harder to reveal our theories as partial, as argument, as value laden, as built rather than given.

Both of us began our research endeavors with a desire to participate in the scholarly community. We wanted to ask questions of scholars in communication and education, to name their assumptions and ours and to explore the effects these/our studies have had on the research participants who were subject to (and the subject of) these research projects. How has the work on whiteness and racism obscured the ways mundane enactments of cultural members (re)create and maintain systems of race? How does the everyday discourse surrounding students (of all sorts) help to institutionalize and naturalize these identities? Our research has been an effort to speak back to, call out, and, at times, celebrate the scholarship that moves us. Indeed, this book is about speaking back, about challenging ourselves as scholars—as researchers, students, and teachers—to imagine and engage in critical, hopeful work.

* * *

In the 2000 issue of *Communication Education,* the editor, Joe Ayres, provided space for two reflections on Ron's "The Critical Life." Ragan

(2000) and Banks and Banks (2000) each articulated their readings, their assessments of Ron's work, offering context and framing to a suspicious academic audience. From Ragan (2000):

My reaction to Editor Joe Ayres's decision to publish this piece, despite my recommendation as a reviewer to reject it, was a disconcerting mix of surprise and pleasure. (p. 229)

The main reason that I recommended rejection of "A Critical Life" was that there was no fit between the piece and the social science criteria (i.e., *Communication Education*'s criteria) for assessing it. (pp. 229–230)

Autoethnography is not a "method" in the sanctioned way that we speak of method in the discipline. It is neither methodical nor systematic, purposefully, and thus it cannot be evaluated by our mainstream paradigm criteria. (p. 230)

Because of Ron's autoethnography, I will think about criticizing and being criticized with new attention to these acts, with aroused awareness of their consequence. (p. 231)

With respect to autoethnography, in general, and to Ron's work, in particular, Ragan's (2000) essay is a mixed bag; she is unclear as to the merit of the work or the method, yet she still finds the piece pedagogical, informing her life as a researcher and teacher. Banks and Banks (2000) are more overtly positive:

Ron Pelias's "The Critical Life" is a bold experiment in evocative writing. It is an autoethnography with attitude. Perhaps this is why it teaches us. (p. 233)

The journal editor asks, "Don't you think it needs some contextualizing?" We did, but we believed the contexts for interpreting and applying an autoethnographic text should be—perhaps can *only* be—supplied by readers, not by the author. (p. 233)

Pelias channels his critique of the generative conditions of his perplexities, while he works out the self-culture dialectic and pursues his questioning of identity, place and power as a situated actor within the communication discipline. (p. 235)

Banks and Banks's (2000) read of Ron's work is that it radically positions the self in relation to culture, positions the self as simultaneously both product and producer of culture, allowing a heuristic view of life within critique.

We contend that Ron's work functions as critical communication pedagogy, as a momentary interruption in the ongoing story of *Communication*

Education, a hitch in the machinery, a novelty in the expected. This moment, this re-vision of how one might conceptualize the doings of everyday academic life, is a tactic, a generative space within a context that resists change and abhors uncertainty. de Certeau might be proud of his effort.

* * *

Thus, critical communication pedagogy is, as we would hope de Certeau (1984) would agree, a tactical form of research practice, in as much as something as sedimented and patterned as research practice can be tactical. It is a response, a recognition of patterns in discourse and thought. Critical communication pedagogy takes as a central principle a commitment to questioning taken-for-granted, sedimented ways of seeing and thinking. It forges alliances and builds new possibilities. In our work, both individually (Fassett, 2003; Warren, 2003) and collectively (Warren & Fassett, 2002; Fassett & Warren, 2004, 2005), we have strived to make our time spent in research matter with respect to our teaching—to make our participants and their lives matter in our own. In part, our desire to understand their lives is a function of our desire to understand our own, to understand how power moves in and through our own discourse as academics. That is, we were driven in part by our desire to not hurt our students, to name and challenge the violence they might encounter as diverse people in a reproductive educational system. In this sense, our research has been tactical, it has been an effort to create spaces for ourselves, our colleagues, and our students to explore how systems of power function, are present in our lives, in our classrooms.

Our desire to make research matter often stems from comments we hear from (and actions we note in) others. For instance, at a conference, we heard a senior professor from an ivy league school say: "Politics plays no part in my classroom—if a white supremacist takes my speech class and becomes a more effective white supremacist, then we've had a successful semester." We witnessed another professor we respected attack a young graduate student, dismissing her effort to define her performance work as research as naïve and misguided. We heard a professor who writes extensively about communication apprehension laugh at the suggestion that he does his work to help others, noting that his scholarship is just "work," that he couldn't care less if it helps the students he assesses in his statistical research. But our desires aren't always motivated by frustration or anxiety; we are often moved by love. We are moved by the colleague who works generously to understand perspectives she doesn't share, the student who asks difficult questions about the moral and ethical value of communication research, and the respondent at conference who willingly and excitedly engages young scholars in conversations about their work, about how their work challenges and extends existing lines of work in our field. Our desire to do critical communication pedagogy is about saying that the reason for, the *why* we research, is often more important than the *what* we research. "To what end?"—the question permeating these pages represents this central component to our vision of critical communication pedagogy. As a respected friend of ours once said, "I don't do work just to get my name in print—I do what I do because it might change the lives of people I care about."

This said, we would do well to remember de Certeau's (1984) caveat: Tactics, because they are ephemeral, are subject to their own institutionalization or co-optation. Radical scholarship, when raised to the status of canon, ceases to be radical. One can and should question the work we both have done, seeking new ways of understanding critical communication pedagogy that frees our work from the constraints we have failed to acknowledge. That we welcome this revision signals our dedication to critical work; because our point is to model and engender reflexivity, it is our hope that others will enter into this conversation with us, taking it into hopeful and productive directions.

Perhaps the most productive spaces we occupy as researchers are those where we selfishly explore something we have written with our students. In their careful and critical readings, we come to see the ways our work has its own limits. During a reading of one of our articles (Warren, 2001c), students found a new and provocative way of understanding a moment of interaction, generating a productive conversation about both that classroom moment and researchers' blind spots. In the article, John recounts how during the crisis following a student's racist comment in class, the student wrote on the chalkboard "I will not say rice burner (yada, yada)" (Warren, 2001c, p. 194). John goes on to address the significance of the expression "rice burner" at some length, as well as the context that made that statement possible. However, John neglected to explore the "(yada, yada)"; in fact, John never saw the construction as problematic during the writing of the article. Upon reflection, the implications of this Jewish allusion are telling for both the content and author of the article and deserving of thorough attention.

We are not suggesting that scholars should measure the relative success or failure of a given work by its capacity to do everything; given the constraints inherent in language, in perception, in values, such expectations are unrealistic and unproductive. A more meaningful focus is to consider how critical communication pedagogy scholars should possess the moral conviction to ask critical questions, the dedication to exploring power in process, even in their own scholarship. Like all tactics, critical communication pedagogy risks co-optation (for instance, each of us has had to make compromises—in our word choice, source selection, publication venue, and so forth—to see some of our work to print). Like all tactics, critical communication pedagogy is necessarily constrained and made possible by the strategies that give rise to it. But critical communication pedagogy scholars do the work anyway. They/we do it because we believe that in it, through it, we might find hope to re-imagine ourselves and our relations with others.

* * *

I must admit, though, my enthusiasm for reading Ron's work—moreover, my reading of Ron's work itself—was shaped, and perhaps nurtured, by a certain amount of suspicion. I found Ron's article in the July 2000 issue of *Communication Education,* but I found Donald C. Shields's critique of "The Critical Life" less than half a year later, in the December 2000 issue of *Communication Monographs.* A very quick response for academics.

Shields (2000) examines what he calls the "theoretical robustness of critical autoethnography" (p. 392), questioning this work's right, Ron's right, to space in the pages of *Communication Education:* "I'm not so worried about whether or not the piece concerns education, but I'm deeply concerned that it doesn't say much about communication" (p. 393). On this basis, Shields reduces various scholars' work to their smallest details, dismissing autoethnographers' efforts, as in Ron's work, as commentary about insignificant daily interactions lacking scholarly rigor (p. 396). In the end, on the basis of his fantasy-theme analysis (interestingly, a comparable method to autoethnography in as much as it involves the collection and interpretation/analysis of data), Shields concludes that autoethnography is "losing its novelty and becoming banal" (p. 416). Unfortunately, because Shields's essay is reductive, dismissive, and defensive, it does not readily invite thoughtful or nuanced discussion about autoethnography as method. However, if tactics are marked by an institution's efforts to squelch them, then Shields's essay stands as evidence of strategy. In his response, he reveals "The Critical Life" for what it is, a critical, destabilizing work that serves to call out our expectations and values as a discipline.

However, what happens if we grant Shields (2000) the worth of his question—does autoethnography have a sustainable future? Might we, rather than question autoethnography's viability, address what it makes possible? We do this here *not* to defend our choices, but to note that autoethnography is a particularly hopeful method in critical communication pedagogy, though surely not the only method one might choose. While Shields offers one answer to the question of autoethnography, we seek here in this book to answer the question through the method, rather than apply standards that will necessitate a particular kind of answer. To discern this method's worth (acknowledging the patriarchal nature of such a question), we ask what it might do for us, especially given that much of this book is written as autoethnographic narratives. Autoethnography (or what H. L. Goodall calls new ethnography)

> is a cultural way of coding academic attempts to author a *self* within a *context* of *others*. It is a way of writing to get to the *truth* of *our* experiences. It is a method of inquiry, scholarly inquiry, that privileges the exploration of a self *in response to questions that can only answered that way,* through the textual construction of, and thoughtful reflection about, the *lived experiences of that self.* (Goodall, 2000, p. 191, emphasis his)

Autoethnography is not a method that answers all questions—no method can answer all questions, which is why we need (why the field as a whole needs) multiple methods and ways of asking and answering questions. Moreover, we might ask whether the desire to assess the worth of auto-ethnography as a method is, however subtly, sexist. Inspired by Cris Mayo (2004), we suggest that efforts to frame a debate around and within the paradigm mandated by Shields only work to normalize and naturalize the measurement, not the ideology that surrounds measuring in the first place. Autoethnography, as we understand it, is a mode of writing that privileges reflexivity—it demands that one slow down the everyday doings of a moment, for us a pedagogical moment, to see the machinery at play within the mundane landscapes of our lives. In other words, when we live our lives, we often fail to see the ways institutions are at play in and through us. This kind of blindness is not individual, but part of the way social systems elide their own mechanisms of power. Autoethnography is a reflexive accounting, one that asks us to slow down, to subject our experiences to critical examination, to expose life's mundane qualities for how they illustrate our participation in power.

Consider our project in this book—to ask what critical communication pedagogy looks like in research and life. This task benefits from writing that locates this argument in moments, in bodies in pedagogy and in research. Autoethnography, as a method, helps us show you—rather than tell you—what we think critical communication pedagogy is. To locate it in the moment, in that moment of articulate contact (Nainby, Warren, & Bollinger, 2003), is to make possible a situated, contextualized accounting of critical communication pedagogy. It is to offer a vision that accounts for how power is at play within the moment of our bodies in contact, our experiences in dialogue, with others. By slowing down moments, exposing them to critical inquiry, we aim to address the strategies (de Certeau, 1984) at play within our lives, within our classrooms, within our pedagogical contexts. We also see this concerted effort as a tactical response to power, an effort to note the mechanisms of power at play on and in our own teacherly, learning bodies. This method, carefully used and crafted, can be a powerful, if ephemeral, tactic—it can serve to assist or uncover power within context. It can address the taken-for-granted; this can be a powerful tool to speaking back to power.

So if this method offers us so much, why silence it? We propose that such moves are strategic efforts to recenter power, to dismiss and erase efforts that disrupt the expected. It is important to note that we do not claim to know the intentions of academics who oppose certain modes of scholarship (though participation in systemic power is rarely about individual intent). Such moves are institutional because the logics that support them are part of our mundane lives, our mundane understandings, our mundane communication. Shields (2000) is interesting in that he represents a patterned way of working to resecure the academic center of power. Through careful analysis and thoughtful reflection, we can see the nature of power illuminated through the pages of our journals.

And, as Ron notes in "The Critical Life," he doesn't really read *Communication Monographs* anyway. Of course, such decisions, while they feel good (and while we share them), work to reinscribe the nature of power itself. And it is the replication of social systems, of institutions, that is really at issue here.

* * *

Why would one do research? Why would one write? We might look to Annie Dillard (1990), who warns,

> One of the few things I know about writing is this: spend it all, shoot it, play it, lose it, all, right away, every time. Do not hoard what seems good for a later place in the book, or for another book; give it, give it all, give it now. The impulse to save something good for a better place later is the signal to spend it now. Something more will arise for later, something better. These things will fill from behind, from beneath, like well water. *Similarly, the impulse to keep to yourself what you have learned is not only shameful, it is destructive. Anything you do not give freely and abundantly becomes lost to you.* You open your safe and find ashes. (pp. 78–79; emphasis ours)

Or Goodall (2000), who addresses the appeal, the intrigue of the new ethnography, of autoethnography:

Therein lie the pull, and the call, of this mystery. When you feel pulled in, called to the mystery of it, you have arrived. You must now begin to write. (p. 8)

Or Stephen King (2000), who has this to say about the writing life, the role of writing in our lives:

> Writing isn't about making money, getting famous, getting dates, getting laid, or making friends. *In the end, it's about enriching the lives of those who will read your work, and enriching your own life, as well.* It's about getting up, getting well and getting over. Getting happy, ok? Getting happy. . . . Writing is magic, as much as the water of life as any other creative art. The water is free. So drink. Drink and be filled up. (pp. 269–270; emphasis ours)

Writing, engaging in the critical research we call for in this book, is more than just something we do as scholars because we have to publish or perish. As Dillard, Goodall, and King suggest, writing is so much more. . . . It is a means of learning, about others and about ourselves; it is a means of becoming, of growing, of giving. We fool ourselves if we focus exclusively on the product of our writing, on the writing itself; that focus masks what writing means for the writer, how she or he is forever changed by the effort of writing. Writing is a process of meaning making, not just for the reader, but also for the writer. bell hooks (1992) once observed, "I came to theory because I was hurting—the pain within me was so intense that I could not go on living. I came to theory desperate, wanting to comprehend—to grasp what was happening around and within me" (p. 1). In a similar way, we seek methods of writing that complicate our lives, that challenge us to look inside ourselves and critically interrogate our participation in power and privilege. Our scholarship, our writing, our theory building is a healing process; it is a place where we can explore the mystery and promise of communication, the depth of our lived experiences, and the meanings we make, necessarily, with one another. It is a talking back (hooks, 1989), a potentially rich tactical response to power.

* * *

My first published autoethnographic essay (Warren, 2001a) was about white identity, about locating the/my self within the soothing/smothering world of privilege. Privilege, so soft yet so limiting. I wrote the essay in four parts, working to articulate how I moved from blindness or unawareness to discerning privilege, to comprehending that privilege, to finally understanding how I was complicit in that privilege. I named the third part, the shift to understanding, "Seeing," an effort to see how we are located in power, how our senses of self are products of (not) seeing the world around us, and how we participate in systems of power. In this condensed except, note how one might see her- or himself as a constituting being, a figure that recognizes how the power of seeking others constitutes the self as well:

I [am] so pissed. Meet us by the big tent, they said. We'll be there around seven, they said. We'll be looking for you, they said. Meet us by the big tent, they said.

I look at my watch—it's 8:00. If I didn't need this night out, I would just go home and leave a nasty message on their machines. *You bastards!* Of course, I would never do that. I would probably work for guilt and sympathy. *Sorry I missed you, I looked for you all for about an hour. We must not have crossed paths. Hope you had a good time.* Yeah, guilt is more my style. I could almost see them, staring at the answering machine with a look of pity for me. Feeling sorry for missing me. That would be good.

I walk by the only big tent I see one more time. The band, a Motown cover group named Jimmy Church Band, echoes "My Girl" as I stroll by the police/first aid stand. A large cop, face slightly sunburned, watches me as I make my way past the tent yet again, searching the crowd. I look almost out of place. This is my first time at Herrinfesta, a local Italian festival in Southern Illinois. . . . The band shifts into "Mustang Sally," a favorite of mine. I stare at them on that stage, watching them work together toward the completion of their song. I stare in part because I am invited to, for they are there for my viewing pleasure. I pause to hear the five African-Americans belt out how Sally should slow her mustang down, and as I take a deep breath, smelling the cooking meats, the fried dough, the smoke from a thousand cigarettes, I see Mark.

As I approach, other faces I know gather. I choose to play it cool. "John! You came!" I smile and reply that I have been looking for them, trying to make it seem like it was an inconvenience, nothing more. We sit, listen to the Motown, watch the people greet each other, eat, and drink beer. Celebration reigns. . . .

Herrinfesta is like nothing I have ever seen before. . . . I look more closely at my surroundings. The dirt area in which I am sitting is carefully groomed—all trash is immediately scooped up by those red-shirted volunteers. Family businesses have their booths set up, each touting local food, owned by local families, offering local hospitality. I am sitting in a large gated area featuring food and music—a gated area only accessible with a smiley face ink stamp that is provided by volunteers who guard the gate and collect the nominal entry fee. . . . As the night progresses, the population of the area in which we are sitting triples, an overwhelming amount of people for Southern Illinois, I think to myself.

As the Motown group finishes their time allotment, I look up to see a balding, pale man in a suit take the mike. The Black performers, now parted by the new presence on the stage, watch as he announces the next band, a group playing seventies music. The presence of that White man's body, in that space, strikes me as almost wrong. Ever since I arrived, that stage was those Black gentlemen's space where they created music and now, with the music stopped and a bare flood light on, the presence of this man in the middle of their space felt wrong—an intrusion. I shake my head and look back at my beer, then glance out over the crowd now gathered. And then I see him. He is standing by the railing, talking with some people. He begins to walk away from me and I adjust in my seat to see more of him, twisting my body to continue my glance. He is there, just up there, can you still see him? I stand, still looking, but he is gone, lost in a sea of bodies—White bodies. This man . . . this man of color, Black, in this sea of White Southern Illinois bodies. Was he real? Did I make him up? I realize that I am dwelling on this man's presence and that now, the Whiteness that surrounds me becomes pronounced. What felt like a mass of bodies, now feels like a mass of White bodies—White bodies in cowboy hats, in jeans and T-shirts, working in booths, dancing on the dirt floor of the gated, protected community.

The realness or fictiveness of that man's body in this place doesn't matter—it doesn't change what I did in that moment of looking, of staring at his body. Through my gaze, I made race matter, while simultaneously unveiling how race always already mattered. In my gaze, I locate that body as different—that body got marked, through my inspection, as meaningful, thus disavowing my own connection with that difference. I marked him as of-color, rendered him a subject in that marking without his consent, like I suspect he has been so rendered before. And through my distancing, I make and reify my own Whiteness: "It is only through that disavowal that [my] whiteness is constituted, and through the institutionalization of that disavowal that [my] whiteness is perpetually—but anxiously—reconstituted" (Butler, 1993, p. 171). So I remade my Whiteness in that little performative moment—I rendered meaningful a legacy of racial discourse and through that act, made race a material, meaningful, and effect-causing reality. . . .

While the disavowal of another as a way to constitute the Self helps to clarify how subjects make and remake their Whiteness, the absence of a disavowal also helps to make race. The act of passing, where all those bodies in cowboy hats and denim sat, danced and drank, remakes race. [Accepting this] racial identity, where I aid and am aided in our collective passing, helps to make Whiteness regardless of whether it is vocalized as such or not. These "stylized," historically informed, "repetitive," performances constitute identity (Butler, 1990b). In these acts, race was not made present—it was made. Racial privilege, racial inequities, and systemic Whiteness were only revealed, in as much as they were caught in the act of creation.

My beer is now flat. I rub my eyes, now irritated by smoke, dust, and the dusk sky turning slowly to night. I feel caught. It's like a mystery where the killer, unaware s/he did it, ends up catching himself or herself. I see myself seeing, seen in the act of protecting my own identity. Like the gated community I am now sitting in, I am protecting myself—working to keep stable my identity. And what's more, I am unsure of what to do about it. I rise, tossing my beer into the trash. I reach my hand into my pocket and pull out tokens for another drink. I am three tokens short. Mary looks up at me—can she see through me? See who I am and what I am doing—see the acts that I have been caught doing? I am the guilty one now.

I'm three short, I say. "Here." She lays three tokens in my hand, and I go in search of refreshment.

Writing this narrative was the most significant part of this essay for me—doing so called on my own need to examine the mundane enactments of how privilege was embedded in my own body, to make the critical implications of my work on whiteness come to matter in tangible ways through me, in me. The writing was pedagogical for me, as I hoped it would be pedagogical for others. As an autoethnographic moment, I sought to slow down this moment, to uncover how and in what ways power was functioning in this communicative moment—it was a moment that could be representative of how race/power/privilege comes to be. As an autoethnographic text, it seeks to pause a moment and reflect, to analyze power in the making.

But I didn't just write this narrative, it didn't just write itself, it wrote me as well; in a sense, I was called forth with the story, born from the fecundity of this research. While much of the process may seem introspective, writing this narrative meant creating, articulating a process of seeing, of how we encounter racial production in the mundane contexts of our lives. I wrote this because I felt these words might grant us (students, teachers, members of this local community, members of the world community, etc.) new ways of thinking about our own taken-for-granted practices.

Critical communication pedagogy is more than the act of research, more than publishing to get a job, finish a degree, receive tenure or promotion; it is about developing a critical vocation, a critical relationship with the world and allowing that positionality to guide and inform our everyday lives. As Shaull (2003) notes in his forward to *Pedagogy of the Oppressed,* "Freire . . . operates on one basic assumption: that [wo/]man's ontological vocation . . . is to be a Subject who acts upon and transforms [her or]his world" (p. 32). We contend in this book that one's desire to engage critical communication pedagogy is inherently Freirean: It is about fulfilling a call to do the work of social justice, it is about learning to listen and see in self-reflexive ways, it is about speaking carefully and humbly and recognizing that it is the job of the critical scholar to open rather than shut doors of possibility, it is about engendering hope in the world rather than dwelling in stubborn immobility. In our writing, we imagine critical communication pedagogy that fulfills Freire's call to us as communicators.

* * *

In the end, Ron's article, carefully placed against and contextualized by the reflective essays by Ragan (2000) and Banks and Banks (2000) in *Communication Education* and criticized by Shields (2000) in *Communication Monographs,* made, for the most part, a relatively quiet foray into the field's collective archive of work. It now functions, as do most articles in the field, as a course reading or a citation within someone's argument. With a brief reprise in Ron Pelias's (2004) book, *A Methodology of the Heart: Evoking Academic and Daily Life,* the article is what it is: a quiet, contemplative piece of poignant scholarship on living, on embodying critique.

In many ways, Ron's essay stands as a rich metaphor for tactical communication—it is a momentary, ephemeral interruption in the everyday doings of a patterned research outlet. This one piece generated a moment of disruption, one that required contextualizing essays and critical response and disavowal. And, after flickering briefly in our disciplinary consciousness, the essay recedes back into the recesses of our lives, to sit alongside the stories we tell our students about the publication of "Sextext" (Corey & Nakayama, 1997) or the Fiske-Carbaugh debates (Carbaugh, 1988, 1991; Fiske, 1990, 1991). The essay's significance will always be a function of the teller, serving as victor or villain accordingly; in any event, these sorts of challenges to the field will undeniably shape scholars' relationships to the discipline, to our collective assumptions, expectations, and values.

Each of us has used Ron's essay to teach the field, to explore what it means to do scholarly work. In her class, Deanna uses it to represent a possible direction in instructional communication research, an indication of shifting paradigms, another instance of scholarship as rhetoric, as pedagogy, as method, as visceral. John uses the piece to illustrate method, asking graduate students to read it as purposeful, legitimate analysis and communication of communication phenomena. Our students have mixed reactions, often taking a great liking to Ron's voice and his perspective or leaving the essay frustrated, feeling let down as he notes the limits of his abilities to live the critical life. And every once in a while, a student comes along who finds the article life changing. In particular, one of our shared students (who completed his M.A. with Deanna and his Ph.D. with John) found so much resonance with the article that he made his license plate CRTLIFE. He teaches the piece at every turn, with every set of students, toward many different ends. He finds Ron's voice compelling and his struggle immediate. For this student—a student who has searched for a way to speak his beliefs; to more fully understand teaching and learning, communication, and the functioning of power; to develop the ability to critically engage in the personal and political of educational life—this essay made possible new directions, new avenues for scholarship that speaks to him in ways other work in our field does not. de Certeau (1984) notes that what power tactics have lies in the "clever *utilization of time,* of the opportunities it presents and also of the play that it introduces into the foundations of power" (pp. 38–39). In this student, we see the meaning and value of Ron's work in the way it generates, in and through the body and mind and language of this young scholar, a possibility of resistance. For this student, Ron's work stands as a metaphor of what might be in critical communication pedagogy.

* * *

It is our hope that this chapter demonstrates that critical communication pedagogy is more than *just* one more area of study we might describe to students as a productive avenue for future research. While it is a research tradition, one we see emerging from the words and arguments of communication and education scholars alike, we also see critical communication pedagogy as more than that. Given its commitment to dialogue, reflexivity, ethics, and hope, critical communication pedagogy is epistemological, a way of knowing; critical communication pedagogy produces knowledge—it makes new ways of seeing and knowing possible.

Critical communication pedagogy is also axiological; it is a value system, an ethic, a way of situating oneself in relation to another. To do critical communication pedagogy is to take a stance of humility; it is to listen with an open heart and a willingness to be wrong. Most difficult about this work is the moment when one's commitments find the bodies, hearts, minds, and spirits of others who may not agree. Too often a "critical" scholar begins from "You know what's wrong with you?" and from never inviting the other's perspective to challenge her or his own. To claim moral, intellectual, political, or social superiority over another does not fit the values of critical communication pedagogy; it prevents true engagement from occurring.

Finally, critical communication pedagogy is ontological; it is and must be a way of being. Our scholarship serves as a guide from which (and by which) we live. It shapes us, gives definition to us, and guides our actions in the various spheres of our lives. To borrow from Freire (1970/2003), critical communication pedagogy is our ontological vocation; we live it because it is in our efforts that we find hope, meaning, and possibility.

5

Compromise and Commitment

Critical Communication Pedagogy as Praxis

This chapter asks: How does critical communication pedagogy look in the classroom? What does it mean to do this work, to take it up in our teaching and studenting bodies, to make it matter in the moment of "articulate contact in the classroom" (Nainby, Warren, & Bollinger, 2003)? This chapter explores our experiences in the classroom, considers how we succeed and, inevitably, fail in our efforts to nurture and sustain critical communication pedagogy. Moreover, we contend that it is dangerous to separate teaching from research, when they are always in tension, in relation, and mutually informing. We have much to learn from both, taken together, and, as Boyer's (Boyer, 1997; The Carnegie Foundation, 1990; Glassick, Huber, & Maeroff, 1997) legacy reminds us, teaching and research are always already connected; we would be wise to understand and explore how each may strengthen or weaken the other. This chapter is about finding the moments in our classrooms, with our students, that demonstrate how we are understanding these connections, these moments where reflection and action intertwine.

We find this approach, this writing, a useful tactic. We hope it interrupts, unsettles our own classroom practice; we hope it generates heuristic spaces for consideration of and dialogue about educational practice. In this exploration, we work to model critical praxis, as described by Freire (1970/2003, 1992) and Lather (1991); in "showing our work," we hope, as Freire might, that these analyses function as a synergy of theory and action. Moreover, we hope that, as Lather suggests, such theoretical and applied work creates generative spaces where we might imagine new and productive perspectives on and approaches to meaningful scholarship.

The Syllabus as Critical Intervention: Safely Vulnerable

Pedagogically sound or not, an hour before my first day teaching Communication Pedagogy, a graduate course for all doctoral and masters students in the School of Communication Studies, I decided I would attempt a very different beginning. I knew others who had done what I was planning to do, but too often the attempts had been exercises, never fulfilled in ways that allow the experience to be more—to be real. I remember one incident in which this kind of activity resulted in the professor taking back her power, forever altering the student-professor relationship in her class. This activity had risks, more than whether we'd succeed at our attempt to design a workable syllabus; to work, it had to be genuine, to proceed irrespective of whether or not I liked the outcome. The students couldn't feel tricked, set up for failure. If this was to succeed, I knew it would have to be honest; the syllabus would have to stick no matter what the students produced. I promised myself and then prepared.

"Good evening," I said as I stared at my new students, my new teachers. Many of the men and women in the room were my graduate teaching assistants, teaching under my supervision as their basic course director. "Tonight, basically, we will be discussing the nature of this class. Here are your syllabi." As I said this last part, I removed 22 bright pink copies of the syllabus I spent days on a few weeks ago . . . then, dramatically, I returned them to my briefcase. I looked at them . . . they looked at me . . . then the briefcase . . . then me again. "I've decided not to give you *this* syllabus." A pause, for effect. "Instead, you will have to design the class yourself. You need to do it all. What course policies do you want, what do you want to read, what do you want to have as assignments, what do you want these next 16 weeks to look like, feel like, be like?" Another pause. "I'm serious; this is a course in communication pedagogy and your work begins right now."

They divided into groups, first to identify the major organizational issues with respect to the syllabus. Then, each group created proposals that would be voted on by the class. They added books, took out others. They chose projects and assignments, many of which were actually on my initial syllabus; other assignments they dropped (the vita project they wanted; the classroom observations they skipped). At times, I felt high. At times, I felt uncomfortable with their choices, feeling that, had I been able to speak on the matter, I might have been able to convince them of their error. But, I let them have the power here, I let the class be theirs, at least as much as it could be. I am reminded of Shor (1996), who described his ideal image of critical education as when his role as teacher was put fully to the service of students' needs; the class moved along their own desires, their own initiative. This felt suspect to me; after all, as an informed member of this community, why did I assume my absence would help here? Yet, I remained in the background.

In three class periods' time, we had a working syllabus. During the whole process, I tried to acknowledge the power I used to get us there—it was me who "gave up power" and they who "received it." I didn't want the fantasy of shared power to go too far; we needed to explore how power played its role in this process. Even taking Shor (1996) to his logical end, this class-room had been about me (and, by necessity, about him) all along. I told them I would not purposefully undermine their choices, that they should tell me if they felt I did. This seemed like a logical compromise; I'd lead from their document and, together, we would evaluate its effectiveness.

Assessment became tricky; we talked about grades, agreeing students could create their own, individual assessment criteria. Around October, one of the students approached me and asked about his grade: "I realize that the assignments we've gotten back don't have grades on them." "Yeah," I replied. "Should I be worried?" he asked. Realizing that this moment was where my pedagogical assumptions and goals met his resistance, we talked about it and I explained I wanted to focus on his work and ideas in process, instead of an end product. He wasn't convinced, but allowed me this manip-ulation of power; I call myself on it, acknowledging my role in his confusion, his frustration. Should I have helped him, holding my desires in reserve in favor of some more collaborative decision-making process?

I wanted this experience to feel more vulnerable than it actually was; truth be told, I felt rather safe in my choices. Students were receptive—as graduate students, they expected less form and more innovation, especially if that inno-vation was within the realm of their own imaginations. The choice to build the course together was not so radical that they lost the ability to predict the daily functioning of the course. The classes flowed pretty smoothly and students seemed empowered by their ability to help shape the environment of their classroom. The end of the semester evaluations were positive; the only critiques were a perceived lack of organization and some individuals' confu-sion as to where they stood in the class, two expected outcomes of the choices I made early in the class. I thought I would feel vulnerable as the teacher. Would they trust me, believe me, find this experience useful or meaningful? In the end, they (apparently) did. This might be the product of my teaching—the dialogic and open way in which I worked to balance my voice and desires with theirs. It might be a product of context—they never saw my vision of the course until they had created their own; it began with them, then grew from there. It might be a product of reproduction—they built what they thought I would want, expect, reward. Who really knows? But, it is, I think, worth wondering why I was so surprised by the safety I felt, worth questioning why I thought this was such a risky choice in the first place.

* * *

When talking with some of my graduate students about the nature of critical approaches to education, I often feel a bit let down, a bit like I've failed to properly communicate what I really mean when I speak of critical communication pedagogy. I know this failure is, in part, a limit of my language—that is, I too am searching for how to do this work, to speak this work, to embody a critical classroom praxis. It is also, in part, a product of my own failures, my own limits with respect to practice, my own necessarily incomplete examples in class and how those fail to make the classroom a transgressive space. It is also, in part, a limit of their location as graduate students, their impatience, their eagerness; I find myself saying to graduate students, again and again, "this stuff takes time." It is also, in part, the nature of power to subvert and subsume resistance, turning it into a tool for the powerful. Yet, when I speak with students, not always but often, I feel disappointed. They are sometimes quick to reduce complex theoretical commitments and ideals into an exercise, an architecture in the classroom, a moment of interaction that, they believe, somehow shows they are critical, that they get it. The problem is that I don't always believe they know what "it" is anymore.

"I put my students in a circle."

"I refused to give grades so public speaking students could really understand what to focus on in my class."

"I told them they'll all get A's if they just stop worrying about assessment and focus on learning."

"I found this race exercise where people stand in a line and move forward and backward depending on their relation to privilege—they moved around and really got it."

"I met with this student and when she objected to her grade, I gave her the grade she wanted but told her she hadn't earned it, that she'd have to live with that!"

"Now I cold call my students—putting them on the spot means they'll read before class."

"I'm critical; I had my students develop their own syllabus."

These interactions, these moments, these specific acts that somehow reflect or embody critical education really do nothing to support learning, nor are they critical communication pedagogy. This doesn't mean that sitting with students in a circle of desks or asking students to engage bodily with issues of race is oppressive or uncritical, but suggests that specific acts, specific interactions, localized moments are *not*, in and of themselves, critical communication pedagogy. They are, in their best light, moments in which students and teachers are able to grasp difficult concepts, engage in complex ideas, and reflect on their own implication within systems of power. But to assume that they abstractly and completely represent critical engagement is to reduce a complicated, fluid understanding of power in communicative interaction to decontextualized component parts. These moments and activities never, by themselves, do the work of critical communication pedagogy; they never, isolated from the larger context of educational practice, subvert anything. An isolated transgression is not always radical nor critical or liberatory.

To take the syllabus building with my students seriously, I must ask several questions about the nature and function of the experience, I must attempt to be honest with myself, knowing that all my interpretations come from this side of the teacher's desk. The quick consensus regarding assignments and grading and the (mostly) positive evaluations of the course suggest to me that the graduate students were able to readily discern the behaviors (i.e., indicates interest in the topic and its relevance to personal experience, well-timed contributions that suggest careful reading of course texts, a willingness to take risks, curiosity about further graduate study or publication) that would complete their performances of "good graduate student" for this class, for me. Of course, I remember from my own schooling experiences that such performances are relatively easy to effect. So many mundane performances, gestures, actions that I, for good and for ill, dismissed as irrelevant or unproductive (e.g., lingering after class to ask a question. . . . just to ask a question, displaying meaningfully marked readings, handing in work early), still gave my professors the impression I was willing to play along, to please. This is not, of course, to suggest that the interest I read in my students was all fake or contrived; rather, it is to suggest that it would be problematic to assume that all students found it liberating to design their own way through this course.

Indeed, I know from subsequent conversations with some of the graduate students who were enrolled in the Communication Pedagogy class that many found the exercise (and, as a result, the course in general) troubling, disconcerting even. This raises another place to investigate, to question: To what degree do such pedagogical initiatives fail to fulfill their promise simply because there is a lack of context, a lack of precedent. The most common first-day process is the reading of the syllabus (what Shor, 1992, describes as "reading the riot act"): the ritual of beginning class, learning about the due dates and required readings, the schedule of what to expect. Altering that seemingly simple schooling mechanism means, for some, a larger disruption than it might appear at first blush. The absence of a clear contract can feel like walking a tightrope without a net: Students can feel much more vulnerable than they appear. And who can blame them? What kind of preparation for this work have they had? Where in the whole process of schooling have they been taught to question their most basic assumptions and values about that schooling? As de Certeau (1984) notes, "there are countless ways of 'making do'" (p. 29), but making do is not always the same as feeling comfortable or understanding the struggle as productive. I trusted my students would survive (and they did), but to assume they were properly prepared for this work (and therefore would make the most of it) was a mistake. And, given that I immediately removed the syllabus and pushed them into this activity, I didn't prepare them for this kind of academic engagement either.

However, I think the syllabus exercise, contrived as it was, did do something productive. I think the exercise gave rise to an opportunity for students to be accountable for their own learning, their own movement through an area of communication practice they already have some knowledge of, even if it is limited to their own schooling histories. It also challenged students to understand communication pedagogy by engaging in it; in another class, the exercise might have seemed awkward, but in a class on pedagogy, it seemed to have a level of relevance that served as a metaphor for the course itself. The project was also an occasion for students to work together to make meaning; in groups, they took on matters of the course that would and did affect all members of the community. Moreover, wherever possible, I tried to make the course about the exercise. I didn't undermine their work by falling back on my own assumptions about the class after we came to consensus on the syllabus; rather, that syllabus (and the process by which we created it) served as a foil and general organizing principle or mission for the class. For better and worse, I used that exercise as a frame for the course and, in the end, evaluated students on how well they fulfilled their own expectations and goals.

As I think back, I'm torn with respect to whether this was, in fact, critical communication pedagogy. On the one hand, I think the experience was incredibly compromised by the limitations of the context, by our shared constraints; yet, on the other hand, it did work toward realizing what I envision as the goals of critical communication pedagogy. Here's how:

- I tried to engender a context where we could explore our educational identities, as teacher and students, as emergent, (re)made through our communication, through the negotiations and decisions regarding our syllabus.

- I introduced our consideration of the syllabus as an exercise of power, as a mechanism of how teachers and students produce, affirm, and resist power in educational contexts.

- I asked us to understand the syllabus as a product of culture, imbued with cultural assumptions about not only our roles as teachers and students but also the purpose, function, and value of an education. Because a cultural product is, in effect, a collaborative product, I also asked students to address questions regarding participation and representation, to consider whether all members of the class should, could, would have voice in the experience.

- The focus on the syllabus was a direct effort to explore how the mundane moments of classroom interaction (i.e., even seemingly benign or traditional first-day rituals) are productive of the social system of education.

- I also invited students to engage the making of the syllabus as an opportunity to reflect on and name the ways they have been disciplined through syllabi in the past. This came out most clearly during the students' discussion of class policies (e.g., with respect to attendance, deadlines, grades).

- This activity made language central, as a productive and meaningful part of defining our roles and obligations in the classroom.

- We had to be reflexive in building the syllabus; we had to force ourselves to question the assumptions we make when entering education. This became especially marked as the class proceeded and we were able to reflect on those moments where we felt constrained by the document we collectively made.

- This activity stands as a model of how theory and practice in critical communication pedagogy gives rise to generative spaces of possibility, even if we choose not to pursue the possibilities we generate.

- In working together to organize the students' participation in the process of knowledge construction, we could and did explore our understandings of both subjectivity and agency—and how instructional communication work often effaces nuanced understandings of both—in the classroom.

- To build a collective sense of what this class could and would be, dialogue was *the* central component of our time in that space. Each of us had to make an effort to listen, to learn from the stories and life lessons we shared.

* * *

I remember leaving that first day of Communication Pedagogy feeling very proud of myself. I remember being so pleased that I was able to generate a space of conflict, a space where folks had to balance their excitement at the prospect of making their own syllabus (and in essence, their own class) and the discomfort at feeling like their professor had left them without the means to understand their own immediate pedagogical future. I remember being so excited that they had to live in that space of tension, feeling neither wholly happy nor lost, but rather, a careful balance of these tensions.

I know that some students felt terribly put off by this classroom environment. I know that, for many, the discomfort may not have been worth it, not worth the lesson I was teaching. I know it was an exercise that was constrained from the beginning. But I believe that these moments of tension, these moments that challenge our expectations, might challenge us to consider how education works its magic on us all, all of schooling's many subjects.

I was, in the end, pretty proud that day. It is really up to us to live up to the potential of that day, to make meaning from that experience. Discomfort can be an ideal means for learning to trouble the familiar; more powerful still is how we act in light of such insights. I know I changed as a result of that experience. Perhaps that, in itself, was useful.

Vic's Story: Resistance Languaged[1]

Eventually every class I observe goes there. I know what will happen before I get there. . . . It's the time in the class where I encounter the KKK. Tom is a young man, very thin and very pale. He often wears old black T-shirts that are faded and worn, displaying a rock band logo from the eighties. He is fairly vocal, takes on racial issues in class—the typically moderately liberal Midwestern young White male, if there ever was one. (Warren & Fassett, 2002, p. 583)

"I just don't think you should have used . . . that word . . . again." Vic's voice is clipped; he's speaking through clenched teeth, jaw and tendons pulsing. "That word" is "faggots" and we state it exactly twice in our article "(Re)Constituting Ethnographic Identities" (Warren & Fassett, 2002). We use it purposefully, and pointedly, and certainly not lightly. And we excerpt those moments here, though it gives rise to that word again.

That's when he brings up the KKK—the extreme example of White racism that is so often called-upon to separate the liberal White antiracist from *those* people, those racists. . . . And so Tom begins. "This one time, I was in Chesterville. I was in this Denny's, and, well, you know that Chesterville is the

KKK base in this area right? So, anyway, I was with my brother and we were going to get Van Halen tickets and we went to this Denny's first. We were sitting close to the door and they came in with their black outfits and those crosses and all, that's how we knew who they were. That and they looked like assholes. Anyway, I was sitting there wearing my Jim Morrison T-shirt and they picked us to talk to. They called us faggots cause we had long hair and then spit on the table. Luckily not on our food though." (Warren & Fassett, 2002, pp. 583–584)

There are eighteen of us—a graduate seminar swollen by deep cuts to the state budget—sitting in a loose circle. At least half don't understand what's happening; the others are markedly uncomfortable, shifting in their seats, looking first at Vic, then at me, and then back to Vic again. He almost never participates in class, except to praise or to punish someone's scholarship; tonight it's mine.

Tonight we have been examining ethical dilemmas in critical and interpretive research methodology—starting with Lindlof's (1995) discussion of Zimmerman's (1987) work with Alcoholics Anonymous and then moving on to other pieces, like Halualani's (2002) study of Hawaiian identity and the poignant moment where she explores her tourist arrival in Hawaii, her *aloha,* as betrayal (p. 146). We move from her work to a discussion of our piece in *Qualitative Inquiry* quoted above, where we explore the uncomfortable tension in believing one is shaping a research study and learning that one is shaped by it as well. It's an unusually poetic sort of piece—we wrote large swaths of it in an almost choral style—but what it does well is illustrate how small repetitions, reiterations shape not only the subjects we, as researchers, attempt to understand but also ourselves as researchers. We point to the discomfort, the anxiety, the desire and revulsion of needing to see certain kinds of communication in our interviews and observations, of needing to see evidence of homophobia or racism or pain, so that we would have something to analyze, to theorize, to complicate, to ameliorate.

I grow both troubled and excited by the details of the story, this story by this very pale thin young man who has often noted his sometimes rocky relationship with his *girl*friend. I grow troubled and excited to watch as he narrates this story, interested in the identities he constructs for us: heterosexual but the victim of homophobia, White but the victim of the KKK. . . . My pen continues writing. There is so much here. I begin to underline key words in the passage I just copied down: Jim Morrison shirt, KKK base, looked like assholes, not on our food though . . . Van Halen tickets, faggots. I am curious about this tale—what does it do, how does it help construct Tom's identity? (Warren & Fassett, 2002, p. 584)

Vic is not "out" with this class, nor is he out with me. He never discusses his personal life, and I don't ask. There's a fair bit of innuendo between us, vague suppositions about our backgrounds and lifestyles, but neither of us clarifies. I suspect he's gay, but I don't ask. I suspect he suspects I'm straight, and I've never worked to complicate that assumption. He thinks I'm too academic, too invested in certain discourses, certain modes of engagement; I don't think he's academic enough, too focused on using scholarship to make the argument he wants to make and not on allowing that work to push back, to shape his writing. I'm tired of being told I'm wrong, told I'm too young, told I'm too scholarly to understand how it is in the "real world." And, in this moment, this classroom, I'm acutely aware that Vic's about to say something he can't take back, something that will forever alter his relationships, with me, with his peers. This would be fine, but he has done so much work to keep his life, his emotions, his feelings to himself.

I've brought this article to the class not because I think I am clever, not because we've been the only researchers who've ever felt this tension before, but because I hope they will see that I am in process too. Too readily, students defer to me as the expert, dispute me as the liberal, deny me as the academic; they are quick to resolve me as someone static, fixed, finished. In writing this article, I tried to get at something that gnaws at me still, and, my hope is that, as a class, we can continue a conversation about ethics that perhaps prepares them in a way my own experiences as a student in methodology courses failed to do. I want to perform this piece for the class, as much for the voicing as the audiencing. Part of this is certainly narcissistic, in that I'm proud of some of the language in this piece, proud of how this scholarly voice resonates in my throat, helping it to sound more like me than other works I've written. But part of this is also purposeful: to illustrate how the voicing or audiencing, more than the reading, of the piece underscores our argument. Vic offers to read a segment of the article to the class with me, standing in for John's voice; it's a strong reading, given he didn't know he would be performing this piece for the class. Though, when he says, "My pen continues writing. There is so much here. I begin to underline key words in the passage I just copied down: Jim Morrison shirt, KKK base, looked like assholes, not on our food though . . . Van Halen tickets," Vic falters and begins again. " I am curious about this tale—what does it do, how does it help construct Tom's identity?"

* * *

"I just don't think you should have used . . . that word . . . again." Vic's voice is clipped; he's speaking through clenched teeth, jaw and tendons pulsing.

I have so many possible responses to the content of his statement; I have many, many more possible responses to his tone, to his means of engagement: "Just who are you anyway?" or "You won't listen to me, why should I listen to you?" or "Kiss my ass." "I'm sorry" is very far from my mind; nasty, unsympathetic retorts are very close. But I know he's reacting to something important, that he's posing a challenge that might function as one of those teachable moments (perhaps for him, perhaps for the others listening in, perhaps for me). I understand he has a right to his claim and a responsibility to express it.

I opt for: "That's an important observation Vic—one I think we should discuss as a class. What do you all suppose is the logic behind that choice?" I imagine we'll explore communication as constitutive, or perhaps how our choices as researchers are no more or less complex than our choices as students or teachers (or parents or children or members of communities . . .), or perhaps what makes this piece (un)reflexive. But instead, Vic answers immediately, "I don't know, but I don't think you should have used that word again—it was totally unnecessary. It doesn't add anything." Adding . . . that's interesting . . . that's precisely the point. . . . All discourse adds; each iteration adds weight and gives substance. Discourse never takes away, never subtracts; even deconstruction leaves building blocks behind.

"Okay. . . . Does everyone agree? What does this language choice mean for the reader? Or the research participant? Or the researcher?" Not surprisingly, no one wants to touch this topic; the students seem content to watch us resolve this between ourselves. Most students' eyes move back and forth, back and forth, as though they're seated at center court; only one or two students look worried, like they'd rather be anywhere else, and one student yawns. "Well, I guess John and I were trying to get at how complicated desire is in ethnographic research, of how terrible it feels to seek to find oppression at work and learn that we're implicated in that oppression. It helps to show that it's honest to feel you might be making things worse when you're wanting to make them better, and that it's frustrating to feel like you're alone when you're not. The repetition just makes it feel worse; it just *makes* it, makes what you're studying."

"Yeah, but you made that point already. You don't need to keep saying it." But he doesn't see that it's the repetition that matters. Maybe John and I haven't called that out enough, haven't done enough to show how troubled we are by it in the writing, but it's the repetition that matters, that gives rise to action or inaction. It's interesting to me that Vic hasn't said he's troubled by the first instance of "that word." We've quoted it as data, does that make that choice sound? Why is it more troubling to him that we should restate it than it is for Tom to have included it in his story or for the KKK figures in that story to have used it in the first place? It's as though he feels that by excising "that word" from our writing, we might eliminate it elsewhere, like J. K. Rowling's witches and wizards, who change the name of the Dark Lord from Voldemort to He-Who-Must-Not-Be-Named; but, as Harry Potter knows, changing Voldemort's name doesn't make him disappear, it just makes him more difficult to discern, to understand.

"But Vic, this work is autoethnographic. . . . We talked about the difference between showing and telling; it's more important for us to evoke the feeling of that desire, that repetition, than it is to just say it. Just saying a claim—"

"What if it had been 'the N word'? I bet you wouldn't have repeated that!"

"I'm pretty sure we would." I'm too quick, too dismissive. "Let's think about the argument, maybe you think we don't do enough to address our intentions—"

"Well maybe it's different if someone is screaming it, spitting it in your ear over and over again while he's kicking the crap out of you—you wouldn't know that!"

And that's it for me. No, I don't know what that's like . . . exactly. But I don't feel like that's the point; the point is to shut me down, and I respond in kind. "Perhaps that's true, but I don't think you're in a position to say what I do or don't know about this. You don't know anything about me."

> Their performances of Whiteness are not their own. . . . I am not reading them, but rather (re)creating them on the page. I am manipulating their words and their bodies to make my ethnographic point. . . . Further, the writing and presentation of those moments serve as another reiteration of Whiteness. That my scholarship, even if it is intended to undermine the structures of Whiteness, reinscribes Whiteness by making it a possible identity. My ethnographic identities are tied to the production of Whiteness, a system of which this paper is now a part. It is the insidious nature of Whiteness to grow stronger under the eye of s/he who critiques it. It is the nature of Whiteness to allow me to find pleasure in finding racism, in uncovering the daily maintenance of power, in the (re)constitution of privilege. And through this, I, with pleasure and pain, reconstitute myself and that which I strive to erase. (Warren & Fassett, 2002, p. 587)

When we return from break, Vic is gone. He's gone the next week too. And when he returns, he doesn't explain his absence; he never speaks of that evening. Once, I try to raise the issue with him, to suggest that he doesn't have to agree with me, he just has to respect me—he can't interrupt me, and he can't try to trump me at the level of personal experience, can't flash an essentialism badge that allows him to understand everything about me, but that prevents me from understanding anything about him . . . or myself.

* * *

This interaction, this mix of justified student anger and justified professor suspicion, resists easy answers, easy ways of awarding blame and victory. Indeed, Vic was right to ask questions, to call attention to places where language meets the skin of his body, the scars (physical or otherwise) that ache when we hear violent (or, "excitable" in Butler's, 1997, sense) speech. Vic needed to call attention to this moment, to ask about ethnographic ethics—it was, after all, the central issue of the essay. Vic's question invites us to investigate the use and power of language in the academy. An honest response, borne of pain, Vic's question made possible an opportunity for us to reflect, in a meaningful way, on the visceral relationship between language and lives.

Of course, the students, those quiet students, had an opportunity too. They could have helped to create dialogue, to open generative spaces in our discussion. Had they answered my call to participate in, to shape, this conversation, their voices could have, might have reframed our sense—Vic's sense, my sense, their own sense—of contest, making the classroom a space where we might carefully and respectfully take up the question of (scholarly) language as oppression. To create meaning, an intellectual community must work together. I would have loved to work with the class to gently account for the wounds our words have wrought, to consider the ways the words in this article reopen them, and the ways in which other words in this article or in our experiences help to heal those hurts. Perhaps there was a way to save my relationship with Vic.

The places where I could have done something are numerous. It is easy to question Vic's motives, Vic's knowledge of my life, of John's life, of the contexts that made this essay possible. Indeed, Vic is an easy target in this moment—the student questioning the teacher in front of the class. How many times do I need to see Hollywood tales of classroom to know that this is not how a student is supposed to act? And, as a young professor, as someone who supports him academically, as a long-time supporter of the very issues he is accusing me of betraying, don't I have a right to be treated at first with compassion? Have I earned nothing from my work that allows me to enter a dialogue about how these ideas came to be on this page, in this argument, at this time? I can just as easily question the members of the class, their willingness and their ability to make this encounter more productive, more meaningful. But how much weight should I expect them to carry? How much do I have a right to expect from them in this moment? What kind of preparation for this kind of work have I given them? What's more, all these questions shift attention away from me and my choices in this moment. My own pride, my own belief that intention matters when it meets his body, my own human response to threat, my own position or location at the nexus of so many different and contradictory cultures make it very difficult to let Vic have this critique without offering a response to it.

Critical communication pedagogy as praxis, as a way of being in the world, in the classroom, means that often there are no easy responses to or understandings of power, of who has it and who doesn't. In this situation, one can see me, the teacher, as the one with the power to make or break this pedagogical moment; I shut down Vic and assert my own sense of what is right, what is truth, what is critical. One could understand Vic, as the "mere" student, as thoroughly powerless, as the victim of my researching/teaching self. Of course, the reverse is also possible. One could understand Vic as claiming authenticity, asserting moral and experiential authority over me and his presumed understanding of my life, my research partner's life, and our intentions. Denied access to our stories, silenced by the voice of evidence of experience, John and I are victimized as well; as Scott (1992) might suggest, such reliance on the power of experience often shuts conversation long before it opens it up. All of these understandings are apt and none of them is adequate.

So what are we to make of this moment, this convergence of forces, these conflicted voices, these voices in conflict, each striving to claim the critical ground? It is clear that irrespective of the sides we were advocating, of who was right in this moment, we both failed to listen. As we have learned to do, as we both teach our students not to do, we both reacted to moments in each other's talk, in each other's approach, that made it hard to listen, to understand why the other was speaking. Vic and I both failed to make time for dialogue and in that instant, we both failed to do, to live, to be critical communication pedagogy.

Truth be told, I believed in the moment that Vic would see my side in this discussion, that if he would just calm down enough to see the evidence, he would understand. Attributing to him a false consciousness (Freire, 1970/2003; Lather, 1991), I failed to question my assumptions. I think I believed, in my assumption that he was gay, that he would see the argument we were making about identity and the power of discursive repetition. In his unwillingness to see my side, I cast him as duped, as blinded by his own social location, as unable to move beyond his own parochial understandings about how scholarship should look and feel. And, in that moment, I committed "a sin of imposition . . . in the name of critical pedagogy" (Lather, 1991, p. 78), by failing to recognize that Vic might have valuable reasons undergirding his perspective, by failing to recognize that Vic might be struggling to make sense of this new information in light of previously sensible ideological frameworks (Lather, 1991), by failing to remember that theory, if it is to be emancipatory, must be dialogic. In the classroom, I failed to see Vic in his full humanity, failed to see that he too had a genuine reason for believing as he believed, seeing as he saw, acting as he acted. I wrote Vic off, and I suspect Vic did the same to me.

However, we cannot judge the power of critical communication pedagogy from moment to moment alone. We must consider the ways this one moment made possible other reflections, other actions; we must consider the ways this moment is metonymic of an ongoing process. Even though I don't really talk to Vic much anymore—he has moved on, out of my care, out of my life to a large extent—my reflections on this and other experiences with him live with me, shape my actions, my choices in and out of the classroom. Though I may not have achieved the end result I (or he) would have preferred, the process itself has meant quite a lot to me. I don't second-guess myself, I don't fret about how to avoid conflict in my classrooms, and I don't try to divorce my feelings about my work from the work itself; however, I do reveal more of how I'm confused, how I don't understand, how I would like to learn more. I still use our essay in class; I use it to show how I, too, am struggling to live a critical life.

* * *

Though I hated every part of it, I'm glad I had this moment with Vic. It allowed me to examine my own practices in the classroom, my own way of interacting with students. And while I still advocate my beliefs, still stand when I think an argument is worthy, I also work to understand how another's perspective might productively illuminate my own, even if that perspective feels challenging or threatening to me. Critical communication pedagogy will not allow easy distinctions between oppressors and oppressed; we are always already both. So, when I look across the table to Beth, when I watch her read my comments on the first draft of her thesis, I wait . . . I want to know what she'll say, how she'll respond. Because I know I will have an opportunity to respond too. We may never fully agree, never fully understand one another, but we can sustain our relationship knowing that we can compromise without being compromised.

Making the Tapes: Lost Translations

My first task as a brand new professor, a beginning assistant professor, was to prepare for the first day of orientation. As a basic course director, I was faced with steering my very first group of TAs through teacher preparation, building with them the ground, the skills, they would need to be successful in their first weeks as new teachers. The context was weird: I would work with more than 40 teaching assistants, many from another college on campus, and staff meetings would be next to impossible. In other words, the 5 days of orientation would be the only certain time I would have with these new teachers. I never saw some of the TAs again, for that entire academic year, due to various scheduling conflicts precluding their attendance at the staff meetings I did hold. These teachers varied in experience—some had as many as 10 years of teaching experience, others had just finished their undergraduate degrees a few days before. Further, the course itself was a new context for me; never before had I been the director of a program that featured a 900-student lecture splitting into small "lab" sections run by the TAs. I taught 300 students at a time, 3 days a week. I would lecture, repeat it twice more, and then the students would attend the small breakout sections. I hated this structure immediately.

The first revision occurred during the summer: I changed the curriculum, bringing it more in line with both the field and the department. I focused the assignments and found a textbook I thought students would find challenging (I would later adopt a more overtly culturally oriented textbook). Subsequent revisions were structural. Still giving mass lectures, I began to meet with both deans and provosts, lobbying to redesign the course in small independently taught sections. After 2 years of difficult negotiations, I received approval of and funding for the course revision. There was, however, one catch. There is always a catch. I needed to create a series of video lectures, on everything from communication models to cultural studies to Monroe's Motivated Sequence. The TAs would show the series in their sections, "so," as one associate dean said with a smile, "the students won't lose access to your expertise."

I have to admit I thought the idea of video lectures was terrible. I found them pedagogically suspect and believed they would undermine both the teaching assistants' authority and their ability to focus on meaning in their lessons (instead of coverage of concepts). I knew the students' hatred for the videos would only be outdone by that of my teaching staff. However, to remove the students from the auditorium, I agreed to this compromise. The video lecture series would only consist of seven brief videos, not 16 weeks of lecture hall time. Further, as the TAs acquired more skill, we could make flexible choices about which videos to "air" and when. It all felt like solving a problem with a problem, but the idea of teaching interpersonal communication to a gathering of 300 was irony I could not stomach.

I wish I had thought to imagine this as a fascinating opportunity to examine my teaching choices as though they were research, a distancing move that would have allowed me to observe how students and TAs talked to me about the lecture series. Students I don't recognize often eye me, often in awkward situations like at the gym or in the restroom; they may ask, "Do you teach at the university?" Or, sometimes I preempt them: "I'm the guy on the IPC 102 videos." Their relief is funny; it is as if I'm a mystery they would wonder about until they'd solved it, like naming "that guy" in a movie or television show. The TAs are somewhat less polite. On the sweet side: "They really are not as bad as I thought they'd be. . . . " Or the less sweet: "I had to tell my students about the mistakes you make on the videos; I don't want them to be misinformed." More than one graduate student-professor relationship has been tried by these kinds of comments. Further, graduate students believe that my outward dislike for the videos and what they represent means I'm open to their criticisms. Yet, when the nasty comments come (recently, I discovered a TA talking about the lack of pedagogical value in them, for instance), they feel like an attack, they feel visceral, they hurt. I don't like the videos to be sure, don't believe in them as a rule, worry about how they frame the TAs in relation to their students; however, when my video-body becomes the object of their discourse, I want to respond in kind, to put their pedagogical bodies at as much risk as I feel. It becomes an eye for an eye, and I hesitate because I know my teeth are sharper than theirs—the consequences are very different if I bite back. And they think I'm friendly, and such retaliation would certainly be surprising.

If this were "just" research, I would certainly have lovely details to share, specific moments to use. Instead, I just have impressions and sore feelings. After all, I made this change to improve the course, to give more responsibility to the TAs. I thought such changes, though compromised, would benefit learning, theirs and their students. But, as happens with critical work in institutional contexts, much is lost in the translation; memory is short and a few years feels like a lifetime ago.

* * *

Critical communication pedagogy offers no magical spells to ward off moments of frustration and hurt. Indeed, we often are blinded to, and by, moments of compromise—they feel like cop-outs, and perhaps sometimes they are. But a key question that remains unanswered centers on the role of action and compromise, especially in institutional contexts like universities. How are we to make sense of administrative actions, which can seem so slow, so contradictory, so conservative? Is it possible for us to understand these actions as critical, transgressive, tactical? Is it critical communication pedagogy to replace a large lecture with smaller sections and video segments? Is that fulfilling some sort of radical promise, some sort of transgressive politics? Is it time for a medal; or perhaps, recognition in the teacher/administrator of the year award show? Should the TAs who have to now teach within this context line up with gifts, placing them on a critical altar celebrating the anniversary of my arrival on campus? Of course not, but, all snarkiness aside, the question remains as to how we understand compromise within the logic of critical theory and communication pedagogy.

In many ways, my video lecture series was an important step forward, even if it was marked by a half step back. I do believe that the TAs who now only know the video lecture series would have hated the "lab/lecture" format even more. Yet, I believe that when my teaching staff complains, they have every right to do so—that they need to be able to talk about what happens in their classroom, to address the injustices they feel when the institution imposes on them, marks their interactions with students, and constrains their teacherly selves. I want for them to expect more and to strive for more. I want for them, though I typically keep this quiet wish to myself, to resist, to find ways out, to seek alternatives. I want for them to want the best pedagogical experience they can get, both for themselves and their students. I want for them to develop critical vocabularies of hope and optimism. I want for them to keep me honest, to help me see new ways of imagining education. I want for them to prevent me from resting, from allowing better to stand in for best. And while I want for them to see compromise as a way to reach a goal, I want for them to reach with all their might, to reach without becoming compromised.

Critical communication pedagogy is social justice, as defined, explored, and implemented within a community of caring and generous believers in freedom, and justice, and love—for all, all the time.

If I had been able to separate, to distance myself from my teaching, I would certainly have lovely details to share, specific moments to use. Instead, I just have impressions and speculations. When the September 11th attack occurred, many believed that such a radical attack would result in major sweeping changes in citizen behavior. Yet, years later we are remarkably the same. Change so rarely occurs in dramatic sweeps; rather, it is often necessarily incremental—it happens slowly and over time. I have a vision for the basic course—one that I hope to be able to effect. But for me to do it, for me to make it happen in a way that advances critical engagement, I have to believe that small changes make a difference, that working with this community to shape and refine this vision will make a difference. So I'll keep my head up when the slings and arrows of justified fortunes come, but as I do, I'll try to keep my ears, my mind, and my heart open to new possibilities, new visions. I'll be compromising without becoming compromised. Compromise is praxis at its best—reflection, hope, action, and theory from a place of engaged participation.

On Doing Critical Communication Pedagogy

When we began this chapter, we wanted to show classroom examples of critical communication pedagogy; instead, we shared flawed examples . . . examples that would, at first blush, appear to show how we have failed in our efforts. Perhaps they illustrate a failure of our imagination—a failure to imagine what could be. Perhaps they illustrate a failure of our practice—that we can't do what we preach, what we claim to do, what we advocate. Perhaps they illustrate a faux modesty, a failure to admit our abilities, to risk looking like braggarts. But this is not all there is to these examples; though these particular moments are complex, and, at times, unflattering, they illustrate a process of critical communication pedagogy.

Often, we are frustrated by other scholars' tendencies to imagine critical theory as a zero-sum game. That is, one either is or is not critical, there is no middle ground, no place for incremental change, no place for working toward a goal, building consensus, or generating dialogue about the issues at stake. Sometimes the academic left participates in the politics of the right—the president calling out the nation, calling all "patriots" to take sides—either you are pro-war or pro-terrorist. Stranger still is when critical theory scholars suddenly sound like Ann Coulter, branding all those who value different forms of inquiry as traitors, those who imagine other ways of moving toward change as unpatriotic. Such academics often claim puritan positions in relation to critical theory—you are either on the side of progress or you are in the way. Nowhere was this more clear than during a recent discussion at an academic conference in which we found out that critical theory can assert as much power as it deconstructs.

* * *

We are seated around a large table—a weird setup for a conference panel, which usually consists of those awful, tailbone-numbing, linked hotel chairs. But seated in large leather chairs, the kind you find in board meetings for major corporations or city councils, we face each other, looking into each other's faces as we discuss the purpose of our work in the classroom, our efforts to make critique matter. In our conversation, we become aware that while we share a common literature base (critical theory), we see that work playing very different roles in our classrooms. As teachers who value critique, but who also value entering conversations with students where they are, we try to avoid making students defensive—that is, even if we don't always succeed, we always try to think of students as good people, good people who are situated in social systems that obscure how power is at play. But not everyone agrees this is how critical work should proceed.

We feel uncomfortable as he begins to speak. He describes a student who is struggling with issues of privilege and power—a white, male student who almost mirrors Audre Lorde's (1984) mythical norm (white, male, Christian, straight, able-bodied, etc.). The story he tells includes little nuance, little space to see this student as a complicated figure within systems that, although he helps to support, he did not design or create and may not fully understand. We are already sorry for this student, afraid of how easy it is to story someone as inhuman. As the story unfolds, we see that the student is trapped, trapped in an argument that he cannot resist or overcome. This student is being authored in this moment and all we can do is listen. The story is predictable: This student told a story in class that represented all the terrible things privilege reproduces (sexism, homophobia, white supremacy). In the end, this student is an echo of systems of power—at best, he is a dupe incapable of critical thought, and at worst, he is a terrible person who actively seeks to harm others. This straw student is left to his own devices, abandoned to the inhumanity he illustrates. He served his purpose in the story by illustrating dominance in everyday life, and so do we. He serves as a reminder of how our own communication can remake power, whether in the classroom or at the conference; as silent witnesses, we do too.

* * *

It is easy to question the student who, within his or her context of privilege, fails to see power at play. The question must, rather than turning that student into a symbol of all things wrong with students as a whole, be about how we can learn from this student—how this student can help us as teachers to develop a more nuanced understanding of the nature of power, of how power comes to play upon and in the hearts and minds and bodies of our students and ourselves. What might be gained from looking at this student as a product of systems of power rather than as a cause? To create scapegoats, to locate evil in particular students, is to reduce complicated norms and structures of power to individual intents; moreover, this act of scapegoating elides our own participation in those norms and structures. This is to say, the road to social justice can be in the service of students or at the expense of students; unreflective self-interest comes at a cost. Without exploring power as subtle, nuanced, and fluid, the hard line will always reduce complex issues to black and white, reduce dialogue to diatribe. If we allow that kind of thinking to alter our perspective, from the lessons we teach to the policies we propose, then we participate in the very intellectual violence we protest as critically informed teacher-scholars.

We have, in this writing, struggled to embody the "critical democrat" (Warren & Hytten, 2004), that figure who strives to take in different perspectives, to listen carefully, to consider how s/he is implicated in what s/he resists. There have been times when students and colleagues have challenged us, called us out, and when we could, we tried to listen to those voices, to heed their call. We do this because we believe that critical communication pedagogy, as a way of being in the world, asks us to encounter the world with open minds and hearts. We try to hear and reflect on how students understand experimental pedagogy; to try to find ways of listening to students who question our abilities, our experiences, our sense of justice; and, in the moment where compromise leaves us making some choices and not others, we try to listen to the voices and concerns of those around us rather than trump their voices with our own. We don't always succeed.

* * *

Critical communication pedagogy can be as much about failure as success, as much about pain as celebration, as much about what happened as what sense we made of it. There is no how-to manual for this work, no set of ten easy steps, five basic building blocks, or seven effective practices to engage in when doing this work. Scholars who try to sell such a manual are hiding something—they are hiding what it means to engage in educational practice: Education, if it is to be successful, must begin in and emerge from a particular community of learners. Anyone who tells you circles and discussion are better than rows and lecture must, by necessity, divorce pedagogical practices from any kind of lived classroom context. The desire to have such mechanical steps to pedagogical practice is about making education easy, finding the answers so we no longer have to remember the questions. And because we are talking about a complex situation (education) and an intricate and reflexive practice (teaching) steeped in rich and local cultural, social, political, and economic contexts (history and time), each new classroom is a new horizon, a new beginning, a fresh start. This is the promise of critical communication pedagogy.

We can only offer this one way of thinking about critical communication pedagogy; no doubt there will be others, emergent from particular settings and local needs. Common to all will be the willingness to critically and hopefully examine the process, the doing of critical reflection, the theorizing from lived experience, and the decision making that is its outcome. We model here how we come to think, to imagine, to put into play the critical ideals we use to frame this book; we work to make these ideals matter—to make them real—in these pages as we examine and theorize from our classroom moments. In the praxis of our lives, in and out of the classrooms, we have only the ability to engage in dialogue, to reflect, and to look toward the next semester and the next student with hope and optimism; the journey is the critical payoff. Engaging today while planning for any number of possible tomorrows is the gift, the mixed blessing, of critical communication pedagogy.

Note

1. See the appendix for a reprint of our essay "(Re)Constituting Ethnographic Identities" (Warren & Fassett, 2002). First published in *Qualitative Inquiry,* this essay serves as a reflective foil from which we theorize critical communication pedagogy in this section. We have included segments here but wanted the original essay to be available in this volume as a reference. Our thanks to Sage for allowing its reprinting here.

6

Nurturing Tension

Sustaining Hopeful Critical Communication Pedagogy

I believe that writing and teaching for social justice can and should be undertaken as nourishment for the educator, and not simply altruistically, not only in the service of the oppressed. (Nainby & Pea, 2003, p. 33)

Friends bust friends out of jails. If that "jail" happens to be constructed out of a narrative of denial, or of a lack of self-awareness, or out of fear or anxiety over the true content of a life, then I believe my ethical purpose is to help my readers find the strength to deal with it. Which is to say to rhetorically craft words to help them explore, to help them create, to help them build a new language pattern for expressing, for liberating, that jailed part of themselves that has become "unsentence-able." (Goodall, 2000, p. 193; emphasis his)

The notion that pedagogy and research are inextricably intertwined is not a new insight; scholars live in this tension every moment of every day, whether or not they understand it as such. While, at times, this tension feels like a competition, a question of which is better than the other or whether one takes time away from the other, it needn't. "Tension" is a misleading word; too often, we take it to mean uncomfortable, conflicted, or awkward. Instead, it would be fruitful to think of tension as relationship, as community, as cooperation. For instance, without the muscles in the front and back halves of our bodies exerting opposing forces, we wouldn't be able to stand, let alone walk or run; without hope, meaningful critique is impossible. Tension, in this sense, is balance. We are all very familiar with tension out of balance—some force pulls at us, demands too much from us, leaves us bent if not broken. Critical scholarship, whether research or pedagogy, can drag us down or give us strength; it doesn't take much to tip the scales. Freire (1970/2003) understood the importance of this balance; hence his assertion of praxis as both reflection and action. To neglect action is to live life as a bystander, complacent, isolated; to neglect reflection is to transgress for the sake of transgression, to live life frenetic, solipsistic, and, again, isolated.

We have struggled a fair bit, in this writing, with our use of the word "pedagogy" (as in the title of this book). Do we mean "critical communication pedagogy" as teaching? Or, do we mean "critical communication pedagogy" as research? Rather than setting these terms against each other as opposites, as antithetical, we have worked to reveal the connective tissue that binds them together; critical communication pedagogy is inherently about teaching and research both. In other words, while research is always pedagogical, whether overtly or covertly, in that it teaches, teaching is always scholarship, in as much as it must explore and respond to students' and teachers' lives.

Autoethnography is well positioned to an analysis of praxis, of balance, of tension. As noted earlier, it is a "method of . . . scholarly inquiry that privileges the exploration of a self *in response to questions that can only be answered that way,* through the textual construction of, and thoughtful reflection about, the *lived experiences of that self*" (Goodall, 2000, p. 191; emphasis his); autoethnography makes possible the exploration of the tensions, contradictions, findings, and fears of our pedagogical work. Autoethnography makes the questions of how one lives the life of critical communication pedagogy answerable—creating space for a voice that demands reflexivity and theorizing of lived experience. And while Goodall doesn't describe autoethnography in Freirean terms, he is most certainly making a claim about praxis; we might transform our worlds, word by word and action by action, by building meaning from careful, concerted reflection on our lives. We teach our students that writing is epistemic; writing is not simply a conduit for communicating what we have learned about some phenomenon or other, but rather a means of coming to understand that phenomenon more fully.

Academic debates about the nature of autoethnography and whether it belongs in the discipline can be counterproductive. Indeed, whether something counts as scholarship or not doesn't advance knowledge as much as it works to divide scholars' attention from the questions we, as a discipline, seek to answer. Autoethnography, as we teach our students, helps uncover particular kinds of communication phenomena. It generates new insights into how power works around/through/in our bodies; it helps us imagine alternate, possible futures. We often joke that when we teach autoethnography as method, students misunderstand it as catharsis, as exorcising demons, as peeking under the bed or in the closet for monsters and finding you've been the monster all along. Indeed, it is tempting to believe that we have to channel our own inner beat poets, that we must alter our senses and open our wounds to engage in this work, that we must dwell in the negative to do our work; so many beautiful and stirring autoethnographic writings seem to support this (Pineau, 2000; Ronai, 1996; Tillman-Healy, 1996; etc.), writings that remind us of how fallible we are, of how we've been fooled, harmed, thwarted, and how we've done the same to others. But what of the happy autoethnographer? Would we read, would we find as compelling, scholarship that celebrates, savors, and sings as we would scholarship that denounces, decries, or bemoans? Perhaps.

In this chapter, we place our examination of our own critical communication practices, our attempts at critical communication pedagogy, within the context of tensive, yet productive, community building. That is, we seek here to move from the introspection of the self to the ideal of community, ultimately suggesting that critical communication pedagogy, when actualized, might be a way of finding healing in the art of teaching.

Remembering

I don't know what happened to Jane (Fassett & Warren, 2005). In fact, it's been so long since I've seen her, I don't even remember her real name. She'll always be Jane to me and that makes me sad, not simply because I've forgotten whether she was a LaShaunda or a Monique or a Melanie, but because there's so much I remember about her that I haven't been able to share in my writing, because she's defined by the questions I asked, by the conversation we had one day at a Subway in Carbondale in 1999. I wish I could know what she went on to do: Is she happy? Did she stay in school? Is she managing a hotel in Atlantic City? Or helping injured athletes stretch out in physical therapy sessions? Has she found someone to love and who will love her? Does she have kids? And really, the answers to these are none of my business, but I'll wonder about them all the same, each and every time I sit at my computer to write. Each and every time I meet a student in class who moves me.

I first met Jane as a student early in my doctoral work; she was enrolled in my Introduction to Speech Communication course, which at Southern Illinois University is a hybrid course all students take, usually in their first or second year. She was enrolled in the Center for Basic Skills, a program to help engender success in provisionally admitted students (often first-generation college students from low-income, inner-city neighborhoods in East St. Louis or the south side of Chicago). Jane was an outstanding member of that class, full of engaged, curious, bright students (however unevenly prepared for college); she was a constant source of support for her peers, and while not always caught up with her reading, she worked to put communication concepts to work in her life. Her final persuasive speech was the most moving I have ever witnessed. Over the holiday, she tried to visit her best friend from high school, who was receiving hospice care for the end-stage of AIDS. Her friend wouldn't allow her in, wouldn't let her say goodbye. Forever altered by that experience, Jane took her final 6 to 8 minutes in that class to persuade us of the importance of telling the people we love how we feel and what they mean to us in every way, every day of our lives. I wonder if Jane remembers our tears—my tears—our rapt attention, our collective celebration of her lesson, and our collective sadness, sense of loss, for her and for ourselves.

It was this moment in that class a year or two prior that led me to ask her for an interview for my dissertation. I remembered she was eloquent, and that she had struggled in her first semester of college; I also remembered she was an A student and articulate. I figured she'd make some thoughtful observations about her experience, and she did (Fassett & Warren, 2005; Warren & Fassett, 2002). What I didn't expect was all the elegant mess, all the calm rage. Did she ever find money to pay the rent? Did she keep going to therapy? What has she found to replace the loneliness? What happened to the other teachers she touched? And what of the teachers who will never remember another thing about her, not even her name?

She sits with me as I write. She asks me about the articles I'm reading; she wants to know what they say and what they mean for her. When I work with graduate teaching assistants, on anything from the difference between meaning and coverage in a lecture to whether they should implement reading quizzes, I think of her; when I teach critical and interpretive research methods, when I talk with students about how to write an interview protocol or how to code their data, I think of her. Jane is the present absence in my classroom; she is the absent presence in my writing.

Save the Crisis for the Holidays

One of my students, Eric, has shown up to take the final early. He's standing in the doorway to my office, but not really standing; he's doubled over and making a low keening sound, though I'm not sure he's even aware he's making a sound. "I can't make it to our final this afternoon. . . . "

"Eric—why don't you sit down? What's wrong?" He's still wearing an emergency room band, and can't quite sit; everything he does is painful, is painfully slow.

"My doctor . . . um . . . thought I might . . . um . . . have meningitis . . . so I had . . . to go . . . to the emergency room . . . last night. They did a . . . spinal tap . . . and I still feel . . . so . . . bad. . . . " It's here when I realize Eric's in all this pain even though he's so drugged up he can't think straight.

"But why are you even here? You could have just called; we could sort all this out when you're feeling better."

"I'm so sorry professor . . . I just feel terrible . . . I want to take the final . . . I can't . . . I can't . . . I've got to do well . . . I'm turning in my grad application. . . . " Eric can't hear me, and, judging by the way he's not calming down, not breathing freely, he shouldn't be here. He should be at home, or perhaps back in the emergency room, but not here.

"Eric. You need to go home. Come back when you're feeling better and you can take the final, okay?" I help him up out of the chair, "Can someone come get you?"

"I called . . . my dad . . . after my other final." Another final?

"Eric, you took a final this morning?" I'm forever amazed at what students will force themselves to do, even when they shouldn't.

"Yeah . . . my professor said I had to take it today. I have . . . to pass . . . her class." I'm forever amazed at what teachers will force students to do, even when they shouldn't.

"Eric, did she *see* you? Did she say that anyway?" He just nods, and heads off, slowly, down the hallway.

* * *

I didn't take a sick day the entire time I was in graduate school. That's not to say I was never sick, never had viruses or bacterial infections, never hurt my back, and never spent days on codeine trying to sit for 3 hours at a desk. That's not to say I never had headaches, or allergies, or deaths in the family. That's not to say I never broke up with anyone, was never hung over, or never tripped over my cat. All this happened to me and more, but I went to class, taught my own classes, completed my readings, wrote my papers.

I went to class on pain relievers when I hurt my back (there is about a week of Performance as Methodology I simply don't remember), I taught public speaking with fluid oozing from torn eardrums—the ear infections making it next to impossible to hear the soft-spoken student in the back, and I made it to class the afternoon I had tests to determine whether the swollen lymph notes in my neck were the result of HIV, lymphoma, or gingivitis. That doesn't make me a hero. That doesn't even make me a good student, though I thought, at the time, that it did.

I wore each of my illnesses like a badge of honor, as did my colleagues: "Are you kidding? Once I hurt my back so bad I had to crawl around my apartment!" "Wow . . . did you know that during prelims, I forgot to eat?" "You know, when I was in graduate school, I lost and regained over 50 pounds . . . twice." "Oh, I wish I had time to read for pleasure. . . . " It's hard to explain . . . but perhaps you understand. . . . It's not so much that these are things to be proud of—I don't think anyone would go there—but more about what we had to sacrifice to achieve our goals. Working hard— a measure of whether one deserves tenure, the Ph.D., the pass on prelims, the admission to the program—in a life of the mind means sacrificing the body . . . or so it seemed. Our own professors, bedraggled and beleaguered at the end of the semester, helped us understand that feast meant famine, spring meant winter. In one of my interviews for the dissertation, a good friend of mine said, "I was told [by my M.A. adviser] that this is what's going to happen to you: They are not going to care that you have a family. Your family is now second. You get used to that now, so that when you get there [you'll be ready]; I didn't know where I was going [for the Ph.D.] at the time. Now, I haven't experienced that completely here, but it creeps out. It creeps out that you are not allowed to go through crisis, I mean, tough shit, move on." Another interviewee put this beautifully, "Yeah, it's kind of like save the crisis for the holidays."

I left graduate school believing that a headache was not a reason to miss class (there's Advil, isn't there?), that babies could and should be planned (tenure first, family later), that some funerals were more important to attend than others ("Your friend's mother died? Were you close?"). I left graduate school believing that other people's sacrifices should mirror my own. That is, until I met students who had sacrificed more. Angela's writings explore her relationship with her teenage daughter, recently diagnosed with a rare bone cancer; as a mother, Angela wants a greater understanding of the optimal level of uncertainty in communication with teens—with her teen—about having a life-threatening illness. Maria wonders whether it is selfish to write a thesis; her family, undocumented immigrants to California's strawberry fields, needs her at home to help care for her brothers and sisters as much as they need her to make enough money to help pay the rent. I haven't read any writings from Jason in some time; his father is living with Alzheimer's disease, and he has decided school can wait. I don't disagree with his choice. We all make meaning from our lives, meaning that doesn't come from a piece of paper signed by the governor and the regents, meaning that doesn't come from when and whether one took a final exam on schedule.

* * *

Loss and sacrifice are, on some level, sensations everyone knows. Such things make us feel like victims, like we've given of ourselves more than we knew we could offer, more than we received in return, like we've given up something valuable and can't ever get it back. Inevitably, loss and sacrifice are also what most of us would identify as isolating events; we tend to see ourselves as living loss and sacrifice alone. During one semester, I remember reading in the newspaper about one of my former students; he threw himself through his dorm room window, dying broken and alone. I remember a sense of loss, a sense of emptiness that I suspected would consume me, mar me, making it impossible to every really continue as I did before. I remember what the first year of my relationship with my partner felt like under the weight of grad school, what it did to us as I engaged in experiences that drew me away from her as I pursued education. Each time I experience loss, feel the pull of sacrifice, I know there are others who are implicated in these moments too; yet, in the moment it feels very much as if the moment is mine alone, as if I am feeling this all by myself.

Of course, as selfish as this is, sacrifice and loss are always already a social experience. Loss, in many ways, is about gain. I lose a quarter on the bus; someone finds it. My grandfather passes; someone new is born into the world. Loss, like any tensive relationship, is also about gain, even if someone else stands to benefit. Sacrifice is also like that. Mothers tell their children the stories of their births, stories of long labors or changed careers, changed lives. Teachers tell students about the hours they spend grading. Students tell teachers about their many responsibilities, their extra jobs, the hours working in the cafeteria in order to pay for tuition. These kinds of sacrifices give rise to results—those for whom we sacrifice gain the knowledge of that gift, the joy of that return.

Loss and sacrifice, if they are to matter—if they are to have meaning—should be remembered, should be acknowledged, should be appreciated. Jane, who gave so much of herself to our relationship with her, to our work, to our understanding of "risk" and "success," who asked that her contribution be made to count, who wanted to be seen in all her humanity, deserves to be remembered. And while we have lost ties with her—have lost her name—we make her loss matter, make it real, make it material in our classrooms by sharing it with our students. When think of the sacrifices we've made, or that Eric has made, we know that while it often feels like sacrifice is a lonely business, it doesn't have to be. And in the act of teaching, in the act of pedagogy in a critical context, we might find space to question why we see such events as isolating. We can undo these tendencies if we make meaning from them, through them, and allow those moments to guide our actions. Jane's speech, her reminder to tell others we love them, teaches us still.

Heroes

I must admit, I begin this part with hesitation. This is the part where I admit a fear I have, a fear that bothers me. It bothers me because I'm sure that others don't worry about this. Perhaps I'm alone in this, in this uncomfortable space of self-reflection, self-doubt, self-critique. Or maybe others feel it too, feel the worry that perhaps . . . perhaps they are also guilty of falling into this trap.

* * *

My high school speech teacher was a hero I grew to worship—I thought he was the coolest teacher in school. I remember when I went into communication in college, I had so hoped he would believe me to be his protégé, his reproduction, his academic child. When I told him I'd earned my Ph.D., he nodded, and then proceeded to ask if I wanted to look at his new car—"It's a Ferrari."

In college, one of the professors in my major took his place. I loved his classes—he was a superstar and I felt like one of the "in" crowd. Having sat in on his grad classes, having visited with him over coffee as if he were a friend, I imagined the joy he would experience when I said I'd followed in his footsteps, followed in his area of research. I learned very quickly the meaning of out of sight, out of mind; he doesn't return my emails.

In grad school, she was one of those professors, just beginning, that you kind of hope to be. They seem put together, confident, able. Yet, early in our interactions, I came to realize that our differences would not allow us to be friends. My respect for her work couldn't compensate for my participation in a critical intellectual tradition she found suspect. In the end, our relationship became empty hellos and strained looks. I tried to convince myself I was better off without her.

* * *

So when I'm teaching, especially graduate students, I find I struggle with the degree to which they seek something in me, something they long for, something that speaks to them. Occasionally, I hear students make comments about my teaching, my research, my persona in the department; I know the degree to which I occupy a popular space on the faculty—I'm on over 31 committees currently, advising 10 through the highest degree our field offers. I remember when my most recent advisee left my office—having only just finished our discussion on what this new relationship would mean—she ran into another advisee. Jokingly, he asked, "Did you get the Warren brand—it's required!" Even in my own office, many years away from my own experiences as a doctoral student, that comment feels quite real; the sting from the iron, hot on my own skin, burns still.

* * *

There is often an unrealistic expectation we place on our heroes—we come to expect so much, dedicate so much energy to our illusions of what the hero does, how the hero acts, what the hero means to us. This kind of pedestal so rarely can bear both the weight of the person, that hero, fragile in her or his own right, just trying to make it through, and the weight of all that pressure, all our expectations, all our demands.

We all know this person, these people—they exist in our imaginations, in our offices, across our campuses. They stand as people who we, on the one hand, wish we were and, on the other, fear we will become. They are everyone and no one—they are us, if anyone. Imagine the figure, that person who you believe—know—walks on water. You know this person—you know, that person that you might bet, indeed, bet your life, walks on water, and if you arranged a test where that person and a pool of water could coexist, you could prove it. You would have made this bet and walked away with a very full wallet. This, of course, would be quite a set of expectations and you can see the eventual (and inevitable) fall that is forthcoming. As a "critical scholar" in the field, you expect that person to always be on the side of the little guy, defending the poor gal crushed under the weight of "hegemony" or "ideology" or "oppression." Yet, when the rubber meets the road, when you need this person, s/he finds precious little time to support your efforts. Feeling quite like the little guy or gal, you will be disappointed, but you will try not to take it personally. You will try, of course, until s/he stops talking to you, seeing in you all the failings of critical possibility. You are soon to be unworthy. And like a child who doesn't understand the way of the world, you will let this hero go. You will have to let this person go in order to save your sense of self, your very worth.

This person never exists in one body—s/he is always a mixture, an amalgam of so many others that come to be within a lifetime. But in small moments, s/he will feel like a whole, a being holding you accountable, even if unfairly. It is funny how when you are faced with someone in this position, you desire to call this person out for her failed hero status. It is much harder to see yourself as this failure though.

* * *

The fact of being a faculty member in a graduate program means I will become the reason some students might come to this university. This is how graduate programs work—they advertise, feature the faculty: "Come to San José State University—Deanna L. Fassett teaches here. . . . " "At Southern Illinois University, we have John T. Warren." It is a fact of life as a professor at these kind of universities. And in my experience, I have had advisees who have come to this university in part to work with me. I can try to justify it away—"They are coming for the program, I'm a bonus," but this is sometimes only a rationalization. The reality is, for some, I'm the reason. This, of course, freaks me out. Not only am I "young" in the field (or at least I used to be), I'm also desperately afraid of letting someone down, of being a failed hero, of being the person I have grown to hate—that figure in my life who disappoints people. I don't want to be anyone's hero; I know that a hero always falls much harder than one expects.

* * *

Of course, I want to recover a sense of humanity here—as I was reminded by a friend, not so long ago, heroes are flesh and blood. They have faults, they have lives that sometimes deliver curve balls and changeups. They don't have the time to be worshiped while they are undergoing family or professional crisis. I know personally that sometimes my wishes, my goals are obstructed by my duties, my obligations. Building heroes leads to disappointment and places unfair expectations on those we claim to love.

* * *

I am a failed hero and I fear I may be alone in this. Perhaps I am a magnet for failure, a person who codependently seeks relationships with those who will mistreat me. Perhaps I mistreat others because I seek to give back to the world the abuses I've endured. Perhaps I am destined to never see the ways I let others down. Perhaps recognizing my failure is a first step to not letting people down in the future. Perhaps the illusion is that I have any control in this at all. Perhaps if I tell people not to make me a hero, they won't and I'll be safe. Perhaps if I tell them this, they will only do it more.

Or, in the end, perhaps this life is a never-ending process of building people up to watch them fall.

Keeping Honest

The TAs and I have been rereading Freire, considering the implications of his work for our classrooms. We're nearing the end of our time, and I'm trying to distill our conversation, to create a temporary sense of closure. "One part of engaging racism, sexism, homophobia, classism, and the like with our students is willingness . . . willingness to engage in difficult conversations in the first place. We can't just write someone off for not believing what we believe, for not voting how we voted, for not living as we do; we have to inquire, understand where those beliefs comes from, and recognize that everyone has good reasons for their beliefs. That's why dialogue is so important." I'm looking at my notes again when I hear:

"I assume that includes your godmother?"

* * *

Working with TAs helps keep me honest. Post graduate school, I weighed over 200 pounds; I hope I never do again. On my five-foot-six-inch frame, this meant huffing and puffing to climb the stairs in the parking garage, having a resting pulse rate too high to donate blood, and a complacent soft expanse of tissue just under my navel that implied prediabetes. There was no real reason for this, no one cause I could point to, not even the sense that I didn't have time to focus on my health. Hurting my back meant giving up running for some time, and starting again at this weight seemed impossible. I'd always enjoyed long-distance running, the sense of accomplishment, the looks on other people's faces when I'd say I ran 5 miles or 10 miles; if I couldn't have that, then what was the point? Still, it was a lot of weight to carry.

Two events happened to change my mind: First, my father was diagnosed with melanoma, and second, Tess, one of the TAs, shared with me her experiences walking the Avon Breast Cancer walk (which was then a 3-day, 60-mile walk), about the rigor of it, about the women walking to honor others, to honor themselves and their survival. It's not like I thought to myself, "Wow, I'd better do something about my life"; I carried these two bits of information around with me for months . . . testing a walk around the neighborhood, using a hand mirror to examine this mole, that mole. One day, Tess gave me a training schedule and suggested we walk 2 days a week, after her class but before mine. But it wasn't until one of the other TAs said, "Wow—you don't really yell at us anymore" that I decided I was making a good decision, and not just for me. And it wasn't until I'd finished walking the Portland Marathon, at about the time running the San Francisco Chronicle Marathon for the first time was only a gleam in my eye, that I learned they'd been taking bets as to when I'd quit exercising. I don't mind. . . . On the contrary, I wonder who lost and how much; I've lost at least 60 pounds. (Though, to be truthful, I've lost and regained the last 10 more than once. . . .)

The TAs' inquiries into my personal life are very discreet. But the TAs do inquire. They ask me about my latest writing, about whether I've done justice to the ideas and situations and crises we explore together, about my tenure dossier and what goes in it, about whether I've found a date for that upcoming wedding, even about how my running (and my grudgingly tolerated diet) is going. I'm very aware that they read me—my moods, my opinions, my actions. They attribute significance to my choices and they consider whether and how those choices have relevance for their own lives. This is not to say I think they're naïve or impressionable, but rather to suggest they read me for consistency and for contradiction, for a sense of whether I, as one TA puts it, "walk the talk." They pay attention to whether I'm late for class (rarely), whether I'm a basket case at finals time (more frustrated and realistic than frantic), whether I'll have a Dr. Pepper or a piece of birthday cake (I do, but usually not both at the same time), and whether I ask of myself what I ask of them. As to that last, I try: I do write lesson plans for each and every class (and I'll hand them over if one of them asks), I do learn my students' names, I do (almost always) return student work within a week, I do write exams that match the content of the course. . . . But there's more to this . . . they also read for whether I engage in critical work, whether I would send them forward where I would fear to tread.

* * *

I know I'm supposed to love my godmother; I know she loves me, in her way. She says she loves me even as she says I'm too old, too busy, too single, too childless, too bookish, too strange, too opinionated. She's of a different era, one where women stay home and raise children; where women might be teachers, but never professors; where it's important to explain that "So-and-So has a lady doctor," or where she might ask, "Have you heard from your friend, that little Oriental gal?" Her most recent visit coincided with ongoing and prominently positioned news stories featuring resistance to San Francisco's, to mayor Gavin Newsom's, push for marriages for gay and lesbian couples. In one report, a protestor proudly displayed his sign reading "Sodomy is sin." On seeing this, my godmother turned to my mom and asked, "What's sodomy?" To which my mother, never one to shy away from such moments, offered a very direct and uneuphemistic definition. I sort of knew where this was going, and then it went there. . . . Turning to us, my godmother asked, "Why would the gays want to marry?" And I didn't want to go there, which is strange, because I so readily go to these places with students. Rather than express surprise at the question, rather than engage in a meaningful response, I offered "Why not?" and went to find my dad, who was watching *CSI* in his room. I may love her, but I don't like her.

The TAs know this story, know that when my godmother visits, I'll be on edge; they know all about the ways in which I have tried to agree to disagree: on abortion, on free speech, on the presidential elections, on marriage equality, on civil rights, on education funding, on what it means to be successful . . . as a woman. . . . And they know it's a place where I commonly fail to practice what I preach about teaching, about living a critical life, about speaking across ideological difference. Mel's "I assume this includes your godmother?" is a gentle nudge, well, a shove really. And he's right. This does include my godmother. And, if I'm to be honest, I must include her.

* * *

Loss and sacrifice. Failure and honesty. Counting on others and being responsive to their needs. In critical communication pedagogy, as in all pedagogy, we interact with, we encounter others. Early in my writing, I was told by advisers and friends that I needed to think about persona, about who I wanted to be for others on the page, about who I wanted them to learn from and about and why. It was, and still is, about audience. The same is true for any performance; from the theatre to the classroom, from the art of teaching to the art of everyday life, the audience matters. We are always in the presence of others when we are teaching.

My first day as a teacher did not go well; I remember being so nervous that I nearly threw up. I lost my train of thought in class and dismissed the students after only 5 minutes. I choked. And while I was able to recover (thanks to good mentors and a supportive community), I learned that teaching, even if it is a seemingly lonely enterprise, is, in fact, a community experience. For within the classroom, I began to think of myself as one of many; my colleagues and friends began to shape my thinking about education, appearing in and through me as I interacted with my students. I could only imagine how to teach by imagining myself as part of a community where they needed me as much as I needed them; we, as a class, functioned as collaborative and not opposing forces, caught in a tensive dance that worked to support the weight of our learning.

Hero-making might very well be an inevitable part of educational life. As teachers, we can both describe instances where we became heroes when we didn't even try, didn't even want that responsibility. Because I respected his distress, his pain more than a policy or a grade, Eric might look upon me as a hero, might feel I have restored some humanity to teaching and learning. Jane might consider me a hero because of my intervention, my efforts to go with her to a counselor, my writing about her in the way I did. In any number of ways, individuals may seek in us something that resonates, that calls out to them, that creates a sense of relational connection.

Critical communication pedagogy is inherently collaborative. It depends on the productive nature of pedagogy itself, that context that demands a sense of accountability and relevance. That is, this work makes us accountable to not only the student in crisis, but the student celebrating her or his successes. It makes us accountable to godmothers, to heroes, to the various loved ones in our lives who expect from us some measure of humanity. When Freire (1970/2003) describes his pedagogy of the oppressed as a relational pedagogy, he imagines our vocation as one of treating others as Subjects, as people of and in the world who have a sense of purpose and hopeful futures to lead. The reasons we are afraid to let others down, the reasons we grieve when we are let down, the reasons we seek not to write others off, and the reasons we strive to live lives of critique and care is because to do so positions us humanely with respect to others. In the moments I use my power as a teacher or researcher to impede or impugn others, I rarely feel critical. But the moments when someone looks at me with gratitude, the moments I hear that some small gesture I gave was met with recognition, the moments I learn I am a meaningful participant in others' lives—these are the moments when I remember that, as individualized as I might feel in any given moment in education, I am always working with others. My critique must build toward a sense of community fulfillment if it is to be part of a vision for critical communication pedagogy.

During an early meeting on our goals and desires for this book, we discussed how we might want to frame critical communication pedagogy. In that meeting, one of us said this book should function as critical nourishment for its readers. That is, could the book supply a sense of purpose for those who need it? Could the book build a spirit of hope in and with the field? Could the book feed the hungry heart seeking a pedagogy of possibility? This book needed to be nourishment, carefully constructed and critically oriented—a fertile place for nurturing roots, for planting flowers of possibility. What garden could sustain that crop?

"The Time Is NO/W," or "Freedom Isn't Free"

"I just feel like I'm being attacked here! You're. . . . This isn't a safe place for me—I feel so alone." This is perhaps the harshest rebuke I've heard; Melody has finally broken the silence, cracking through the collective fake-niceness and fear and confusion. We've been sitting here in this staff meeting for over an hour and a half; I've spent every minute perched, all bristly, on the edge of my chair, and it isn't until Melody names the discomfort that I realize I've been tearing my cuticles back, systematically, until each is raw pink skin.

It's been like this in the TA community since the election. Not everyone voted for Kerry/Edwards, and that matters very much to a few members of our insular community. This community, this family of sorts, has gathered together to celebrate holidays and graduations, coffees and study groups; now we're suffering from what Melody's partner Keri has named "post-partisan depression." This includes me. I'm moping around the office and not doing a very good job of following up on students' requests to discuss the election's outcome in class; I feel raw, disappointed, self-righteous, indignant, perplexed. So, I'm not proactive when I ought to be; I leave for the National Communication Association conference, leave Lacey in charge of the staff meeting that will happen while I am away, leave it all behind for friends and stuffed pizza and the Sears Tower and some clarity, perhaps. It's almost Thanksgiving when I discover what I've been is lost, lax, lazy.

Melody and I see each other in the hall after class: "Hey Deanna, maybe you've already heard this, but I couldn't go to the staff meeting on last Tuesday."

"Uh . . . ok, what happened?" This is unusual, though not necessarily cause for alarm—Melody could have been sick, or caught without wheels or whatever.

"Nobody told you yet?" This, however, is stranger still. Why should someone have told me anything? And if it was an emergency, shouldn't someone have called me on my cell?

"No . . . maybe you should tell me what happened."

"I just couldn't go. I mean, I can't believe you left Lacey in charge of the meeting." This is only sort of true. Lacey was in my office when I was compiling a list of announcements to make to the TAs; I asked her to shepherd the first half-hour or so of the meeting to make things easy. I try to explain this, even though I'm still not sure why I'm explaining anything: "I asked her to make a couple of announcements while I was away—weren't Chris and Marcus leading a session on how to use debate in the classroom?"

"Oh, I don't know. . . . You'll have to ask someone else how that went. I just couldn't be around *her*. . . . " And this is just when I know something is wrong. Everything clicks into place: One of my colleagues saying one of the debates got out of hand in the graduate argumentation seminar; the sudden appearance of bold, blue "Kerry/Edwards" shirts on a few of the TAs; the passionate positions on the various party platform issues and the stilted, monosyllabic responses. . . . "*Her?*"

"I just don't feel safe; I mean, I can't believe it. . . . It's all too. . . . Lacey just tossed off that she voted for 'W' and she just doesn't get it. I can't . . . I can't be around people who are saying I'm garbage just because I want my marriage recognized. I'm sick of her 'God loves everybody but gays and lesbians' crap. . . . " And everything makes sense again, but that doesn't make me feel any better. At least at this point in Lacey's life, marriage is for one man and one woman; it is sanctioned by God, not by Gavin Newsom. Melody, who has been an outspoken advocate for marriage equality, is willing to make this her Stonewall Riots, her Montgomery bus boycott; for her, this is not about God, but rather about civil rights, about protecting her union, her family. I can't blame either of them; each has good reasons for believing as she does. And while I agree with one perspective and not another, that's not the point; how I voted doesn't help me in this situation any more than it's helped them. But frankly, I'm really pissed off at them both, and I don't feel like I should say that either. I'm tempted to make the Solomon-like decision of firing them both unless they can learn to get along, or, at the very least, attend their required staff meetings. I don't get to play favorites; I don't get to help one TA at the expense of another or imply I care about one more than another. Each is a forever-evolving collection of strengths and limitations—as are we all—and as tempting as it is to focus on the product—getting along and playing nice—I take it to be my responsibility to help them understand the process—learning to speak across, find meaning in, and draw strength from what feels like profound ideological differences. More to the point, while they can choose their friends and lovers, they can't choose their family, their colleagues, or their students.

"I just feel like I'm being attacked here! You're. . . . This isn't a safe place for me—I feel so alone." Melody's rebuke in our staff meeting will stay with me forever; it was hard to hear, in part because of all the work this community engages in to support and understand diversity in all its forms. Melody's partner Keri is a regular character in the department, often sitting in on classes and attending department functions; many of us in this TA community work to challenge heteronormativity and homophobia in our classrooms and in our research. We've celebrated her wedding, and traveled with her on her journey to self-discovery. But that's not what we're thinking about today, and it's not hard to see why. The overwhelming majority of the meeting has consisted of dancing around the unsaid, the present absence that holds honest dialogue at bay. I was fortunate enough to invite our colleague and friend Keith Nainby to the meeting; I've asked him to discuss one of his favorite topics, how to create community in critical work. He's gentle with them, allowing them to raise the specter of the election or vent their hurt feelings on their own. He foregrounds our work with students, work that evolves from commitments we share (even as they manifest differently in each of us). Keith tells the story of exploring identity with his students in a "speech, self, and society" course, how they used Garfinkel's (1967) study of Agnes to explore transgendered identity. Agnes, the subject of Garfinkel's most famous ethnomethodological study, stands as a question for medical science—the paradoxical figure that is a woman with a penis—the purpose of the study is to see how Agnes successfully accomplishes the passing of woman given her biological makeup. When several of his students expressed concern that they would have to accept that identity in order to pass an upcoming assignment, he reminded them that they needn't agree, but that they might explore how their faith shapes their identity, how those values and experiences shape their interactions with others, opening and closing off dialogue.

Marcus tells the group that he works to engage diversity in the classroom; one example he shares is an impromptu speaking activity that includes topics ranging from "violence on television" to "whether the course text should be required" to "gay marriage."

Melody interrupts, "Marriage equality."

When Marcus keeps speaking, Melody stops him . . . raising her voice loud enough for people in the hallway to hear—"MARRIAGE EQUALITY."

"Alright, alright . . . marriage equality." Marcus crosses his arms, slumps in his chair, and the meeting falls into silence.

Melody breaks the silence, "I just feel like I'm being attacked here! You're. . . . This isn't a safe place for me—I feel so alone." And though I'm not sure we all know exactly what she means, how she feels, we are sharing the experience. "I can't talk about this. . . . I. . . . Ever since the election, I just feel like nobody cares. That I'm garbage, that my whole life is garbage. . . . Conservatives are so narrow-minded, so. . . . "—

"*Some* conservatives. . . . " Marcus asserts himself; it's clear he's been looking for a place to catch Melody, to prove a point of his own.

Melody continues, "I just want to feel like I belong, and I don't know whether I belong here anymore. I feel alone, and I'm sorry for bringing all this up."

Other TAs fill the silence: "You know, I don't always like what I learn from you Melody, but you keep it real, you help me see things I would never see otherwise, and I thank you for that." "I can't change how you feel Melody, but I hope you know we care about you." "I think I don't do a very good job of thinking about how I'm privileged. There are so many things I don't have to think about, haven't had to think about because I'm like the majority. You help me with that, but that has to be tiring." Melody doesn't seem satisfied.

I add: "I hope you understand that I appreciate each of you—that's when I agree with you and when I don't. We don't have to see eye to eye to do good work in the classroom. I can name something I've learned from each of you right now, and I'll bet each of you can do the same. And I'm proud of you for engaging in a very difficult conversation. Here's the thing: Part of our hard work, part of our community building will have to involve speaking with each other, sustaining community, even when we disagree. We have to speak to each other, we have to find meaning with each other, even when that's across what feels like an intractable divide. But we've started to do that today."

And then Keith reminds us of one of the most important insights I've heard about living the critical life: While critical work can be draining, can draw us to finding fault, to demonizing people on the other side of the critical turn, it can also be a source of strength. We can take critical work to be an opportunity, a way to find common ground, to understand each other better. Our critical work must nourish us; how else can we nourish others?

Melody, a realist, pushes back: "I don't know how to do that. I'm not sure that's even possible."

Perhaps she's right. But I don't agree. I take heart in what I do every day; I don't focus on the negative, and I don't ignore it either. I believe all people are basically good, that they understand love and pain and confusion, and that they're capable of empathy, change and growth. I believe we must nurture ourselves and each other, and no, that's not easy. But I don't agree with Melody, and that's okay. . . . I respect her all the same.

Subject: Help!

The TAs have a listserv. While most of the time this is a convenience to both them and me (they use it to arrange holiday dinners and office clean-up times, to ask each other questions about how to teach audience analysis or Monroe's Motivated Sequence, and so forth; I use it mostly to remind them about important deadlines or what to prepare for the upcoming staff meeting), it's maddening to read some of the information they post. Most frustrating are the messages that should be for me alone, should be sent "off list" and instead are sent out to everyone: special scheduling needs, requests for extended time to complete assessment reports, acknowledgement emails (like "Hey Deanna, thanks for sending that; I'll see you at your office hours on Monday!"). I even try to help, in my emails, by reminding folk to reply to me off list at their convenience. But it's so much more convenient to reply to the list; I even fall prey to this now and again. In these moments, I honestly think the listserv is a pain in the ass.

I've started to wonder whether the listserv is sentient, or rather, whether some imp has it hostage, putting our posts to spammy ill will, but the odd thing is that, sometimes, the right message finds the right audience. Now, I check my email pretty frequently—far more than anyone should, in my opinion—but that's an acceptable tradeoff for being able to do my writing at home. But today, I've found something important in my inbox, nestled among the usual array of emails from Nigerian diplomats, impotency professionals, and lonely young women all named "Sexy Christy." It's a strand of emails, variously titled: "Help," "Oh shit—please disregard," and "Re: Oh shit—please disregard." They're from the TA listserv.

When I first open the email "Help," I think it will be important because it will have something to do with the sender's public speaking classroom, that she needs my counsel about an incomplete or is having trouble getting a video camera for the upcoming persuasive speech round; I think it might be important because it has something to do with the classroom, with teaching. Instead, I find the sender in distress: "Deanna, I was wondering if you could help me with something difficult. My best friend just found out he's HIV-positive. Anyway, I know you've walked the Silicon Valley AIDS walk, and I was hoping you could point us in some direction. He's pretty freaked out, and I guess I am too." It's a beautiful email in a way—simple and direct. I look to see when she sent it—yesterday. Oh . . . I hate to let emails like that linger, all that time just gives rise to doubt, to needless worry. The next email, "Oh shit—please disregard," gives me pause. Oh, no . . . oh, she didn't send it to the listserv. . . . And she has, and she's figured that out for herself: "Hey everybody, I'm so sorry—that was supposed to go to Deanna. Just disregard, ok?" But there are other emails here as well: one from a TA who lost his brother to AIDS some years back, and another who is active with a variety of HIV-positive support groups for both gay and straight young people in San José. Each is offering advice, places to go, experiences with loving friends with HIV, experiences with protecting themselves (and not protecting themselves as well as they should). I add my own voice to this chorus, but already, I am so proud that I wasn't the first to speak . . . or the last.

This email is important because it does have something to do with the classroom, with teaching; it just isn't a direct or obvious connection like how to plan a lesson or when to turn in grades.

* * *

Loss and sacrifice. Failure and honesty. Recognition and communion. Building critical communication pedagogy is like building a carefully crafted house of cards. It is fragile, it is subject to the winds and the quakes from those who fail to see the work, the care that went into crafting it. It takes time, patience, and a gentle but purposeful touch. It requires vision and demands tending, compromise, and sacrifice, knowing that, at any turn, one can knock down, you yourself can knock down, progress. For the cards to form a house, to make a foundation from which one might imagine a future, one needs to be able to see the cards in tension, how each rests against, balances on the others, how each card makes possible other cards.

In our academic careers, we have sought to find collaborators to help support our work—to identify those folks across the country who, within their classrooms or their research, work to build spaces of social justice and community. At conferences, we meet up, participate in panel discussions, and commune with each other, listening to their stories and their experiences. As we take them in, we gain nourishment from them as we strive to gain sustenance for the journey back to our own classrooms. At the National Communication Association conference, we have each been involved in a number of panels that are variously titled "Pedagogies of. . . . " For instance, "Pedagogies of Silence," "Pedagogies of Growth," or "Pedagogies of Violence." These panels are quite powerful, but often consist of similar folks sharing tales and ideas that build toward the theme. As a presenter and audience member in these sessions, I take from their voices a sense of myself, a sense of what I could be, could do, could imagine in my own classrooms. One particular member of this panel has become a kind of kindred spirit to me—a person I go to, share with, and regenerate from; she has welcomed me and my pedagogical visions with a kind of care and attention that makes me more whole. Indeed, just knowing she is out there doing her work helps me believe in myself as a teacher. I hope she too gains a kind of sustenance from me.

In this way, both of us have sought out mentors in the field, people who can provide support for our paths, for our journeys. A mentor is a very different figure than a hero: A mentor supports while a hero stands on high; a mentor gains as much from the other as the other gains from her or him, but a hero lacks the ability to share, lacks the ability to see the other in her or his humanity. During the writing of this book, we have come to understand what it means to be a mentor to each other, of each being that opposing force that helps the other stand, that helps the other bear the weight of her or his experiences. Only half joking, we observe that we are in the perfect complementary relationship, each providing what the other is missing. One sees details, the other sees patterns; one see the trees, the other the forest. Indeed, we sometimes joke that Deanna is the teacher who likes to research; John the researcher who likes to teach. And in many ways, this meets a kind of experiential truth: John is at a research institution in the Midwest, Deanna is at a teaching university on the West Coast. Enjoying these tensions, we have used this metaphor to organize our time, build our arguments, and generate the words and ideas that fill these pages. Yet, the writing of this book also frustrates that clean division. Indeed, we are both dedicated to the classroom—we both entered the academy because we love to teach. We both remain committed to the idea and practice of research as a way of being and growing as teachers. We have tried to trouble what counts as *simply* pedagogy or *simply* research in this chapter because we know in our own practice that such distinctions are superficial and only work to again marginalize teaching and research about teaching. Deanna is a good teacher only because she researches; John is a good researcher only because he teaches. And in that balance (not balance of details against vision—a false dichotomy—but rather harmony between the moments of living critical communication pedagogy) is the potential to build that fragile, yet worthy, scholarly house of cards.

Of course, the moment that house of cards becomes real, becomes worth it all, is in the moment when we see Eric, in pain, and send him home, in moments of kindness and healing, in moments that illustrate that even in institutional contexts, there is hope and humanity. It is worth it in the moment when a graduate student poses a seemingly innocent question about my godmother, asking me to be accountable to her, in moments that recognize I am worthy of being questioned, that my humanity is at stake and that I am worth the time and effort. Most meaningful of all are those moments where community members come together to regroup, to heal. Even in the midst of Melody's hurt, in the moment where she feels so at risk, so much the target, the community tries to build a moment of healing. In the moment of exploring the implications of HIV, on our TA listserv, we see fellow community members respond with care, compassion, and uncompromising love; we see the true meaning of critical communication pedagogy as a way of being. Here, in the tensions between hurt and compassion, the community reminds itself of why they are there, why they are working together, why each of them and all of them matter. These moments are better than the best final essay, the best performance on the exam, the best oral presentation. These moments heal us, make us all better people because we learned from them.

In the end, we argue teaching is research, research is teaching not only because we believe it is true—each informs our lives—but because, together, these two practices, like opposing sides of a sheet of paper, need each other to survive. It is only in the tension between them that we come to imagine our lives as members of communities, scholarly and otherwise.

* * *

Loss and sacrifice. Failure and honesty. Recognition and communion. Joy.

During finals week, we never have time to call each other; living in different states, different time zones, we find there are few opportunities to connect. Which is, in many ways, sad. Sad because, for every finals week, we have small moments where we remember, where we are honest with ourselves, where we savor the heroic moments of semester's end. In these moments, we remember we love our jobs, love what our jobs allow us to do, rejoice in what our institutions make possible. In these last few moments, we draw the joy of teaching, the possibilities we have built, and the learning we have shared with our community to a close. As students and colleagues move on, we find our roles shift, that we have lost a voice that calls us out or helps us heal. During these changes, during these closings, we often wish we could share these experiences with each other, to make meaning of these gifts from our departing friends. We must share these moments, document them, account for them. Our calls to each other would certainly include those moments when someone gave us a small gift because we did something we really don't remember, when someone remembered us years later, when someone shares with us what meaning s/he has made from our work together. Those moments of joy, those moments that make getting to school worth it, those small gestures are glue for that fragile card house in which we've placed our lives. And those unexpected moments give us the stamina to keep building, keep imagining what is next to come.

Conclusion

Grappling With Contradictions

Mentoring, in and Through the Critical Turnoff

"It's another case of the critical turnoff. . . ." I feel very sage, very clever as I say this, but Meg is not amused. Tendrils of smoke swirl up around her face, her furrowed eyebrows, and off in the direction of the Central States Communication Association's conference hotel's piano bar where attendees are enjoying an especially loud version of a Motown classic. She shakes out her match—"I guess I don't get what that means. . . . I'm teaching intercultural . . . we're going to have to talk about power, about privilege . . . and I keep having to get up on this soapbox. If I don't point out how they're not getting it, how they're just reproducing racism and sexism and homophobia, then I don't know who will." It's the point in the conference where everyone has had just a bit too much—too much to drink, too much to say, too much to process—and all I really want to do is talk about something else . . . something fun . . . something unrelated to school. But now I have to account for myself, to explain what I mean, to keep professing even when I'm supposed to be off the clock: "The critical turnoff. . . . It's like people interested in critical theory get so caught up in *the critical imperative,* in what they feel is just or purposeful or meaningful that they can't see they're turning people off. Nobody wants to hear they're hurting others . . . even if you say they don't mean to, that's still a pretty tough sell. . . . " And I'm pretty sure Meg knows what that means, though it's hard to tell from the top of my soapbox.

* * *

We end this book by asking the question of what it means to be a mentor, an adviser, a person in the world who attempts to guide others through the messy wilderness of critical inquiry in communication pedagogy. We ask about how to do this in ways that keep the stakes high, the potential tangible, and the tread light. We end here with a view into the process—for that is, in the end, what we have tried to articulate. We have tried in this book to avoid, as much as we could, the prescriptive detailing of what one should do, how one should research, or what position one should take in particular studies or arguments. We have described what we called a critical paradigm shift in the field, named a series of critical commitments, given examples of applying critical theory, examined both reflexivity and praxis as exemplified in research and teaching, and defended a philosophy of research and teaching as mutually constitutive; however, we have not given specific values to believe, specific stances to take, specific politics to advance. We have shown how we struggle in doing this work, how we assume the stances we take, how we engage politics in the classroom as we do, and how we try to position ourselves in relation to the others in our lives. If anything, we have shown how to struggle, how to grapple with the ideas and issues that working with, living in, critical scholarship demands of you.

In this final thought, this final collage of words, we ask how specifically one might imagine mentoring in/through this paradigm. Often mentoring in our lives takes the form of advising, but often it is much less formal, occurring in places and times we least expect it. We reflect here on those professors who mentored us as well. Indeed, you, the reader, will mentor, are mentoring, the students, teachers, family members, and friends around you. For instance, we have long considered each other mentors, even though we completed our degrees at about the same time and occupy similar positions in the academy. Mentoring needs no specific role, no specific place in the hierarchy of academic or social life. We try here to imagine what mentoring might, could, should look like within this logic. And we end with mentoring for very specific reasons; we believe that mentoring, the act of working collaboratively with our mentors and mentees, provides the kind of dialogue that makes this paradigm worthwhile. In the act of collaboration, in the moment of community with students and teachers, we see the true potential of living the critical life; yet, in the critical life, as Pelias (2000) suggests, one can feel bogged down with the weight of critique. Here, we consider the role of mentoring and again try to model the process, a means of living and working within critical communication pedagogy. After all, we cannot define critical communication pedagogy as what happens only in the classroom or within the pages of our journals and books; sometimes it occurs in a hotel bar, surrounded by conference attendees and cigarette smoke, with kind folks like Meg and her friends.

* * *

I can't help but think of my own adviser, who sat across from me in her office as I proposed what I wanted to do for my dissertation and said, "I've read all the critical pedagogy crap I want to read." At the time I felt caught, trapped in between my adviser's seemingly idiosyncratic desires and my own ideological commitments. It never occurred to me that she might be right, that there might already be enough sanctimonious, holier-than-thou critical work, and that I might do better to walk a different path. At the time, I felt she was asking me to walk a conventional path, an unreflective path, and perhaps she was; but, as I work with my own advisees, I finally see her meaning: There is quite enough work that focuses on critique and not hope, enough research on teaching that begins on the intellectual equivalent of "You know what's wrong with you?" I've spent years harboring resentment regarding her power, her ability to shut me down in that moment, but with each passing year, and with each new graduate student advisee, I come to realize something of the truth in her words: I cannot abide more work that casts students or teachers as judgmental dopes. But then, how might a caring, critical educator (who demands critique and change, but also hope and possibility) begin to effectively mentor students and teachers who want to follow this path?

* * *

I remember thinking that advising and mentoring grad students would be easy.

My first year in the department, I'd had a very good experience, been very productive, taught challenging and popular seminars, and been asked to serve on many graduate committees. I even perfected the proper pose for sitting in defenses—asking the hard questions, demonstrating that I had read and engaged in the document. I would be the member who asks *the* question, the one that cuts to the heart of the matter.

When I earned "graduate faculty" status early, I remember others telling me to be wary, to not jump too quickly, but advising my own students seemed a choice reward. And doesn't "early" sound good? Sound sexy? Sound like something you would want as a young assistant professor? So I jumped, landing in the middle of something I did not expect.

Every adviser is, by necessity, marked by her or his mentors. My own adviser was sharp—sharp with her mind, her wit, her critique. She is respected for her ability to cut to the quick, to find what underlies the argument and strike it into relief. As I think about my own mentoring style, I have tried to do this—to cut to the chase early and guide students toward making their arguments—to be sharp myself. But I also wanted to do something none of my own mentors had done for me—I wanted to be the good friend, supportive, unthreatening. In my own education, I chose advisers I respected, but that meant making them heroes, putting them on high pedestals, forever casting about for their approval and fearing I'd come up short. But in working to be the kind, personal adviser, I fear students cast me as easy. If I'm too informal or too jolly, they don't always take me seriously; requests become suggestions. How must the jolly seem when I ask them to make profound revisions before their dissertation can go to committee? Perhaps it feels like a paradox: How do they know who I am in a given moment? How do they balance the shifting power relations, the mystery of who I am and who I'm trying to be?

* * *

"Here's what I think . . . if you can't trust my advice, then I think you need to choose an adviser you can trust." Even as I say this, I realize that's not precisely what I mean to say, but I'm tired, tired of being second-guessed and challenged about whether I'm really asking for reasonable changes to this student's prospectus or whether I'm asking him to "write the book now." Rather than explore how these changes are meaningful or why they're justified, I've taken that grappling off the table; I've made this conversation about power, about whether he'll need to find another adviser.

* * *

I admit that I have a bias—that when I'm working with students in my office, I have particular directions, paths I want them to chart. I guess this is not such a big surprise, as everyone has learned from someone. My former graduate adviser and I share many research interests—she begat me, in a sense, and I will inevitably begat others. However, this bothers me more than I suspect it bothers some others; as a "critical" adviser, I believe in searching out the passions they have, not just reiterating my own. Further, I specifically frame my job as a guide and facilitator, not a sage, never the kind of person who uses graduate students to further my own research goals.

Yet, when Lana is in my office to discuss her dissertation, I push her to find a theoretical frame for her work. She offers a few choices, but as I listen to her, I find she really needs something more complex, something more. . . I hand her Garfinkel (1967) and Fenstermaker and West (2002); the ethnomethodological frame will help her see her participants' sense making and allow her to articulate how gender is constructed in moments of interaction. When she leaves, I feel like a good adviser; Lana is genuinely grateful (or at least appears to be). Of course ethnomethodology is only a side note in the qualitative methods course she took from me, not really a subject she would have had the time or ability to investigate until now. Of course, I like ethnomethodology because of its similarity to performativity, the major theoretical frame I use. Of course, that connection will have the chance to grow as we proceed, improving my own scholarship. And, of course, as a consequence, this dissertation went from hers to mine. And I did it all under the premise of "critical" advising. Suddenly, I suspect my abilities, turned off by my own shortsightedness.

* * *

I want to call all my advisees to apologize, to explain that if I had only known more when I was working with them, I would have done a much better job. There are many famous renderings of this sort of story, told by people who have been working with students much longer than I have. But still I wonder, what sort of "job" would I aspire to "do"? In the end, I have seen students to completion of their masters' degrees, to employment in community colleges, to continued graduate study in doctoral programs. I have seen them ask critical questions of themselves and their own students, and of that I am impressed (and sometimes a bit surprised). On the other hand, I wonder whether I have shown them my grappling, my struggling, enough? Of when I didn't know whether a prospectus meeting was a work-in-progress, roll-up-your-sleeves meeting or a meeting to defend the first three chapters of the thesis? Of when I didn't know how do draw out that deeper analysis, the one that really did justice to their data? Of when I couldn't think of a silky way to reveal my vulnerability so I simply cast the issue in black and white: Either trust me or find someone you trust.

* * *

The soapbox is a common trope in my work with graduate teaching assistants, especially as they come to explore power and justice with their own students; sometimes I have the sense that the soapbox is their bully pulpit for promoting social change, but at other times, I wonder whether the soapbox is really more of a bludgeoning tool, a means of battering students into particular lines of thinking or ways of seeing their lives and their connections with others.

It's natural for Meg to want to stand on her soapbox, to call out, to call down from the mountaintop that her students need to pay attention, to see how their communicative actions and inactions shape the lives and experiences of others, to see how they build, and may therefore also change, racism, sexism, heterosexism, classism, ageism, ableism, and other forms of oppression. And for some students, students like I was or like Meg is, that's enough. But what of the vast majority of students who have heard all the critical pedagogy crap-political correctness-bleeding heart liberal humanism they can stand?

Freire (1970/2003) argued that a pedagogy of the oppressed was just that: a pedagogy *of,* not *for,* not *on,* not *to.* In arguing for a midwife model of teaching and learning (what Shor, 1992, and others have called a problem-posing pedagogy), where teachers work to draw out what students already know rather than deposit knowledge into them, fully formed, Freire articulated a means for the critical project. Freire knew the challenge of drawing people in and drawing them out, when the temptation is to demystify, to tear down, to push in, to rupture.

* * *

How do we reveal the machinery of social oppression in a way that illuminates and enlivens students, that doesn't eclipse their sense of agency by suggesting there's little they can do to effect material change to their lives? In our own research, we spend considerable time trying not to make our argument sound like a personal attack. That is, when we write on culture, gender, sexuality, privilege, power, oppression, and the ways systems of power are products of ongoing, mundane, communicative acts in which we all participate, we strive to not create a straw argument, just telling people they are bad human beings who oppress with each and every act. As our mothers taught us, you get more bees with honey. To this end, we have designed our research to shed light on the systems of oppression and privilege that have created us as subjects, to ask how we each are products (and, thus, producers) of social processes, to balance individual agency with the systemic nature of power.

As we work with students, we ask similar questions of our own practice. That is, it feels too easy to simply tell students to repeat our own vision of the world, to just fit within our own ideological commitments. What we try to do is more Freirean, building from their own voices and desires, posing problems back to them, asking them to theorize their own positions.

At a recent conference, we both sat in the bar with a new doctoral student who was feeling blue about her position in her department. We became the subject of her story because we were not a risky audience, neither of us her current faculty. She spoke of feeling out of place, about feeling at odds with her students and her professors. In our "critical" way, we listened patiently, posing questions back to her about her assumptions, about how she was positioning her new faculty, about expectations, about how coded messages from faculty are not uncommon and may be offered as a way of pushing her to be better, to do more, to achieve. She nodded and then shifted topics.

Later, we wondered whether we had just reinscribed her location, making her more accustomed to or helping her find peace with this marginalized location. On the one hand, we believe that her faculty does like her, does believe in her. On the other hand, we see her hurt, feeling incompetent. And though we didn't mean to, we worked to make sure she stayed there.

But this suggests the difficulty of advising, of trying to be a mentor who can meet the needs of critically minded, intelligent, and socially aware students. It suggests the lack of models for doing it well. If in that moment again, would we make different choices? Probably not. Why? Why would we do this reproductive work if we now see its potential violence? Because, like our own disciplinary mothers and fathers, we are the product of complex, historical social systems that emerge through (and must be reenvisioned through) communication. To be critical advisers, we must take seriously the pedagogy of advising and allow ourselves to be as changed as by our relationships as our students are; this has yet to be fully explored. This failure to account for the relationship between adviser and advisee, the failure to write about it in ways that do it justice and help create practices that give rise to compassion and accountability, is to reproduce the status quo. Seeing that student nod convinced us there must be other ways.

How do we reveal the machinery of social oppression in a way that illuminates and enlivens students, that doesn't eclipse their sense of agency by suggesting there's little they can do to effect material change to their lives? We don't know. And that's the problem.

* * *

I think it was when my Butler and Scott (1992) volume *Feminists Theorize the Political* disappeared that I realized, with some reluctance, that perhaps some of my books were, in fact, being stolen. Now I don't mean that my loving graduate students, my advisees, my scholars-in-training, secretly broke in to my office, *Mission Impossible* style, and stole my tattered copy of Butler and Scott, though it does make me laugh to think of them in my office at 3 AM holding up my book laughing and cheering their liberation of my property. In my mind, I see these students standing in my office, stocking hats pulled low on their foreheads, swinging precariously from high tensile wires, flashlights gleaming, searching for seemingly obscure texts that fulfill their academic desires. Part of me revels in this image.

I suspect, though, that it is most often an accident: They see a book that might help them with an idea, they ask to borrow it, they use it, they put it on a pile of books in their own offices and, as time moves on, they forget it is mine. It eases into their own collection; it becomes familiar enough to pass as something that has always been there, as something that should be there. Five years from now, they will pick it up and, upon seeing my name on the front page, realize that it was once mine and that, after all these years, they forgot to return it to me. Maybe horrified, maybe amused, they will realize that they could send it to me, but they will fear the awkwardness of it, the weirdness that such a gesture might create. Such fears may just prevent them from doing it. Quietly, they will place it back on their shelf and never speak of it again, even when they see me at conferences and reunions.

Much of mentoring is like this. I think mentoring is about offering up some sense of ourselves with the awareness that we might not get it back. Every time I lend a book out to a graduate student, I do so knowing that it might not make it back home, that that piece of myself may never return. I remember the last time I lent a book, my copy of Schlosser's (2002) *Fast Food Nation*, to a student. I remember thinking, "Wow . . . I'll be surprised if Josh actually returns this, even with his promise." The book is still MIA and, even after sending a couple of vaguely threatening emails, I suspect the book is gone for good. So why loan the book in the first place? On some level, I lent Schlosser because I'd read it and I believed Josh would find use in it. I wanted others to know its secrets, its lessons. And there is the desire that with that book, a part of myself will be known too. Wishful thinking, perhaps, but I like the idea of him making that book and those ideas a part of his way of seeing. So the book is gone and I've stopped trying to get it back.

When I think about mentoring, on some level, I have come to see that I've taken much more from others than I have given. I think about a professor from college I really admired, I really loved. I based my syllabus on hers, borrowing some of her language to describe the kind of classroom I wanted to create. In using that syllabus, I steal from her, using that idea to facilitate my teaching. Indeed, I have stolen many assignments from former professors— a favorite of us both is the "weekly writing," stolen from Lenore Langsdorf, a beloved grad school mentor. I have also stolen much less tangible items:

forms of address (I prefer John because I was convinced by an undergrad professor that such choices generate different kinds of respect from students), classroom interaction styles (reading-centered, discussion-style formats), and advising styles (based in part on interactions I had with professors who were not my advisers). In these moments, I have stolen, borrowed ideals I now hold quite dear to myself; they are part of how I define myself. Perhaps the borrowed book, once of my collection and now on someone else's shelf, represents a kind of need fulfilled. Perhaps, on some level, someone just needed something more than I could provide by myself.

That said, let me be clear that while, on some level, I really do love the images of my *Mission Impossible* students dangling from wires in search of scholarship or of the moment when they realize they have borrowed a book of mine forever, in the moment, it really ticks me off. It is in the moment of going to the bookshelf and seeing the book's absence, knowing it should be just there—right there between Bordo's (1999) *The Male Body* and Cleto's (1999) edited book *Camp*. It should be there, but it is not. The empty space, hidden by shifting shelves, is nevertheless there and, without the book, I must turn to Amazon.com to replace, again, this missing book. I struggle with the dissonance of knowing that my book is now missing in action, of knowing that this gift (my Butler and Scott volume, for instance) was not my choice, and loving that these students wanted that gift in the first place. How do I reconcile the desire to provide what I need for the students in my life while also wanting, desiring, and coveting my own "stuff"? It is hard to feel good about Butler and Scott's new home when I miss it.

To my advisees: If you have the Butler and Scott book, you can keep it. As if you needed my permission. . . . I bought a new one this morning.

* * *

Tonight, I participated in a beautiful graduation ceremony. I always walk away from each of these ceremonies feeling loved, feeling as though I make a difference in the lives of real people with real goals and possibilities. But this year is different; this evening I have hooded my first two graduate students, and they will go away. They will go away and make fresh starts in new locales with new advisers and new lines of research. They have taken what they will from me, and my hope is that they've taken more of the good than the bad, and they will make what they will of it.

Once I've removed my regalia back in the office, hanging it carefully so I won't have to dry clean it for next year, I start to cry. I won't be their adviser anymore. Some advisees are hard to say goodbye to, especially when it's not exactly goodbye; they move on to other programs and encounter new ideas and new professors and new ways of being scholars and teachers. You run into these students at conferences, but they're no longer your students; they're someone else's. You know they're becoming your colleagues, but that's an awkward transition because you still have so many more things you want to say, so much more advice you have to give. With each year, with each graduate student, you learn more and more that you would have done better, that you would share now, if only you knew how.

* * *

Grappling is trying, with all your might, to hold on to the shifting, the contingent, the liquid nature of critical inquiry, the ebb and flow of power, the evaporating "it" that you saw right before it disappeared. We grapple because that, in the end, is what we have—only the process of investigation remains. We grapple, we seek, we try to love the process and believe that it, in the end, is the point of the critical journey we undertake.

Critical communication pedagogy is ultimately about the journey, rarely the destination. Indeed, most "critical" books and articles we've read (and some we've written) disappoint in the end, for they usually offer some final thought that never quite seems to do enough, never seems to respond to the problem they've set out to address. Indeed, this book may now fit that description, not quite doing enough for you, the reader, now that we've reached the end. But what we hope you have, is a process of inquiry, a method of doing and reflecting, and a reason for engaging in that work in the first place. We are inspired by the work we have read, moved by the people we've met, and overwhelmed at the potential of our (and your) scholarly lives. From Jane to Vic, from Meg to Melody, we have found joy in our work, relevance in our quest, and hope in the conversations we've shared. May all your journeys reward, all your questions matter, and all your hopes grow. Critical communication pedagogy is what we make it—may we all build a better tomorrow by listening to each other and imagining our futures together.

* * *

"So you can see the critical turnoff all around you—just look at all the professors who say they're critical and then reproduce all the screwed up power-laden political bullshit they claim to challenge. . . . "

"Do you mean Profes—"

"Ugh . . . I can't talk about it, Meg. . . I don't want to get into who does what; you know who they are, and it doesn't help either of us to dwell on the specifics except to strive to be more consistent than they are, to practice what we write about and share with our students." Of course I want to name names; it's a conference and, as with most conferences, we've both seen our unfair share of dysfunctional faculty advances, parries, and dodges. But that's not the point. The point is calling out our own inconsistencies, calling out the places where we're trying to "get it" and just don't, yet.

"Here's what I try to do, but I'm not sure it's the only way. It's just the way I can figure out right now, at this point in my life. I try to show my students how systems are really relationships between people that become rigid and 'thing-like' over time, and then I try to show how we—myself included—buy into those systems even when they hurt us and others. It's like trying to show the architecture of power, and if I can do that, then I don't have to get on a soapbox, because my students can explore how they're shaped by that architecture—and how they work to create that architecture—themselves." Meg seems satisfied by this answer, as though I'm just as sage and clever as I sometimes think I am. And, while this answer sometimes satisfies me, I'm still uncomfortable. Meg lights another cigarette, and offers one to me, "So all I have to do is show them the architecture, then I can offer my perspective as one of many." "Yes," I say, but I know it's not that easy.

I can want to model a process and fail in so many possible ways. That I've failed in these ways does not, however, mean that the process is a failure. Failure is uncomfortable, but it is also generative; it is also productive. That I articulate my struggle is what matters. But can Meg see that I, too, am struggling?

Appendix

Included here is our essay "(Re)Constituting Ethnographic Identities," first published in *Qualitative Inquiry* (Warren & Fassett, 2002). We have included it here to illuminate and extend our analysis in Chapter 5. Does reading the article, in its entirety, shape your understanding of Vic's story? How does reading it influence your assessment of our effort to include, explore, and draw implications from his story?

This essay was our first article-length exploration of many of the issues and questions that gave rise to this book: What are our roles, our goals, our obligations as we enter the intersections of pedagogical and methodological contexts? When, how should we act, and in what way does such action help or hurt those others in our lives, those folks we come into contact with as we live our scholarly lives?

This essay does not answer these questions—indeed, we felt we left so much unsaid, so much unexplored, that we wrote this book; but, as a first installment of our consideration of critical communication pedagogy as reflexivity and praxis, pedagogy and method, we felt including it as an appendix here might provide some clarification as to our own history with these critical ideas.

(Re)Constituting Ethnographic Identities[1]

This paper begins with a study of others, but like most, tells us more about ourselves. It's funny that way. We began, both of us, with the need for dissertation topics. What to do, what to write, what will get us done and off to some new place, some new beginning, somewhere else. We both began in the site/sight of others, the qualitative quest—go into the field, go to the people, go to those 'others' and study them, figure them out, and then report back (and, by the way, make some original contribution to the discipline along the way). Yet, as we reflect back on the projects we undertook, the people we studied, the questions we asked, we find that we learned the most about who we are, what we do, and what we need to do and write as ethical, cultural studies informed, scholars.

Both: At this point . . .

DLF: just a year and a half after defense, I would say that much of my difficulty stems from my positionality within my own discipline . . . perhaps this is why we're in a time and place where we're contemplating the self in relation to the others we study . . .

Both: At this point . . .

JTW: just months after completing the dissertation, I would say that much of my difficulty stems from my positionality within the research agenda . . . perhaps this is why we're in a time and place where we're contemplating the self in relation to the others we study . . .

Both: At this point . . .

We're getting ahead of ourselves. This project, this paper, has three interrelated goals. First, we strive to document what it means to be scholars in communication who struggle, with some success and some frustration, to write and live the academic life with an allegiance to the philosophy of cultural studies—to do scholarship that acknowledges the political nature of research, always foregrounding our speaking and listening bodies as the basis of our reading of others. Second, we aim to uncover the mechanisms—the political, cultural, social mechanisms—that are at work in producing social identities. This is to say, our effort here is to argue that the "subjects" we study are performative accomplishments—that their subjectivities are historical products in an ongoing process of (re)creation. The constructs of "educational risk" or "whiteness" are not natural nor neutral, but rather unnatural, strategic, normalized performatives—they are constituted again and again to maintain political and social power. Third, we consider how these constructs of "the other" get reified through our research while constituting our authoring selves. Thus, we argue here that cultural studies bestows a gift upon qualitative research: the responsibility of reflexivity and the reminder that our research, of how we write it, of whom is its subject, and of whom we subject it to, constitutes the authorial self as well as the participants' identities themselves. Not only are we a performative accomplishment of our research, just as are our participants/co-researchers/subjects, but we continue to reiterate their/our problematic identifiers even as we struggle to resist the baggage those constructs carry.

Both: I came to my dissertation . . .

DLF: alternating between apathy and resistance—apathy because I knew if I followed the steps I could finish, and resistance because I've been wanting to do something I cannot fully articulate and I don't find exemplars in my field. This is complicated by the tensive relationship I hold with the subject matter of my dissertation.

JTW: I struggle between feeling like a critical cultural scholar working to undermine the power of racism, while also feeling like an opportunist banking on the latest academic fad.

Both: I study education from the perspective of a communication scholar.

JTW: I see my dissertation in the crossroads of several bodies of literature, bodies of researchers, and, of course, the bodies of my research participants. In this two-year ethnographic study considering the performance of whiteness in the classroom, I have struggled to maintain a balance between traditional critical performance ethnography and more experimental forms of scholarship, knowing that each fall victim of suspicion in the field at large.

DLF: I see my dissertation relegated to the periphery of my discipline, strewn about the "wrong side of the tracks," to a messy place scholars can avoid if only we speed up, stick to the map, and keep moving. In my interviews, I have struggled to maintain a balance between helping students and teachers succeed in the existing educational system and inviting those folks to help challenge and change that very system, knowing that, by flaunting order and convention, I risk further ghettoizing my research and their lives.

Both: On the one hand,

DLF: One could say that I study at-risk students. More specifically, one could say that I study how students come to be construed as "at-risk" or "successful." And still more specifically, I study how such constructions come to challenge or sustain more global, cultural values regarding the nature of education, of studenting and of teaching.

JTW: One could say that I study whiteness. More specifically, one could say I that I study how students come to and reproduce whiteness as an identity, levying power over others.

Both: On the other hand . . .

DLF: One could say I study the art of researching, of seeing how others get constructed by the act of research. How we are co-constituted in the research project? The articulation of "at-risk" in my research remakes risk each and every time I write it. Even as I try to address and challenge notions of "at-riskness," I restate, remake, and, thus, reinscribe risk. I struggle with deconstruction, knowing that I am laying theoretical bricks as fast as I can tear them down.

JTW: One could say I study the art of researching, of seeing how others get constructed by the act of research. The naming of "whiteness" in my work not only serves as a deconstructive move, but also remakes privilege, theirs and mine, through that voicing.

What's in a name? People look at us, saying, "You look like a John." "You look like a Deanna." "Your name fits you." But the name is not who we are—it is just a sense making device, allowing us ease at distinguishing between each other. Yet something happens in the repetition—something that makes the name more than just a way of distinguishing us. The name takes on a power of its own, making it somehow a part of us. It becomes us—our bodies, our faces, our voices, our expressions seem to capture the name, to make the name an almost essential part of us. Names have this power—they grow in symbolic power until our bodies and our names become indistinguishable.

Names carry social and political power too. We hear names like "Barbie" or "Ken" and our minds fill with implications, often creating self-fulfilling prophecies in which we create and situate those people into pre-established categories. "His name is Ken, can you imagine a better name?" The current crisis surrounding September 11th comes to our minds as we hear of children being born with the name "Osama," knowing the power of such naming to bring about the social power of shaping who those children will be as they grow up with that signifier. Names shape us.

One might say that the act of naming, the act of connecting and repeating an identity with a linguistic symbol, helps to constitute who we are. The act of naming, the act of making John's and Deanna's, so shapes us that we fail to understand ourselves outside of that construction. It becomes so normalized, so much a part of the mundane nature of who we are that it is impossible to imagine ourselves outside of that frame of mind. And if a name can have this power, we wonder what the naming of race or academic achievement might do to who we are—[what] might those labels, the repetition, the sedimentation, the normalization of whiteness or riskness, do to how we interact with each other? What's in a name? Names don't simply hold or identify power; they are power.

Both: We encounter scholarly others.

JTW: "Abolish" the white race?

DLF: The subjects were determined to be "at risk"?

JTW: To choose blackness or brownness as a way of politically disidentifying with white privilege?

DLF: At risk of what? Of not passing a class? Of not finding a job? Of not living a fulfilling life?

JTW: We are whites who have been "transformed" by our experiences? Who gets to claim they can abolish their own race and still have the luxury of being taken seriously?

DLF: Locus of control? Compliance gaining? Verbal aggressiveness? Who gets to choose which traits and states amount to a whole human?

JTW: Choose blackness? Choose brownness? Choice?

DLF: The students were observed . . . Who observed them? Why? To what end?

Both: Isn't there another way?

DLF: I grow cautious of the dangers of passive voice constructions.

JTW: I grow cautious of the dangers of assuming my whiteness is the same kind of choice as whether to spread butter or cream cheese on my morning bagel.

DLF: I grow cautious of the dangers of treating students like objects. I grow cautious of erasing my voice in my research, as if I am not there. As if this is not me reading them. As if I am not there.

JTW: I grow cautious of the dangers of treating performance as pretend, as not-real, as the always already false. I grow cautious of researchers, activists, performers, scholars asking me to abolish whiteness—to abolish that identity which is so integral to who I am. To abolish my whiteness as if I am throwing out an old shirt. As if I can stop doing that which [is] in my tissues, not as some essential quality or attribute, but in my tissues through each and every act I have done, continue to do, and know I will do in the future. Only whiteness can have the gall to suggest that one can suddenly refuse to do what has made it powerful—that is the ultimate institution of power. To deny it while still getting the privilege it provides.

DLF: So much of what I [have] written is for my peers, for people who have been conducting research on locus of control, on verbal aggressiveness, on communication apprehension. I question their work; I ask them to step outside themselves, outside of their research, to consider other ways of seeing. Who am I to judge them? What right do I have to say this? Am I Cassandra or the court jester?

JTW: I grow cautious of the dangers of erasing the power of performance as a metaphor for racial constitution.

DLF: I grow cautious of the dangers of erasing the power of performance as a metaphor for educational success and failure.

Both: Isn't there another way?

Performance has a long tradition of dwelling in the realm of pretense. It is considered fake, the inauthentic carved out of "real" life. Yet it is the metaphor of performance, and the kinds of rehearsal processes that it embodies, that draws us to this theoretical frame. That is, how can the notion of multiple, embodied, and socially practiced repetitions allow us to see how we perform our daily lives. On whose scripts do we rely? What levels of difficulty do we have when we try to negotiate our performances of self with others?

Recently, one of the authors was caught and questioned in the everyday maintenance of his/her performance of self. In his/her office, a queer student poses the question: "Are you gay too?" The queer-identified professor, caught in the everyday slippages of performance, is faced with the consequences of his/her performances of sexuality. How does the professor respond? How does this professor, a straight-appearing but bisexual-identifying woman in a monogamous heterosexual relationship, negotiate the complexities of *this* performance of self? How does she respond? Who she "really is" is complicated, fuzzy, always a negotiation of time, place, and circumstance. What we "really" have are the performances—who we are is the performance of self, the repetition of identity that gets cast and recast before self and others. The question, "Are you gay too?," is an appeal to "truth," but the question itself is really more telling than any answer.

Looking at identity through the lens of the performative means understanding how who we are is a continuing process of acts—a consequence of multiple actions, namings, and significations. The educationally successful student is born not at that subject's literal birth, but through a process of naming—a process that is influenced by economics, history, race, gender, and other political classifications. They/we are created through schooling and social processes that maintain the production of identities. The student we cheer as successful is successful precisely because of the cheers, the constant naming of her/him as such, and the perpetuation of certain characteristics over others. In the same logic, the white subject is born into a complicated system of race—a system that has echoes of past violence, past struggles, and past privileges. They/we are not born at the literal birth, but are made through performative repetitions, the repeated messages of who they/we are. Even skin color, a fact that is often assumed to be biological, is a performative accomplishment—it is the product of social norms that have, through highly regulated sexual politics, produced a skin pigment that carries the political signifier of privilege.

Our identities are a product of repetition, of a continual process of recasting subjectivity until those names, those categories, become so normalized that they fail to seem like we created them in the first place. It is the power of the acts to feel so sedimented, so natural, that demands a performative analysis—only a performative analysis that examines how identities get created and maintained through performance that can shed light how inequalities are sustained through daily actions.

JTW: I am in an interview. The thrill of the ethnographic enterprise rises in my blood, pushing me toward the end of my chair, pushing me. The Diet Coke in my hand feels cold, a small drop of condensation falls from a plastic indention, falls from the slightly scuffed container, falls on to my hand. I smile and look at her, my interviewee. Karen, her brown straight hair teasing her shoulders, has her legs crossed, her kind face smiling at me. Karen is a thirty-something-year-old student in the class I am observing and has agreed to spend some time with me, answering some questions. I look at my notes: "So, Karen? How do you think the class understands culture?" I look up, the question asked, the tape rolling, the process underway. Karen shifts in her seat, uncrossing and re-crossing her legs. "I think this class understands culture in politically correct terms. Uh, in terms of accepting people's ethnicity, other's, uhm, values. And you know, I probably mentioned at the beginning of class, I'm not very politically correct. Don't aspire to be."

DLF: A pretty, dark-eyed woman has been tracking the conversation while sipping a Diet Coke. I can tell she is paying attention because her posture changes ever so subtlety when one speaker's statement gives way to the next. I have asked this group of students to discuss what characteristics make up a good student. There are several people at the table, more women than men, more white than not, and each appears to be participating if not with zeal then with gameful courtesy. Just when the rest of the folks in the room seem comfortable with the idea that anyone can be successful in school if she or he works hard, the dark-eyed woman sets down her Diet Coke and suggests, somewhat tentatively at first, ". . . but even if everyone worked hard then there is still going to be a couple of people that are going to get pushed aside—if everyone is trying to get up there, as you get older, competition gets harder, and you get pushed back." This gives me some pause.

JTW: I am startled. I kind of blink at her, still smiling but blinking in a confused blur. "What does politically correct mean to you?" I know it is a loaded question and I tell her that, yet it had to be asked, I had to ask it, had to and so I did: "What does politically correct mean to you?" Karen begins talking. "Politically correct to me means that I'm not really entitled to any of my own opinions because they might offend someone else." Karen continues but I am no longer listening, no longer hearing her voice. I look at her in what feels like slow motion. I see her lips move and yet all I hear is the first line. I look down to the recorder which is still turning and am relieved that it will catch what I can't. I smile, nodding, picking up just words and phrases: "the kids in our class go out and get bombed, I go home and take care of children . . . I'm involved in church, we're just totally different . . . The whole notion of politically correct that plays itself out in the multicultural thing that we are taught is that it is okay for me to offend you, but don't you dare offend me . . ." She continues in what will amount to thirty some pages of transcript, this nice woman who I no longer feel I know, no longer want to know. I want to interrupt this interview, but I'm gathering. The critique comes later—after a careful ethnographic process. Bad ethnography is when we rush to judgment. So I wait, I nod, I record, I transcribe, I code, with anticipation of critique . . . later.

DLF: At first, I was pleased to hear a cynical view, someone with suspicion akin to my own. Then, as I considered her words more carefully, I began to wonder: Who pushes? This pusher is not as simple as you or me, but then again this pusher *is* as complicated as you and me. Each of us is a part of this system of pushing, either through action or inaction; what does it mean when such a young, bright, friendly woman assumes that success is limited and gatekeeping is normal? Furthermore, what does it mean that I allowed the comment to pass by unnoticed, unchallenged?

JTW: I smile as she continues talking, knowing that this moment, this little moment will be a spotlight of the dissertation, a powerful moment. The uneasiness of the interview begins to fade as I anticipate the possibilities. I smile, I nod, I record, I anticipate critique. I am witnessing whiteness in the process of creation, a remarking of privilege, a maintenance of domination. A spotlight in the dissertation.

DLF: Ahh . . . but I do notice. I rush—to my notes, to my adviser's office, to my computer—to capture the moment, to articulate the best instance of something I'd long suspected, to demonstrate that we do, in fact, limit our understandings of, and thus our possibilities for, educational reform through our own talk. One . . . brief . . . moment . . . of . . . clarity . . . of . . . order . . . of proof . . . And in that moment, I mistake the clarity for truth, for engagement, for understanding.

Both: Isn't there another way?

DLF: We interview.

JTW: We collect.

DLF: We transcribe.

JTW: Fieldnotes—only 200 pages of text.

DLF: How much does it cost to transcribe that?

JTW: We code.

DLF: We code.

Both: Will you double check this for me—intercoder reliability? Why yes I will!

If we use scare quotes, does that make it all right? If we call attention to the construction, the normalization of that naming process, does it alleviate the problem? Are we off the hook now? Can we rest easy in the belief that we are the critical ones, that we are the ones who know better?

We believe two things about categories and the labels we use to describe those we study. First, most of them predate us. That is, we did not choose "academic risk" or "whiteness" as ways of separating some people from others. They are, in many ways, outside our immediate control. In fact, it was the labels that in many ways drew us to the issues involved in those struggles: the needs of "at-risk students" or the unearned privilege embedded in "whiteness." Yet, only once we invest ourselves in those particular areas of research do we begin to see the ways that the label, the name, the identity itself is problematic. Then, we find we lack the language to undo the power of the label—now the label that drew us to those ideas constrains our ability to resist its power.

Second, those labels do have a usefulness that is not easy (nor necessarily desirable) to erase. Scholars talk about identity markers (gender, race, sexuality, etc.) as performative identities—that is, we enact these identities through language and gesture, sediment them through time until they appear to predate the label. Thus, gender is a process, a performance we learn and continue to enact throughout our lives until we naturalize those actions, failing to understand that it is through the acts themselves that identity is created and maintained. In this logic, we begin to think our actions stem from gender. This is the complete internalization of these norms, these now normalized acts. However, even as those scholars discuss identity as performatives, they nevertheless acknowledge the real effects those performances have in our daily lives. The failure to do our race or sexuality right results in punitive consequences ranging from subtle looks to physical violence. Within this frame, the use and examination of identity within and through these labels serves a productive purpose—it is a way of examining how we, through our language choices, separate people. It is a way of examining how, through naming, we levy power in unjust and unequal ways.

As scholars who believe each of these principles to be true, we find that the labels themselves chafe us, rubbing us raw as we struggle to undermine the stability of these categories. We complain over steaming cups of coffee, over turkey sandwiches at lunch, and over beers late in the evening, searching for a new way of speaking, a new way of talking about these identities. Our fear is simple: if we believe that identity is maintained through the repetition of naming, through the reiteration of category systems that preserve the inequities of power, then each and every time we use "at-risk" or "whiteness" in our writing, in our teaching, in our discourse, we recreate and maintain both systems of power. An article on riskness or academic success in education, even if it seeks to question the damage that such a label can do to a child, inevitably recreates the very idea, the very possibility of that identity. Our research is caught in a paradox; it is . . . a critical project that seeks to expose power systems, while simultaneously remaking and maintaining that power.

So, what good do our scare quotes "really" do?

DLF: I'm not sure where to begin.

JTW: Eventually every class I observe goes there. I know what will happen before I get there.

DLF: I keep at it though, trying first one tack, and then another.

Both: It's the time in the

DLF: interview

JTW: class

Both: where I encounter

JTW: the KKK.

DLF: A student who tells me she's suicidal. I took her to Subway for a sandwich. She had so much to say. Jane was a former student of mine, a hotel management major, a young, black and Italian, woman with a 2.8 GPA and some difficulty petitioning into regular admission status.

JTW: Tom is a young man, very thin and very pale. He often wears old black T-shirts that are faded and worn, displaying a rock band logo from the eighties. He is fairly vocal, takes on racial issues in class— the typical moderately liberal Midwestern young white male, if there ever was one.

DLF: Jane is bright and friendly, plays basketball like she's on fire even though she's only five feet tall.

JTW: That's when he brings up the KKK—the extreme example of white racism that is so often called upon to separate the liberal white anti-racist from *those* people, those racists. Often when the KKK is brought up in class, the students would do one of two things in order to construct themselves as 'not-them.' First, there is often a pitch change, a raising of the pitch with a twist of southern dialect. This nonverbal marking not only places racism geographically south of them, but also relies on common assumptions about the ignorant south, the stupid southern racists. Second, the KKK stories have to be larger than life, the most extreme. The bigger the separation from mundane everyday life, the more the KKK gets framed as the easily recognizable antithesis of themselves. Thus, they get constructed as the sympathetic white wo/man who is astonished and angered by this example of racism. Additionally, the KKK serves as an active example of racism, localizing racism to a single intentional act—that KKK guy did this, said that, hurt them—and allows systemic racism to be obscured, hidden.

DLF: I don't know what to do when she says, "I'm evil and it doesn't do anything but stress me out." I think she's joking: smiling, I ask what she means by evil. She says, "I don't know if you want to delete this, but I'm kind of semi-suicidal." And so, where should I begin?

JTW: And so Tom begins.

DLF: In many ways I was well-prepared for qualitative research. I understood how to write questions, how to establish a rapport in an interview, how to sift carefully through the finer details to find the big picture. And yet, in so many other ways, I was wholly unprepared, left vulnerable. You might say I had just enough knowledge to be dangerous. I remember once, hearing someone at a conference ask Dwight Conquergood a question about how to exit the ethnographic site, how to know when or how to leave. I remember thinking I wouldn't need to worry about this; I wasn't going into *the field*, so to speak, I was going to talk with some people and learn about their lives. It was going to be a clean kind of qualitative research. No one would need me, and I could keep my distance. I wanted so desperately for Jane to be in jest, to be teasing me, tastelessly, but she wasn't. I had invited her to talk, and she had something important to say.

JTW: "This one time, I was in Chesterville. I was in this Denny's and, well, you know that Chesterville is the KKK base in this area, right? So anyway, I was with my brother and we were going to get Van Halen tickets and we went to this Denny's first. We were sitting close to the door and they came in with their black outfits and those crosses and all, that's how we knew who they were. That and they looked like assholes. Anyway, I was sitting there wearing my Jim Morrison T-shirt and they picked us to talk to. They called us faggots cause we had long hair and then spit on the table. Luckily not on our food though. They sat in the back and a friend of mine had to serve them. He said they were bad tippers. They left him like three pennies pushed into their mashed potatoes. That's worse than not getting a tip!"

DLF: How shall I write Jane in this moment? How shall I write myself? I do recall, with some strangled sense of pride, that I attempted to take care of Jane first. She told me about her best friend's recent death, her sense of isolation, her overwhelming sense of dread in the face of innumerable obligations—financial, professional, scholastic, interpersonal, familial. I wish I could say the interview was farthest from my mind, but I was acutely aware of the tape recorder, of her vulnerability, of my inexperience, of my professional obligation. Professional obligation? What is my professional obligation in these sorts of instances? Once she'd shown me a picture of her friend and wiped the tears from her eyes, I gulped back my own [tears] and asked whether she'd like to continue with the interview. Brightening, she said "sure." We each took a deep breath and continued. If I say I went with her to see a counselor, does it redeem me from worrying about whether I'd have to erase the interview?

JTW: My hand is quickly trying to get down the story Tom tells, the sweat from the plastic of the pencil makes it occasionally slip. I grow both troubled and excited by the details of the story, this story by this very pale thin young man who has often noted his sometimes rocky relationship with his *girl*friend. I grow troubled and excited to watch as he narrates this story, interested in the identities he constructs for us: heterosexual but the victim of homophobia, white but the victim of the KKK. He is the target and subject of KKK discourse, but can tell it in a way that still allows him to discuss the quality of their tip. My pen continues writing. There is so much here. I begin to underline key words in the passage I just copied down: Jim Morrison shirt, KKK base, looked like assholes, not on our food though, bad tippers, Van Halen tickets, faggots. I am curious about this tale—what does it do, how does it help construct Tom's identity? How does it construct the anti-racist white guy that is also the victim? Further, how does it make non-white folks feel to hear these stories about the KKK and their white victims?

DLF: As I write about education, or students, or teachers, or "at-riskness," or whatever it is that seems to be my purview anymore, I can't do it in the same way I used to. I used to write energetic essays about what labels might mean, a dispassionate-passionate account of my own sense of others' lives. It's not that simple anymore. I am a part of what I study. On one level, this is as simple as how we understand risk. Risk is not an amalgam of traits, of race plus sexuality plus school inequities equals increased likelihood of failure; risk is instead a metaphoric understanding scholars apply to make the painful, the difficult less so—less painful, less personal, less visceral. But, if I render Jane's life in rich detail, to what extent do I re-create all the stereotypes of the at-risk student? Jane's from a poor background, she's biracial, she's small; her life has been marked by tragedy, by family crises, by disruption. That doesn't do her justice.

JTW: As I walked back to my office that day, I was smiling. I was happy to have good data for my study, for my dissertation, for some conference paper, for the ears of someone who might hear it and think

I was smart. I was happy about seeing, marking, and deconstructing racist talk. I was happy. I was smiling. Further, I was happy that this moment uncovered how white subjects are performative accomplishments, how this KKK performance by this white student worked to recreate whiteness. This performance, this one reiteration of racist discourse, worked to make whiteness meaningful. And with that moment, I could mark the making of whiteness. The ethnographic subject in the making. Yes, I was happy. And I smiled.

DLF: I started out my dissertation writing about at-risk students. I wanted to know whether they thought of themselves in that way, and what the consequences of such a discourse might have for how they understand themselves as producers and products of the American educational system. But rather than write a dissertation about "them," I decided I would have to write one about "us." Meaning, I would need to think seriously about how I am implicated in the very phenomena that I study. I wonder if I did that?

JTW: I started out wanting to writing a dissertation about white students and racism. I wanted to know how they came to be who I saw in front of me. I wanted to see them in the making. But, I also felt the need to consider myself as an agent in this process. I wonder if I did that?

Both: To begin seeing them making themselves. To begin to see the making of

JTW: whiteness

DLF: success

JTW: race

DLF: risk

Both: subjectivity.

DLF: Theirs

JTW: and ours.

Often, we dream of graduate school. We dream of sitting in a doctoral seminar, studying philosophy of communication. Our professor draws on the board a stick figure to suggest a person, a living body who is connected to whatever topic we are studying that day. We know this script, we know where she is going and we revel in her presentation. She always draws ears on her stick figures, little half circles to suggest that the person hears, that the person experiences sound. This is her effort to undermine the visual-centric orientation of the academy. And when she draws those ears, providing the story of why she does this, we smile and enjoy the retelling of a favorite story.

These dreams of graduate school, those moments in that room, remind us of our first time—our first foray into finding new ways of hearing. What those meetings did for us, like perhaps anyone's experience in graduate school, was to ask us to rethink, to rehear a given issue. The ability to hear something in a different way, to re-imagine that sound with the urgency of possibility, is a skill, a talent, a desire we long for. Under the sedimented weight of history, we crave the ability to ask questions in ways that encourage folks not only to rethink solutions to whatever problems we address, but to also rehear the very subject of the conversation. We desire a language that undermines the stability of the category even as we address it. We long to capture the feeling in our graduate seminar—the feeling of freedom when we come to the epiphany that if we can rehear, we can imagine new possibilities.

JTW: I am sitting on my mother's couch. The sunlight occasionally breaks through the tree outside the three large windows from which I can look out onto the front lawn and the neighborhood street I used to play on when I was young. I am proofing the pages of my dissertation which I brought with me just in case I might have a spare minute during my visit home. My mother enters and we chat about my dissertation. She is supportive, interested, caring—a good mother. I can tell she is not quite sure what it is that I do, not quite sure she buys all this research on whiteness, on racism through the lens of the privileged. She picks up the first few pages and reads a narrative, a performative piece about whiteness as it manifests in a conference panel.

DLF: I am sitting in my new office, trying frantically to write a conference paper that I should have written some time ago. But this is nothing new. As a new professor, I'm teaching four classes, cultivating relationships with students and faculty, attending various departmental and university-wide committee meetings, and attempting to get published; I am quickly becoming an expert on the eleventh hour accomplishment.

JTW: When she has read the first several pages, my mother asks me what I am sure was simple question, yet when I am this deep in the project, I am very bad at answering these kinds of questions. I find I am defensive, worried that anyone might find a hole where I have so much at stake. She notes that she doesn't agree with my reading of this moment, noting that maybe I am making too much of all of this. "Aren't you taking this a bit too far?" I look up, her face is warm and loving, but curious and insightful. There is more to her question than a simple critique of academic masturbation. There is more, something that matters.

DLF: I look at the abstract for the paper—something I wrote nearly a half a year ago, in a different mindset, in a different place—and I attempt to make good on my promises. I recall how thrilled I was at the idea of this project. I would describe how students create at-riskness in the moment; that is to say, I would describe how at-risk students recreate their risk through everyday performative accomplishments. All I would need to do is examine my interviews with students whom the university has identified as at-risk; I would look for moments in their communication that help to keep them at-risk. Maybe they would speak in non-standard English; maybe they wouldn't place value in higher education; maybe they would reveal their lack of preparation. I really wanted this paper to be that simple.

JTW: In my ethnographic research, I have spent a great deal of time studying "subjects" who appear or self-identify as white. I have published what they did, how they did it, and what *I* think it means. I have critiqued their speech, their actions, and their privilege. And while I have also written about my own privilege, I realize that I have spent very little time reflecting on how I have been constituted in this research site—that my ethnographic self is inexorably tied to the work I do. That as a white scholar who reads whiteness on the bodies and actions of others, I have come to see whiteness and privilege on others, but failed to see how the repeated acts of researching, of writing, and of presenting research works to remake me as an ethnographer. I am constituted as ethnographer just as they are constituted as participants.

DLF: I recall that I asked my research participants whether they thought of themselves as at-risk students. To be truthful, I first asked students if they had heard of the term, and then what they thought it might mean. These folks seemed to know what this meant; they also did not hesitate to offer a sense of themselves as either at risk or not. I am pleased to hear students challenge the researchers' criteria; they did not readily equate demographic traits with their possibilities for change and growth. Some students immediately observed that they were at risk in the same sense as anyone—we are always already subject to perils unknown. Other students felt that they were not at risk; they were individuals who cannot be lumped in with a crowd—everyone addresses challenges in her or his own way.

JTW: But the question my mother asks me is more than simply reflecting on how I am constituted as a researcher, on how I am constituted as a particular kind of ethnographer who does and argues a particular kind of scholarly point. Rather, her question suggests that my reading of them matters—that I am implicated in this work, never neutral. That it too is a form of creation, a form of making. That their performances of whiteness are not their own. That I am not reading them, but rather (re)creating them on the page. I am manipulating their words and their bodies in order to make my ethnographic point. This is not to erase the ways these white students actively created their own privilege in these classrooms, but rather to insist that I am implicated in that production. Further, the writing and presentation of those moments serve as another reiteration of whiteness. That my scholarship, even if it is intended to undermine the structures of whiteness, reinscribes whiteness by making it a possible identity. My ethnographic identities are tied to the production of whiteness, a system in which this paper is now a part. It is the insidious nature of whiteness to grow stronger under the eye of s/he who critiques it. It is the nature of whiteness to allow me to feel pleasure in finding racism, in uncovering the daily maintenance of power, in the (re)constitution of privilege. And through this, I, with pleasure and pain, reconstitute myself and that which I strive to erase.

DLF: This gives me pause. Was I an at-risk student? In some ways yes and, in some ways, no. While I did not meet all of the standard demographic criteria, I can certainly think of times in my life when I struggled to survive in education. And it occurs to me: If I want to learn about how at-riskness is accomplished in everyday moments, I should look at myself. Even as I attempt to deconstruct dilapidated models of educational failure, I repair them in my own assumptions, in my own critique, in my own discourse. And so I attempt to pluck a tensive path between engaging the other in the hope of social meaning and challenging discursive practices by breathing life into them, reinflating them in hopes of helping them explode.

Both: How can one undermine

JTW: whiteness

DLF: risk

Both: without simultaneously reconstructing it?

This paper ends where it began. It begins with one of us a year and a half after defense, with the other just months after completing the dissertation. It begins and ends here, where we again meet to reconstitute ourselves, our subjects, our participants, our identities as academic agents working toward social justice, toward articulating a space in the overlap of qualitative research and cultural studies. It is in that space where we feel the freedom of an academic language that privileges the experiential, the communicative, the critical, the performative.

This essay begins and ends with more questions than answers. Those questions leave us asking what to do now, now that we had said this. Paulo Freire once wrote that "changing language is part of the process of changing the world." We hear his plea; we embrace what we feel is the power behind that ideal—to change the ways in which we conceptualize the problem opens it up to possibility. It is a changed world we desire: an educational system where we hurt students less, a social world where we inflict less racial violence upon one another. We desire that end. And it is to that end that we look at how our research works to remake and rebuild the very oppressive structures we seek to undermine. We ask these questions because to realize our own participation in these systems of power only leaves us as researchers accountable for fostering a new language that serves possibility.

And we *do not* think this project is without possibility. We *do not* think we are forever trapped in confines of our language, our bodily actions, or our sedimented ways of thinking and being. For it is exactly the performative power of identity that makes change possible. That is, if we think of identity, those labels and structures which constitute us, as performative accomplishments, then we must also accept the possibility that they can be created differently. But how? How does one go about this project in a way that does not work against us? We can't hope to answer this question for everyone, but we can at least point to this essay, this articulation as a way of changing our language, our talk about how subjectivity is constituted. We believe that the idea that identity is reconstituted and rebuilt through each utterance can be, if we allow it to be, a moment of strength. The notion of rebuilding identity from the sedimented remains of history means that we can, with analysis and reflexivity, rebuild those categories in different ways. We can do this remaking, this reconstituting, with subtle changes—those subtle complexities that can undermine the simplicity of racial category systems, denying the "this or that" logic of race or risk. It is in the reconstitution, the rearticulation of these identity categories that lie the possibility of imagining new ways of relating to each other. The most damning thing one can do to these naturalized structures is point out the constructedness. It is through this altered way of thinking that we hope this analysis begins; it is with this possibility that we offer this critique. And with that possibility comes the hope of less violence, for this paper does end with the hope that by locating the making of social difference we might foster a new way of seeing how systems of oppression and domination persist. This paper began as a study of others, but like most, tells us more about ourselves. It *is* funny that way.

Note

1. We originally performed this essay at the 2000 National Communication Association summer conference on cultural politics. We have maintained much of the form and style to reflect that moment, that time. As with all essays that are constructed at a particular historical time, social positions change and degrees are earned. However, we maintain the voice of the moment here, working to capture the struggle we encountered in trying to articulate our researching selves. We based the dialogical form of this essay on a performative essay performed by Kirk Fuoss and Randall Hill at the 1999 National Communication Association annual convention on a panel entitled "Rehearsing History: Roundtable on Performance Historiography." Inspired by their mixture of voices, we gratefully acknowledge their influence in the conception and writing of this essay.

Influential Sources

Butler, J. (1993). *Bodies that matter: On the discursive limits of "sex."* New York: Routledge.

Conquergood, D. (1991). Rethinking ethnography: Towards a critical cultural politics. *Communication Monographs, 58,* 179–194.

Denzin, N. K. (1997). *Interpretative ethnography: Ethnographic practices for the 21st century.* Thousand Oaks, CA: Sage.

During, S. (Ed.). (1993). *The cultural studies reader.* New York: Routledge.

Ellis, C., & Bochner, A. P. (Eds.). (1996). *Composing ethnography: Alternative forms of qualitative writing.* Walnut Creek, CA: AltaMira Press.

Freire, P. (1992). *Pedagogy of hope: Reliving* Pedagogy of the Oppressed. New York: Continuum.

Garfinkel, H. (1967). *Studies in ethnomethodology*. Cambridge, UK: Polity Press.

Giroux, H. A. (Ed.). (1991). *Postmodernism, feminism, and cultural politics: Redrawing educational boundaries*. Albany: SUNY Press.

Goodall, H. L. (2000). *Writing the new ethnography*. Walnut Creek, CA: AltaMira Press.

Hill, M. (Ed.). (1997). *Whiteness: A critical reader*. New York: NYU Press.

hooks, b. (1994). *Teaching to transgress: Education as the practice of freedom*. New York: Routledge.

McLaren, P. (1993). *Schooling as a ritual performance: Towards a political economy of educational symbols and gestures* (2nd ed.). New York: Routledge.

Nakayama, T. K., & Martin, J. N. (1999). *Whiteness: The communication of social identity*. Thousands Oaks, CA: Sage.

Parker, A., & Sedgwick, E. K. (Eds.). (1995). *Performativity and performance*. New York: Routledge.

Pelias, R. J. (1999). *Writing performance: Poeticizing the researcher's body*. Carbondale: Southern Illinois University Press.

Pollock, D. (1998). Performative writing. In P. Phalen & J. Lane (Eds.), *The ends of performance* (pp. 73–103). New York: NYU Press.

Swadener, B., & Lubeck, S. (1995). *Children and families "at-promise": Deconstructing the discourse of risk*. Albany: SUNY Press.

Warren, J. T. (2001). Doing whiteness: On the performative dimensions of race in the classroom. *Communication Education, 50,* 91–108.

References

Alexander, B. K. (2004). Racializing identity: Performance, pedagogy, and regret. *Cultural Studies ↔ Critical Methodologies, 4,* 12–28.

Banks, S. P., & Banks, A. (2000). Reading "the critical life": Autoethnography as pedagogy. *Communication Education, 49,* 233–238.

Baringer, D. K., & McCroskey, J. C. (2000). Immediacy in the classroom: Student immediacy. *Communication Education, 49,* 178–187.

Baudrillard, J. (1994). *Simulacra and simulation.* Ann Arbor: The University of Michigan Press. (Original work published 1981)

Bazerman, C. (1987). Codifying the social science style: The APA Publication Manual as behaviorist rhetoric. In J. S. Nelson, A. Megill, & D. N. McCloskey (Eds.), *The rhetoric of the human sciences* (pp. 125–144). Madison: University of Wisconsin Press.

Bennett, J. A. (2003). Love me gender: Normative homosexuality and 'ex-gay' performativity in reparative therapy narratives. *Text and Performance Quarterly, 23,* 331–352.

Bohman, J. (1991). *New philosophy of social science.* Cambridge: MIT Press.

Bordo, S. (1993). *Unbearable weight: Feminism, Western culture, and the body.* Berkeley: University of California Press.

Bordo, S. (1999). *The male body: A new look at men in public and in private.* New York: Farrar, Straus & Giroux.

Bourdieu, P. (1991). *Outline of a theory of practice.* Cambridge, UK: Cambridge University Press.

Boyer, E. (1997). *Scholarship reconsidered: Priorities of the professoriate.* San Francisco: Jossey-Bass.

Buber, M. (1996). *I and thou.* New York: Simon & Schuster. (Original work published 1923)

Buell, C. (2004). Models of mentoring in communication. *Communication Education, 53,* 56–74.

Burroughs, N. F., Kearney, P., & Plax, T. G. (1989). Compliance resistance in the college classroom. *Communication Education, 38,* 214–229.

Butler, J. (1990a). *Gender trouble: Feminism and the subversion of identity.* New York: Routledge.

Butler, J. (1990b). Performative acts and gender constitution: An essay in phenomenology and feminist theory. In S. E. Case (Ed.), *Performing feminisms: Feminist critical theory and theatre* (pp. 270–282). Baltimore, MD: Johns Hopkins University Press.

Butler, J. (1993). *Bodies that matter: On the discursive limits of "sex."* New York: Routledge.

Butler, J. (1997). *Excitable speech: A politics of the performative.* New York: Routledge.

Butler, J., & Scott, J. W. (Eds.). (1992). *Feminists theorize the political.* New York: Routledge.

Carbaugh, D. (1988). *Talking American: Cultural discourses on* Donahue. Stamford, CT: Ablex.

Carbaugh, D. (1991). Communication and cultural interpretation. *Quarterly Journal of Speech, 77,* 336–342.

Carger, C. L. (1996). *Of borders and dreams: A Mexican-American experience of urban education.* New York: Teachers College Press.

The Carnegie Foundation for the Advancement of Teaching. (1990). *Campus life: In search of community.* Princeton, NJ: The Carnegie Foundation for the Advancement of Teaching.

Certeau, M. de (1984). *The practice of everyday life.* Berkeley: University of California Press.

Cleto, F. (Ed.). (1999). *Camp: Queer aesthetics and the performing subject: A reader.* Ann Arbor: University of Michigan Press.

Cooks, L. (2003). Pedagogy, performance and positionality: Teaching about whiteness in interracial communication. *Communication Education, 52,* 245–258.

Cooks, L., & Sun, C. (2002). Constructing gender pedagogies: Desire and resistance in the "alternative" classroom. *Communication Education, 51,* 293–310.

Corey, F. C., & Nakayama, T. K. (1997). Sextext. *Text and Performance Quarterly, 17,* 66–77.

Corrigan, P. R. D. (1991). The making of the boy: Meditations on what grammar school did with, to, and for my body. In H. A. Giroux (Ed.), *Postmodernism, feminism, and cultural politics: Redrawing educational boundaries* (pp. 196–216). Albany: State University of New York Press.

Crow, B. K. (1988). Conversational performance and the performance of conversations. *The Drama Review, 32,* 23–54.

Delpit, L. (1995). *Other people's children: Cultural conflict in the classroom.* New York: The New Press.

Dewey, J. (1938). *Experience and education.* New York: Collier.

Dewey, J. (1944). *Democracy and education: An introduction to the philosophy of education.* New York: The Free Press. (Original work published 1916)

Dillard, A. (1990). *The writing life.* New York: Harper & Row.

Elbow, P. (1973). *Writing without teachers.* Oxford, UK: Oxford University Press.

Ellis, C. (1995). *Final negotiations: A story of love, loss and chronic illness.* Philadelphia: Temple University Press.

Ellsworth, E. (1989). Why doesn't this feel empowering? *Harvard Educational Review, 59*, 297–324.

Fassett, D. L. (2003). On defining at-risk: The role of educational ritual in constructions of success and failure. *Basic Communication Course Annual, 15*, 41–82.

Fassett, D. L., & Warren, J. T. (2004). "You get pushed back": The strategic rhetoric of educational success and failure in higher education. *Communication Education, 53*, 21–39.

Fassett, D. L., & Warren, J. T. (2005). The strategic rhetoric of an educational identity: Interviewing Jane. *Communication and Critical/Cultural Studies, 2*, 238–256.

Fausto-Sterling, A. (1987). Society writes biology, biology constructs gender. *Dædalus, 116*, 61–76.

Fenstermaker, S., & West, C. (Eds.). (2002). *Doing gender, doing difference: Inequality, power and institutional change.* New York: Routledge.

Fine, M. (1991). *Framing dropouts: Notes on the politics of an urban public high school.* Albany: State University of New York Press.

Fiske, J. (1990). Review of *Talking American: Cultural Discourses on* Donahue by D. Carbaugh. *Quarterly Journal of Speech, 76*, 450–451.

Fiske, J. (1991). Writing ethnographies: Contribution to a dialogue. *Quarterly Journal of Speech, 77*, 330–335.

Foucault, M. (1970). *The order of things: An archeology of the human sciences.* New York: Random House.

Foucault, M. (1977). *Discipline and punish: The birth of the prison.* New York: Random House.

Foucault, M. (1980). *Power/knowledge: Selected interviews and other writings 1972–1977* (C. Gordon, Ed.). New York: Pantheon Books.

Frankenberg, R. (1993). *White women, race matters: The social construction of whiteness.* Minneapolis: University of Minnesota Press.

Freire, P. (1992). *Pedagogy of hope: Reliving* Pedagogy of the Oppressed. New York: Continuum.

Freire, P. (2003). *Pedagogy of the oppressed: 30th anniversary edition.* New York: Continuum. (Original work published 1970)

Freire, P., & Macedo, D. P. (1995). A dialogue: Culture, language, and race. *Harvard Educational Review, 65*, 377–402.

Garfinkel, H. (1967). *Studies in ethnomethodology.* Cambridge, UK: Polity.

Gingrich-Philbrook, C. (1998). Disciplinary violation as gender violation: The stigmatized masculine voice of performance studies. *Communication Theory, 8*, 203–220.

Giroux, H. A. (2003). Spectacles of race and pedagogies of denial: Anti-black racist pedagogy under the reign of neoliberalism. *Communication Education, 52*, 191–212.

Giroux, H. A., & Shannon, P. (1997). Cultural studies and pedagogy as performative practice: Toward an introduction. In H. A. Giroux & P. Shannon (Eds.), *Education and cultural studies: Toward a performative practice* (pp. 1–9). New York: Routledge.

Glassick, C. E., Huber, M. T., & Maeroff, G. I. (1997). *Scholarship assessed: Evaluation of the professoriate.* San Francisco: Jossey-Bass.

Goodall, H. L., Jr. (2000). *Writing the new ethnography.* Walnut Creek, CA: AltaMira Press.

Goodall, H. L., Jr. (2004). Narrative ethnography as applied communication research. *Journal of Applied Communication Research, 32,* 185–194.

Gray, P. H. (1998, February 14). Calling the cops. *American Communication Journal, 1.2.* Retrieved May 17, 1999, from http://www.americancomm.org/~aca/acjdata/v011/Iss2/special/gray.htm

Halualani, R. T. (2002). *In the name of Hawaiians: Native identities and cultural politics.* Minneapolis: University of Minnesota Press.

Heidegger, M. (1962). *Being and time.* New York: Harper & Row.

Heinz, B. (2002). Enga(y)ging the discipline: Sexual minorities and communication studies. *Communication Education, 51,* 95–104.

Hendrix, K. G., Jackson, R. L., II, & Warren, J. R. (2003). Shifting academic landscapes: Exploring co-identities, identity negotiation, and critical progressive pedagogy. *Communication Education, 52,* 177–190.

Hill, S. E., Bahniuk, M. H., & Dobos, J. (1989). The impact of mentoring and collegial support on faculty success: An analysis of support behavior, information adequacy, and communication apprehension. *Communication Education, 38,* 15–34.

hooks, b. (1989). *Talking back: Thinking feminist, thinking black.* Boston: South End Press.

hooks, b. (1992). Theory as liberatory practice. *Yale Journal of Law and Feminism, 12,* 1–12.

hooks, b. (1994). *Teaching to transgress: Education as the practice of freedom.* New York: Routledge.

Irving, O., & Martin, J. (1982). Withitness: The confusing variable. *American Educational Research Journal, 19,* 313–319.

Johnson, G. M. (1994). An ecological framework for conceptualizing educational risk. *Urban Education, 29,* 34–49.

Johnson, G., Staton, A., & Jorgenson-Earp, C. (1995). An ecological perspective on the transition of new university freshmen. *Communication Education, 44,* 336–352.

Jones, S. H. (1998). *Kaleidoscope notes: Writing women's music and organizational culture.* Walnut Creek, CA: AltaMira Press.

Kearney, P., Plax, T. G., & Burroughs, N. F. (1991). An attributional analysis of college students' resistance decisions. *Communication Education, 40,* 325–342.

Kearney, P., Plax, T. G., Richmond, V. P., & McCroskey, J. C. (1984). Power in the classroom: Part IV. Alternatives to discipline. In R. N. Bostrom (Ed.), *Communication yearbook 8* (pp. 724–746). Beverly Hills, CA: Sage.

Kearney, P., Plax, T. G., Richmond, V. P., & McCroskey, J. C. (1985). Power in the classroom: Part III. Teacher communication techniques and messages. *Communication Education, 34,* 19–28.

Kellett, P. M., & Goodall, H. L., Jr. (1999). The death of discourse in our own (chat) room: "Sextext," skillful discussion, and virtual communities. In D. Slayden &

R. K. Whillock (Eds.), *Soundbite culture: The death of discourse in a wired world* (pp. 155–190). Thousand Oaks, CA: Sage.

King, S. (2000). *On writing: A memoir of the craft.* New York: Scribner.

Kozol, J. (1991). *Savage inequalities: Children in America's schools.* New York: Crown.

Kozol, J. (1995). *Amazing grace: The lives of children and the conscience of a nation.* New York: Crown.

Kozol, J. (2000). *Ordinary resurrections: Children in the years of hope.* New York: Crown.

Kuhn, T. (1996). *The structure of scientific revolutions* (3rd ed.). Chicago: University of Chicago Press.

Lakoff, G., & Johnson, M. (1980). *Metaphors we live by.* Chicago: University of Chicago Press.

Langsdorf, L. (1994). Why phenomenology in communication research? *Human Studies, 17,* 1–8.

Lather, P. (1991). *Getting smart: Feminist research and pedagogy with/in the postmodern.* New York: Routledge.

Lee, C. R., Levine, T. R., & Cambra, R. (1997). Resisting compliance in the multicultural classroom. *Communication Education, 46,* 229–243.

Lindlof, T. R. (1995). *Qualitative communication research methods.* Thousand Oaks, CA: Sage.

Lindlof, T. R., & Taylor, B. C. (2002). *Qualitative communication research methods* (2nd ed.). Thousand Oaks, CA: Sage.

Lorde, A. (1984). *Sister outsider.* Freedom, CA: Crossing Press.

Martin, J. N., & Davis, O. I. (2001). Conceptual foundations for teaching about whiteness in an intercultural communication class. *Communication Education, 50,* 298–315.

Mayo, C. (2004). The tolerance that dare not speak its name. In M. Boler (Ed.), *Democratic dialogue in education: Troubling speech, disturbing silence* (pp. 33–47). New York: Peter Lang.

McCroskey, J. C., & Richmond, V. P. (1983). Power in the classroom: Part I. Teacher and student perceptions. *Communication Education, 32,* 175–184.

McCroskey, J. C., Richmond, V. P., Plax, T. G., & Kearney, P. (1985). Power in the classroom: Part V. Behavior alternation techniques, communication training and learning. *Communication Education, 34,* 214–226.

McIntosh, P. (1988). *White privilege and male privilege: A personal account of coming to see correspondences through work in women's studies* (Working Paper No. 189). Wellesley, MA: Wellesley College Center for Research on Women.

McIntyre, A. (1997). *Making meaning of whiteness: Exploring racial identity with white teachers.* Albany: State University of New York Press.

McLaren, P. (1993). *Schooling as ritual performance: Toward a political economy of educational symbols and gestures* (2nd ed.). London: Routledge.

McLaren, P. (1994). *Life in schools: An introduction to critical pedagogy in the foundations of education* (2nd ed.). White Plains, NY: Longman.

McLaren, P. (1997). Decentering whiteness. *Multicultural Education, 5,* 4–11.

McLaren, P. (1999). *Schooling as ritual performance: Toward a political economy of educational symbols and gestures* (3rd ed.). Boston: Rowman & Littlefield.

Mottet, T. P., Beebe, S. A., Raffeld, P. C., & Medlock, A. L. (2004). The effects of student verbal and nonverbal responsiveness on teacher self-efficacy and job satisfaction. *Communication Education, 53,* 150–164.

Nainby, K. E., & Pea, J. B. (2003). Immobility in mobility: Narratives of social class, education and paralysis. *Educational Foundations, 17,* 19–36.

Nainby, K. E., Warren, J. T., & Bollinger, C. M. (2003). Articulating contact in the classroom: Toward a constitutive focus in critical pedagogy. *Language and Intercultural Communication, 3,* 198–212.

Nakayama, T. K., & Krizek, R. L. (1995). Whiteness: A strategic rhetoric. *Quarterly Journal of Speech, 81,* 291–309.

Pacanowsky, M. (1988). Slouching to Chicago. *Quarterly Journal of Speech, 74,* 453–468.

Parks, M. R. (1998, February 14). Where does scholarship begin? *American Communication Journal, 1.* Retrieved May 17, 1999, from http://www.american-comm.org/~aca/acjdata/v011/Iss2/special/parks.htm

Pelias, R. J. (1999). *Writing performance: Poeticizing the researcher's body.* Carbondale: Southern Illinois University Press.

Pelias, R. J. (2000). The critical life. *Communication Education, 49,* 220–228.

Pelias, R. J. (2004). *A methodology of the heart: Evoking academic and daily life.* Walnut Creek, CA: AltaMira Press.

Pineau, E. L. (1994). Teaching is performance: Reconceptualizing a problematic metaphor. *American Educational Research Journal, 31,* 3–25.

Pineau, E. L. (2000). *Nursing mother* and articulating absence. *Text and Performance Quarterly, 20,* 1–19.

Plax, T. G., Kearney, P., McCroskey, J. C., & Richmond, V. P. (1986). Power in the classroom: Part VI. Verbal control strategies, nonverbal immediacy and affective learning. *Communication Education, 35,* 43–55.

Pollner, M. (1991). Left of ethnomethodology: The rise and decline of radical reflexivity. *American Sociological Review, 56,* 370–380.

Ragan, S. L. (2000). The critical life: An exercise in applying inapplicable critical standards. *Communication Education, 49,* 229–232.

Richmond, V. P., & McCroskey, J. C. (1984). Power in the classroom: Part II. Power and learning. *Communication Education, 33,* 125–136.

Richmond, V. P., McCroskey, J. C., Kearney, P., & Plax, T. G. (1987). Power in the classroom: Part VII. Linking behavior alteration techniques to cognitive learning. *Communication Education, 36,* 1–12.

Ronai, C. R. (1996). My mother is mentally retarded. In C. Ellis & A. P. Bochner (Eds.), *Composing ethnography: Alternative forms of qualitative writing* (pp. 109–131). Walnut Creek, CA: AltaMira Press.

Rosenfeld, L. B., & Richman, J. M. (1999). Supportive communication and school outcomes: Part II. Academically "at-risk" low-income high school students. *Communication Education, 48,* 294–307.

Rosenfeld, L. B., Richman, J. M., & Bowen, G. L. (1998). Supportive communication and school outcomes for academically "at-risk" and other low-income middle school students. *Communication Education, 47,* 309–325.

Rosow, L. (1989). Arthur: A tale of disempowerment. *Phi Delta Kappan, 71,* 194–199.

Ryan, W. (1976). *Blaming the victim.* New York: Random House.

Sacks, H. (1989). *Harvey Sacks lectures 1964–1965* (G. Jefferson, Ed.). Norwell, MA: Kluwer Academic Publishers.

Schegloff, E. A. (1984). On some gestures' relation to talk. In J. M. Atkinson & J. Heritage (Eds.), *Structures of social action: Studies in conversation analysis* (pp. 266–296). New York: Cambridge University Press.

Schlosser, E. (2002). *Fast food nation: The dark side of the all-American meal.* New York: Harper & Row

Schrodt, P., Cawyer, C. S., & Sanders, R. (2003). An examination of academic mentoring behaviors and new faculty members' satisfaction with socialization and tenure and promotion processes. *Communication Education, 52,* 17–30.

Scott, J. W. (1992). Experience. In J. Butler & J. W. Scott (Eds.), *Feminists theorize the political* (pp. 22–40). New York: Routledge.

Shaull, R. (2003). Foreword. In P. Freire, *Pedagogy of the oppressed—30th anniversary edition* (pp. 29–34). New York: Continuum.

Shields, D. C. (2000). Symbolic convergence and special communication theories: Sensing and examining dis/enchantment with the theoretical robustness of critical autoethnography. *Communication Monographs, 67,* 392–421.

Shor, I. (1980). *Critical teaching and everyday life.* Chicago: University of Chicago Press.

Shor, I. (1992). *Empowering education: Critical teaching for social change.* Chicago: University of Chicago Press.

Shor, I. (1996). *When students have power: Negotiating authority in a critical pedagogy.* Chicago: University of Chicago Press.

Shugart, H. A. (2001). Parody as subversive performance: Denaturalizing gender and reconstituting desire in *Ellen. Text and Performance Quarterly, 21,* 95–113.

Spano, S. J. (2001). *Public dialogue and participatory democracy: The Cupertino Project.* Creskill, NJ: Hampton Press.

Sprague, J. (1992). Expanding the research agenda for instructional communication: Raising some unasked questions. *Communication Education, 41,* 1–25.

Sprague, J. (1993). Retrieving the research agenda for communication education: Asking the pedagogical questions that are "embarrassments to theory." *Communication Education, 42,* 106–122.

Sprague, J. (1994). Ontology, politics, and instructional communication research: Why we can't just "agree to disagree" about power. *Communication Education, 43,* 273–290.

Sprague, J. (2002). *Communication Education:* The spiral continues. *Communication Education, 51,* 337–354.

Stewart, J. (1995). *Language as articulate contact: Toward a post-semiotic philosophy of communication.* Albany: State University of New York Press.

Stucky, N. (1988). Unnatural acts: Performing natural conversation. *Literature in Performance, 8,* 28–39.

Teven, J. J., & McCroskey, J. C. (1997). The relationship of perceived teacher caring with student learning and teacher evaluation. *Communication Education, 46,* 1–10.

Thompson, A. (2003). Tiffany, friend to people of color: White investments in antiracism. *International Journal of Qualitative Studies in Education, 16,* 7–30.

Tillman-Healy, L. M. (1996). A secret life in the culture of thinness: Reflections on body, food and bulimia. In C. Ellis & A. P. Bochner (Eds.), *Composing ethnography: Alternative forms of qualitative writing* (pp. 76–108). Walnut Creek, CA: AltaMira Press.

Turner, V. (1982). *From ritual to theatre: The human seriousness of play.* Baltimore, MD: Johns Hopkins University Press.

Warren, J. T. (2001a). Absence for whom? An autoethnography of white subjectivity. *Cultural Studies ←→ Critical Methodologies, 1,* 36–49.

Warren, J. T. (2001b). Doing whiteness: On the performative dimensions of race in the classroom. *Communication Education, 50,* 91–108.

Warren, J. T. (2001c). The social drama of a "rice burner": A (re)constitution of whiteness. *Western Journal of Communication, 65,* 184–205.

Warren, J. T. (2003). *Performing purity: Whiteness, pedagogy and the reconstitution of power.* New York: Peter Lang.

Warren, J. T. (2005). Bodily excess and the desire for absence: Whiteness and the making of (raced) educational subjectivities. In B. K. Alexander, G. L. Anderson, & B. P. Gallegos (Eds.), *Performance theories in education: Power, pedagogy and the politics of identity* (pp. 83–104). Mahwah, NJ: Lawrence Erlbaum.

Warren, J. T., & Fassett, D. L. (2002). (Re)Constituting ethnographic identities. *Qualitative Inquiry, 8,* 575–590.

Warren, J. T., & Fassett, D. L. (2004). Spiritually drained, sexually denied and metaphorically erased: Toward an engaged pedagogy of the mind, body, and spirit. In D. Denton & W. Ashton (Eds.), *Teaching from the heart: Tales of spirituality, action and pedagogy* (pp. 21–30). New York: Peter Lang.

Warren, J. T., & Hytten, K. (2004). The faces of whiteness: Pitfalls and the critical democrat. *Communication Education, 53,* 321–340.

Wendt, T. (1998, February 14). The ways and means of knowing: The "problem" of scholarship in a postmodern world. *American Communication Journal, 1.* Retrieved May 17, 1999, from http://www.americancomm.org/~aca/acjdata/v011/Iss2/special/wendt.htm

West, C., & Fenstermaker, S. (1995). Doing difference. *Gender and Society, 9,* 8–37.

Wink, J. (2005). *Critical pedagogy: Notes from the real world* (3rd ed.). New York: Addison-Wesley Longman.

Wood, A. F., & Fassett, D. L. (2003). Remote control: Identity, power and technology in the communication classroom. *Communication Education, 52,* 286–296.

Zimmerman, S. (1987, May). *Al-Anon communication and culture.* Paper presented at the annual meeting of the International Communication Association, Montreal.

Index

About the Authors

Deanna L. Fassett received her Ph.D. in Speech Communication from Southern Illinois University, Carbondale. She is Associate Professor of Communication Studies at San José State University. She has published essays in several education and communication studies journals, including *Communication and Critical/Cultural Studies, Communication Education, Multicultural Education,* and *Qualitative Inquiry.*

John T. Warren received his Ph.D. in Speech Communication and Performance Studies from Southern Illinois University, Carbondale, where he is currently an associate professor. His publications include the books *Performing Purity: Whiteness, Pedagogy and the Reconstitution of Power* and *Casting Gender: Women and Performance in Intercultural Contexts,* as well as essays in several education and communication studies journals, including *Educational Theory, Communication Education,* and *Communication and Critical/Cultural Studies.*